GAMBLERS & GANGSTERS

FORT WORTH'S JACKSBORO HIGHWAY IN THE 1940S & 1950S

by

Ann Arnold

EAKIN PRESS Fort Worth, Texas

To L.

We gambled on each other and won.

FIRST EDITION

Copyright © 1998
By Ann Arnold

Published in the United States of America
By Eakin Press
An Imprint of Wild Horse Media Group
P.O. Box 331779
Fort Worth, Texas 76163
www.EakinPress.com

2 3 4 5 6 7 8 9

1-57168-250-3

Library of Congress Catologing-in-Publication Data

Arnold, Ann, 1932-
    Gamblers and gangsters : Fort Worth's Jacksboro Highway in the 1940s and 1950s / by
Ann Arnold.
        p.   cm.
    Includes bibliographical references and index.
    ISBN 1-57168-250-3 (alk. paper)
    1. Fort Worth (Tex.)—History—20th century—Anecdotes.   2. Criminals—Texas—
Fort Worth—History—20th century—Anecdotes.   3. Fort Worth (Tex.)—Biography—
Anecdotes.   I. Title.
F394.F7A75   1998
976.4'5315—dc21   98-28262
                                                                                                              CIP

Contents

Foreword   v

Acknowledgments   vi

Introduction   vii

Chapter 1   Introducing Hell's Half Acre   1

Chapter 2   They Called it "Thunder Road"   10

Chapter 3   Search Begins for "Hidden Gambling"   17

Chapter 4   The Killing Begins   24

Chapter 5   Enter the Grand Jury   32

Chapter 6   Meet John B. Honts, the New Prosecutor   39

Chapter 7   Stopping the Rolls of the Dice   48

Chapter 8   Evans Livestock Company: "Heifers for Sale"   59

Chapter 9   Deuces Were Wild   68

Chapter 10   Murder, Made for the Movies   73

Chapter 11   Blood Made Him Sick, But He Killed Anyway   79

Chapter 12   Little Gambling House on the Hill   84

Chapter 13   "Tincy": Meaner Than a Junkyard Dog   93

Chapter 14   No Chamber of Commerce
             Type Gambling Machines   107

Chapter 15   And the Killin' Goes On   117

Chapter 16   Miscellaneous Murders   122

Chapter 17   Good Guys Wear White Hats   133

Chapter 18   Here Comes the Tax Man   145

Chapter 19   The Michigan Connection   151

Chapter 20   Crime, a Family Tradition   155

Chapter 21   Big Bands at the Casino   162

Chapter 22   The Other Side of Town   174

Appendix A: Indictment Who's Who   177

Appendix B: Browning Legal Documents   181

Appendix C: Final Grand Jury Report   197

Summary of Indictments   202
Summary of Gangland Slayings   203
Endnotes   205
Bibliography   213
Index   215

Foreword

A few years ago, I headed west out of downtown on Jacksboro Highway to witness the demolition of the Four Deuces. As a member of the Fort Worth Landmarks Commission, I had called Pat Kirkwood to find out if there was any way to save the building and the amazing history it represented. Pat told me about his many efforts to keep his father's storied club standing, all to no avail. After no takers came forward to meet Pat's double or nothing coin flip for the club, and the bulldozer went to work, it struck me that the chapter had finally closed on Fort Worth's gambling traditions. But somebody needed to write the book.

From the earliest days of the cattle drives through town, Fort Worth embraced, if not with open arms, then certainly with an open palm, the profit and excitement of illegal entertainment. The crime and corruption which followed it were simply the costs of doing business. The men and women who made their livings in, or off of, the backrooms, bars and gambling houses contributed much to the character and folklore of the city. From the good bad guys to the bad good guys, their stories are compelling, fascinating, sometimes amusing and often tragic.

Ann Arnold has captured a period in Fort Worth's not too recent history with the keen eye of a speakeasy lookout. She dispels the myth that the old Hell's Half Acre had been shut down by the early part of the century. The Acre just changed shape, scattered around town and carried on for another fifty years. With her book, Ann has given us the real stories behind some of our wildest local legends. We may not always be proud of them, but the stories needed to be written. They are too much a part of Fort Worth to let them fade from memory.

QUENTIN MCGOWN

Acknowledgments

After reading Rick Selcer's intriguing and informative *Hell's Half Acre*, I remembered my early years in Fort Worth. Based on newspaper reports (few people had television then) it seemed every time we turned around we read of a body being discovered in a shallow grave near Lake Worth. Gambling was fairly open, but arrests were few. My interest piqued, I searched for a book on that period of Fort Worth history. There was none. Old newspaper accounts of the 1951 grand jury led me to many interesting people who shared their firsthand memories with me. Thanks to the following for making this book possible:

Kenneth Adcock, Sam Atchley, Bob Bolen, Wayne Brown, George Campbell, Bill Fairley, Al "Cotton" Farmer, J. D. Farmer, Howard Fender, Carl Freund, Herbert Hopkins, R. R. Howerton, Carroll Hubbard, Pat Kirkwood, B. M. Kudlaty, Louie Lancer, Joan Loicano, Byron Matthews, Twain Morrow, Bobby Morton, Harley Pershing, Jim Piland, Leon Rausch, Ben Rubin, Perry Sandifer, Carol Stanley, Cecil Stoker, Louis Tassione, B. J. Walton, George Wilderspin, Madeline Williams, and Donna Young were most helpful.

Jim Gordon, son of amusement columnist Jack Gordon, generously shared his late father's materials. Henry Wright allowed photographer Sargent Hill access to former sheriff Harlon Wright's photographs. Thanks to all three.

A very special thank you goes to Dr. Gerald Saxon and his staff at the Special Collections Division, University of Texas, Arlington, for their splendid efforts in searching for old newspaper files and photographs.

And of course I thank my husband, whose support is the wind beneath my wings.

Introduction

Fort Worth has been described as a gentle land populated by a gentle people. They endured the floods of the 1940s and the severe drought of the 1950s by pulling together as a community. More blue-collar than the larger city to the east, Fort Worthians' values centered on home and family. Most went to school or work on weekdays, and church on Sundays. Baptists and Methodists were larger in number, but the first church built was the First Christian (Disciples of Christ).

Few homes had air conditioning, and in the warmer months people sat out on the porch or in the backyard to keep cool. Children roller-skated on sidewalks in front of their houses. Boys rode bicycles to sandlots in nearby parks. Arlington Heights, North Side, Polytechnic Heights, Riverside, and South Side were nice neighborhoods in which to raise families.

Fort Worthians read about crime and vice in the newspapers, but it rarely touched them personally. There was a dichotomy between "us" and "them"—gamblers and gangsters lived in one domain and everyday citizens lived in another.

People not involved in entertainment or gambling rarely encountered the underworld. They had no reason to be fearful. The first many neighbors knew of the double lives of men killed in gangland slayings was when they read about it in the newspapers.

If it can be said that any criminals have class, these men of past decades had class. They were concerned about the welfare of their families, and except for their particular area of crime, were law-abiding citizens. For example, notorious gangster Tincy Eggleston, commenting on a newly installed traffic light at a school crossing, said, "That's the best thing that ever happened. Some little kid was going to get killed trying to cross this road."[1] The fact that this statement was made while Eggleston was in the custody of Dallas County deputies as a suspect in a murder, nicely summarizes the era covered in this book—gamblers and gangsters in the 1940s and 1950s.

Chapter 1

Introducing
Hell's Half Acre

Ten-year-old Bobby had a sore throat and didn't go to school Wednesday, November 22, 1950. About 9:15 that morning he felt better and decided to go down to the kitchen. He was on the stairs when the house shook so violently he almost lost his balance. Earthquake! But Fort Worth, Texas, wasn't earthquake country. In the 1950s it was gambler and gangster country. Bobby's neighbors, gambler Nelson Harris and his pregnant wife, Juanita, who lived at 3105 Wingate, had just been blown to bits by a car bomb. The bomb also blew the lid off the most open secret in town. Unknowingly, Nelson Harris was a martyr. Because of his death, citizens realized crime and corruption were serious problems that could no longer be swept under the municipal rug that had been covering vice for quite a long time.

* * *

After the Civil War, Fort Worth became the stopping place for cattle drives plodding north to railroad centers. The typical cowboy, dry from herding up to a thousand ornery longhorns, and rich with a month's pay, sought a little "R and R" in Fort Worth's Hell's Half Acre. First he might take a bath in a real tub, then strap on his gun and head for the south end of town. In the numerous saloons, drinks were guzzled and cards were shuffled. Brothel madams eagerly accommodated, but most required their customers to remove their boots first.

For a night or two the cowboy caroused. Out of money, but with a wide grin on his weathered face, he departed, driving steers across swollen rivers and hostile Indian territory.

City fathers and merchants also had wide grins on their faces. They counted the cash and waited for the next herd to hit town. For over thirty years in the struggling outpost on the Trinity, vice and jail fines produced a large part of Fort Worth's economic base.

Finally, when things got too wild, and the Acre's money wasn't so important, the townspeople demanded law and order. Women and clergy led the effort to make the streets safe for decent, God-fearing people. Vice became less open, but as author Richard Selcer concluded in his book of the same name, Hell's Half Acre "did not really die in 1900 or 1901."[1] Some would say it was reincarnated as the Jacksboro Highway. In the 1940s and 1950s that five-mile strip rivaled the earlier legendary south end of town in matters of vice and political corruption.

A 1917 Fort Worth telephone directory listed 178 saloons and sixteen churches. During the 1920s, Cowtown had its share of boot-leggers and speakeasies. After repeal of the Eighteenth Amendment, the Texas Legislature voted to restrict the sale of hard liquor.

In November 1935 the Tarrant County district attorney conferred with local police chiefs and the sheriff, ordering all establishments selling whiskey to shut down. Even though law permitted alcohol prescriptions to be filled at drugstores, more liquor was dispensed out the back door than over the counter.

Fort Worth Press columnist Jack Gordon visited the downtown State Bar on November 23 to commiserate with the bartender. Gordon pulled a flask of "drug store toddy" from his hip pocket, explaining he had a touch of influenza, but when two West Texans walked in and ordered whiskey, the bartender dolefully offered beer.

Places selling bootleg whiskey during Prohibition thrived, and many bootleggers ran clubs. The law allowed a private club to sell mixed drinks to its members, which created an elitist atmosphere. Country clubs carefully screened new members. Night clubs were less discriminating. Two things were required to join: Applicants had to be breathing, and have money to pay for the drinks. Owners greased the palms of dirty cops to stay in business.

In addition to the dance floor and bar, many clubs had a back room for further entertainment. Payoffs to law "nonenforcement" officers also covered illegal gambling, but cost more.

One resident recalled as a seven-year-old going with her father, a high school teacher, to a cafe on the Jacksboro Highway: "I was too small to reach the slot machine so I stood on a wooden milk rack and played my quarter's worth of nickels."[2] Another woman, the daughter of a coin machine company operator, told of having her own slot machine when she was a child. "I was the most popular kid on my block,"[3] she laughed. Her grandmother also had her own slot machine.

It is impossible to write of Fort Worth in those days without placing Amon G. Carter in the center of things. When Carter came to his adopted city he changed more than his address. He hated his first name, Giles. Even G. Amon Carter was repugnant, so he switched to Amon G. Those who knew what the "G" stood for would more likely refer to God the Father as "Pop" than to voice the hated name. Intimidated by his explosive temper, employees referred to him by his other name, "Amon the Terrible," when safely out of his hearing range.

The fast-talking, fast-walking dynamo regularly put in eighteen-hour days and, after a twenty-minute nap, could work the remaining six hours. With an ever-present Robert Burns panatela clinched in his teeth, which he waved vigorously like an orchestra conductor's baton, he directed the civic and cultural life of the city.

Carter, publisher of the *Fort Worth Star-Telegram,* controlled the city as if he were its anointed king. His power over civic, commercial, and political spheres extended into far West Texas. To him, farm and ranch news was as important as the New London school blast that killed more than 500 people. From the mayor down to the owner of the corner drug store, none dared oppose or anger him. He truly loved his chosen city, and was an unabashed promoter of Fort Worth. Through his efforts the city became known on Pennsylvania Avenue and Wall Street.

By Carter's rules, reporters were forbidden to air local dirty linen in public. Thus, if prominent citizens were caught in awkward situations, not one word of it was printed in the *Star-Telegram.* It was okay to write about the scandalous conduct of the King of England and Mrs. Simpson, but not about the wealthy, married Fort

Worth woman who showered expensive gifts on the handsome, single sheriff.

Carter's home away from home was the Fort Worth Club. This elite gathering place for movers and shakers was established in 1885. Across the street from the *Star-Telegram*, the club was housed in its own twelve-story building. In addition to the five dining areas and members-only bar, suites were available. Sid Richardson lived there, and Carter also maintained a suite. Will Rogers always stayed at the Fort Worth Club when he was in town.

The Club's stated purpose was to provide an opportunity for business and professional men to socialize while working to bring growth to the city. Carter and other city lions could eat, get a haircut or a massage, gamble, read the *Wall Street Journal* or the *Oil and Gas Journal*, all at the same place. Carter held the office of club president for more than thirty-five years. There the publisher and his cohorts debated deals bringing the biggest industries to Fort Worth. The scheme to bring the first Casa Manana was hatched at the Club.

The year 1936 was an important one for Texas. The once independent Republic celebrated its centennial. Four major cities, Houston, Dallas, San Antonio, and Fort Worth were considered for the official centennial site. Carter believed San Antonio or Houston, both historically important, would win the prize. But times were hard and Dallas had more money to build the exhibits. Dallas won.

Carter's general response to disappointment was to mutter "goddamn." Only from him it came out "gawddamn." When Dallas got the centennial, Amon Carter seethed anger. Those within earshot in the newsroom swore he broke his own record of consecutive "gawddamns." He planned to do something about it.

The city fathers and Carter drafted a proposal for PWA money to build a coliseum, auditorium, and buildings to house a livestock exposition. James Farley presented the idea to the president as "Amon's cowshed." The mulish publisher objected. "Now, gawd-damnit, it's not a cowshed, it's . . ."[4] He twisted arms, including Roosevelt's, until he got approval for a livestock pavilion. Carter raised $1 million for the project.

Significantly, Carter also planned an entertainment center as part of the complex. At $1,000 a day, he hired New York showman William Samuel Rosenberg to produce an extravaganza that would put Dallas to shame. Better known as Billy Rose, Rosenberg created the original and fabulous Casa Manana.

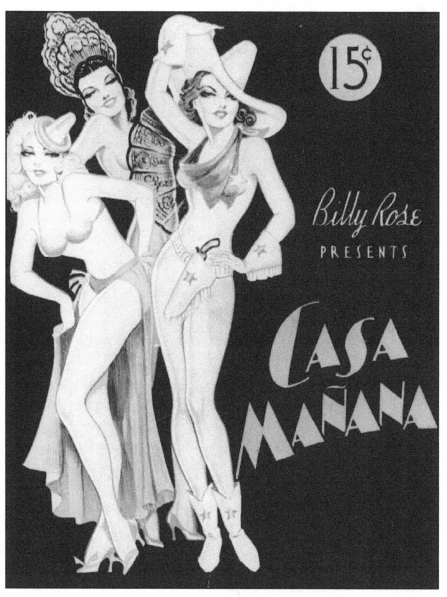

Fort Worth had never seen anything like it, or as much of it.
—From the William E. Jary Casa Manana collection.

A dance teacher from nearby Weatherford auditioned for the chorus line. He turned her down and advised her to forget show business. Her name was Mary Martin. Twenty years and many Broadway hits later, Martin played to a standing-room-only crowd at Will Rogers Auditorium, with ticket prices ranging from $2.00 to $4.00.

Rose hired an array of characters. Diminutive John Fox, once the model for Buster Brown shoes, and seven-foot-four Dave Ballard, were cast in the show. An Amazonian woman who bent nails between her fingers was joined by a seventy-five-year-old bareback rider. To these Rose added a sixteen-piece, all-monkey band. Some four thousand people came nightly to see and be seen. Some wore jewel-draped gowns and tuxedoes, while others wore overalls and cotton print dresses.

Octogenarian J. D. Farmer chuckled as he recalled an encounter with the famous Mr. Rose. J. D. was a teenager learning to box when Sully Montgomery, his coach, insisted he take dancing lessons to increase his skill in the ring. Those lessons allowed the young man to substitute as a dancer in one of the Casa Manana shows. The dancers were paid $30 a week. They balked at getting paid so much less than other performers. J. D. was elected to present their grievances to the boss.

Farmer went to Rose's office in the Worth Hotel. He could hardly see the great, but short, New Yorker standing behind the desk. "What can I do for you?" the showman asked.

Mustering up all his courage, the youth said, "You can give us all a raise, the dancers, the stage hands, everybody."

"Can't do that."

"Well, who do you think can put on the show tonight? Give us more money or we're going to the movies instead of working."

Rose responded, "You could be fired for this."

"Fine. Everybody's still going to the picture show tonight."

That afternoon Rose arrived at the rehearsal to make an important announcement. "After looking at the books," he said, "I've come to the conclusion all my good show girls, my dancers, everybody, is getting a 10% raise."

J. D. spoke up. "Mr. Rose, that's only three dollars. We're going to the movies."

"Did I say 10 percent? Let's make it 20 percent and we'll have no more talk about going to the picture show."[5]

Boyce House, who later wrote memorable books on Texas, was

in charge of publicity. Casa Manana became the talk of the nation. A New York drama critic suggested copying the bigger-than-life extravaganza and placing it in Central Park. Damon Runyon, the Hearst newspaper columnist, wrote, "If you took the Polo Grounds and converted it into a cafe and then added the best Ziegfeld scenic effects, you might get something approximating *Casa Manana*."[6]

The production made Billy Rose the man of the hour. The little impresario, standing a mere 5'1" if he stretched, was always self-conscious about his lack of height. He would have been extremely pleased with 6' James Caan's portrayal of him in the movie, *Funny Girl.*

Casa Manana's successful exhibition was dubbed the "Frontier Fiesta." In the next three years Fannie Brice (Mrs. Rose), Eddie Cantor, Edgar Bergen, Ray Bolger, and Sally Rand and her "nude ranch" girls, graced the stage.

Sally's "nude ranch" act was advertised as the only educational exhibit on the grounds. Eighteen pretty girls, dressed in cowboy boots, hats, green bandanas and little else, wowed the customers. Texans had never seen anything like it, or as much of it. They came from all over the state to ogle the leggy beauties.

Sally's act was, of course, more illusion than nudity. Trained in classical dance, her graceful movements set her apart from other strip teasers. She wore a flesh-colored body suit on the hot stage, perspiring as she performed. One of the orchestra member's claimed "she stank,"[7] and he wasn't talking about her artistry.

When off-stage Miss Rand spoke to PTA groups and opened the baseball season by throwing out the first ball. Speaking at a luncheon for advertising professionals, she said they were in the same business, "selling white space."

The famous dancer possessed a keen sense of humor. When *Star-Telegram* reporter C. L. Richhard went to her dressing room for an interview, he knocked and was told to enter. According to reports, "He found Sally, naked, lying on her stomach reading the Bible. Sally stretched, rolled over, and shyly covered her *mons venus* with Psalms 35:17."[8]

Another attraction was the Rosebuds at the Pioneer Palace. Ben Rubin, owner of a local dress factory, was called upon to supply the Rosebuds' costumes. These dancers, six ladies weighing from 215 to 340 pounds, were dressed in ruffled little girl dresses and big red ribbons in their hair.

The stage was built over the bar. The first time the hefty women did their act, the foundation beams cracked. Bartenders and patrons scattered. No one was hurt, but the stage had to be reinforced. The show was a hit the two years it ran.

Casa Manana entertained audiences until the beginning of World War II. Twenty-two years later a new Casa, a theater in the round, was built on the site. It began its own tradition of bringing Broadway musicals to Texas. Part of the metal wheel which allowed the original stage to rotate is still in place. It is buried under the Equestrian Center, next door to the theater.

Much has been written about Rose's musical productions, but the food service was almost as lavish. Catered by a New York corporation, show-goers dined on a $1.00 dinner or splurged on the $1.70 prime steak. The cost included a seafood cocktail as appetizer, salad, dessert and coffee. A glass of champagne cost sixty cents and beer went for a quarter.

In addition to the Casa Manana extravaganza, gambling, open bars, and night clubs sprang up to entertain those looking for a good time. City fathers closed their eyes. The unofficial motto of the chamber of commerce was, "Let them go to the State Fair in Dallas to be educated, but come to Fort Worth to have fun."

Open gambling was allowed as long as it was run by locals. City and county lawmen clamped down on efforts by Dallas or other "foreign" operators to establish themselves in the city. At the same time, and for the right amount of money, they protected the home boys.

Amon Carter liked to gamble. He could be found at the $100 window of Arlington Downs and other race tracks, or at the roulette tables. But his favorite form of gambling was a good game of poker. He often hosted high dollar games at his 1220 Broad Street home or Suite 10G of the Fort Worth Club.

With his tremendous store of energy, he could play cards for forty-eight hours at a time, winning more often than he lost. If Carter knew a fellow player was over-extended, he would privately return the man's money.

His generosity was not totally benevolent. Josh Cosden, of Cosden Oil, lost $15,000 in a crap game and paid by check. The publisher refused to cash the check. A Standard Oil executive lost over $1,000. However, "Later, he asked civic favors of both men and they paid their gambling debts, but in Amon's coin."[9]

* * *

World War II preparations began about the time Billy Rose left town. Consolidated Aircraft Corporation built "the bomber plant" on the far west side of the city. Tarrant Field, adjoining the plant, trained pilots to fly the B-24 and B-36 bombers. The city experienced a boom unlike any since the cattle drives of the late 1800s, or the oil days of the 1920s. Money poured in, along with people eager to spend it. The population mushroomed from 177,662 in 1940 to 278,778 a decade later. Beer joints, motels, and night clubs on the Jacksboro Highway stayed open, sometimes illegally, around the clock to serve the crowds.

A district attorney said Fort Worth was known as "Little Chicago." In the 1950s gambling and gangland slayings were frequent events. Reporter Mack Williams wrote, "Crime became organized, mean, and played for big stakes."[10]

Honor among thieves was a myth. Gamblers robbed other gamblers. After all, what gambler would file charges when he himself was awaiting trial for a crime? Gang lords with shotguns and submachine guns battled over money and turf.

When someone got too big for his britches, he just disappeared, leaving police to find his abandoned, blood-soaked car in a parking lot somewhere. Usually within a few days or weeks they would get an anonymous tip and find what was left of the unfortunate person in a well or shallow grave. Former Police Chief R. R. Howerton, ninety-three years old, recalling that period in the city, said, "Those were wild and wooly times."[11]

It took twenty years and events such as the Nelson Harris bombing for the clergy and city fathers to change "Little Chicago" back to "Cowtown."

Chapter 2

They Called it
"Thunder Road"

At midcentury, in the three and a half miles separating gambler Tiffin Hall's Mexican Inn Cafe from gambler Lester Hutt's Skyline Drive Motel, the Jacksboro Highway sported eighteen eating places, six liquor stores, seven night clubs, and ten motels, or, as they were called in those days, tourist courts. All were eager to capture the business and money of visitors and locals.

Nestled among this array was the 2222 Club owned by gambler William C. Kirkwood, and the plush 3939 Club run by Hutt and Benny Binion's friend Bert Wakefield. A real estate office belonged to gambler H. D. "Red" Oden. Off the 5100 block of the highway, in the village of Sansom Park, five gamblers lived within a three block area.

Beyond Roberts Cut Off Road toward Lake Worth and Azle was a popular final resting place for gangsters taken for a "ride." No wonder the Jacksboro Highway was called "Thunder Road." It held the title of the toughest, wildest piece of real estate in Texas.

Just outside the city limits, during holidays such as the Fourth of July and New Year's, fireworks stands popped up like weeds after a spring rain. If someone had carelessly tossed a live cigarette, the resulting explosion could have blown the water right out of Lake Worth. With gasoline at only $.17 a gallon in 1954, thrill seekers drove out to the Jacksboro Highway to buy cherry bombs, Black Cat firecrackers, and Roman candles.

The highway had no regular residences. People who ran the various clubs lived in the few houses near their businesses. There was no reason to have a grocery store. Over the hillside to the east was Fort Worth's North Side. Eventually the community of River Oaks developed to the west of the strip.

Beyond the Casino Ballroom, toward Jacksboro, the counties were dry. Prevailing attitudes about alcohol in these rural counties fattened the wallets of more than one entrepreneur. Texas Highway 199 reached from Fort Worth to dry West Texas. Bootleggers loaded up their big, high-powered Buicks, Cadillacs, and Lincolns on the Jacksboro Highway before making the 200 to 300 mile run to counties where even beer sales were illegal. It was such a common sight that any automobile with a trunk loaded down was considered a bootlegger's car.

West Texans came in to sell cattle, get drunk, maybe land in jail, sober up, get provisions, and head back to the ranch. Oil field roughnecks with money to spend were welcomed.

Ladies' companionship was plentiful and "no-tell" motels were nearby. "Let's spend an hour at the Tower" was the slogan among the rednecks and roughnecks. Others claimed there was more sex on the parking lot of the Albatross Club than in any of the tourist courts along the highway.

Revelers could drink and dance at the Barrel, the Black Cat, the Casino, the Coconut Grove, Massey's, the Rocket, the Skyliner, or the Showboat. Tex Beneke got his start playing on the strip. Harry James and Benny Goodman entertained crowds at the more upscale clubs, and a skinny kid from New Jersey named Sinatra came to town with Tommy Dorsey.

At one of the better clubs, the dining and dancing was merely a cover for the gambling. One young couple stopped in for dinner and the bouncer, a brute of a man dressed in a tuxedo, inquired if they had reservations. They replied they did not. "Sorry, we're full up," he said. Seeing that it was early in the dinner hour and only two tables were occupied, they questioned the need for reservations. The bouncer got right in the face of the young man and repeated, "I *said* we're full up." The couple may not have realized having reservations was the entry code, but they understood a menacing look when they saw one and took their business elsewhere.

Diners who had "reservations" were led past a rack of parted coats in the cloakroom and through a locked door leading to the gambling area. Blackjack, craps, and roulette were available for the "diners."

Another story tells of the time the father of a member of a dance band, dressed in boots, jeans, and a Stetson, stopped by with a message for his son. Within ninety seconds after getting out of a battered old pickup, the gambling equipment was collapsed into recesses in the floor, the floor moved back into place, and all of it covered with an area rug that matched the decor. The lookout had mistaken him for an undercover Texas Ranger and sounded the alarm.

In the 1940s defense plant workers and those from the Armour and Swift meat packing houses mingled with bootleggers, gamblers, politicians, and prostitutes. The beer was cold; the action was hot. After the war, well into the fifties, it was the place for anyone seeking a little adventure.

Slot machines and marble boards, also called pinball machines, were in plain sight. Back room card and dice games could easily be found. For the high rollers, the Four Deuces (2222) and the 3939 Club were the places with the action. A *Dallas Morning News* reporter, out for a story, played at several places. In two of the clubs he visited, he was recognized as a reporter and still shot craps and placed bets on horses. Alas, he was turned away from the 2222 Club. He didn't look rich enough.

In reminiscing about the "good old bad days," Pat Kirkwood, who grew up at 2222 Jacksboro Highway, said he would gauge the economy from the roof of his father's gambling joint. "If it was a three-ambulance evening, money was a little tight."[1] Seven or eight ambulance calls meant people were partying and cash registers were ringing.

A Carswell Air Force sergeant told his recruits if they got into trouble on the Jacksboro Highway they were on their own. It was too rough for him.

Leon Rausch, former singer with the famous Bob Wills and his Texas Playboys, told of after-hours on the highway. He said dancers and musicians made their way to all-night clubs, and although drinking was against the law after curfew, they smuggled in liquor and the merriment continued until dawn. He admitted he didn't hang around much because it was too tough for him.

A guitar player recalled the time a fight started on the dance floor and bottles flew onto the bandstand. To escape, the musicians used a microphone stand to break a window, then crawled to the safety of the parking lot.

Before he hit the big time, Willie Nelson sang at a place that stretched chicken wire across the bandstand, protecting musicians from unruly customers and flying objects.

Another musician told of a drunken cowboy, complete with ten-gallon hat, who got overly obnoxious. The bouncer decked him and ordered him to leave, but the cowboy crawled around looking for his hat. Thinking he found it, he started to put a spittoon on his head, but the bouncer took pity on him and helped him and his hat to the door. Such was life on the highway.

Others who worked or played on the strip remembered its heyday. "They weren't all killers, they just loved to fight. . . .The further you went, the badder it got. You could get into anything you were big enough to handle." One man said, "I'd drive my wrecker out to pick up their cars, and I'd take pictures of the murder victims for the sheriff's office."[2]

Associated Press writer Mike Cochran related this story of Jacksboro justice:

> At roughly 2:30 one morning, a Jacksboro Highway club owner who demands anonymity left the Scoreboard Lounge after attending a wedding party for a friend. In the parking lot, two punks stuck a knife at his throat, took his money and his ring, roughed him up and left him lying on the ground.
>
> "We ought to kill you," one said.
>
> "You damn sure should," the victim gasped.
>
> The assailants laughed and left.
>
> Later, after paying $250 to a stoolie, the club owner tracked down one of the muggers outside a beer joint. Luring him into his darkened car, he "extracted" an eyeball and a substantial number of teeth and shot off both of the guy's kneecaps. Then he dumped him in front of a hospital and drove away.[3]

When asked if he knew the identity of the club owner, Pat Kirkwood said he knew two or three that were mean enough, but declined to name names.[4]

Attorney Byron Matthews told of the brawniness of Elmer Sharp. "Nobody ever whipped him . . . he was just tough." Another

Jacksboro Highway character Elmer Sharp
—Courtesy of Fort Worth Star-Telegram Photograph Collection,
The University of Texas at Arlington Libraries

chimed, "Elmer Sharp was so tough he wrestled his pet bear. But his mama was tougher."[5]

The name "Elmer Sharp" drew responses that ranged from grins to guffaws. Then the stories would roll. "One time a guy shot him six times. Elmer beat him up so bad he was hospitalized longer than Elmer."[6]

Sharp was a short, pudgy, muscle man. If he had been part of the Mafia he would have been an enforcer. He operated a "private club" out of the garage of his home on the Jacksboro Highway. It opened after midnight and stayed open until the last customer left. Elmer didn't bother with legalities like a liquor license, but the law didn't seem to mind. After playing gigs at the various clubs on the highway, musicians wandered over to Elmer's for a few drinks.

At his place a customer would put a $10 bill on the bar and order a beer. According to a retired defense attorney who knew Elmer well, the customer was told, "You got more beer coming." If anyone insisted on his change, Elmer came out from behind the bar and "convinced" the man he didn't really want his change *or* another beer.

Asher Rone hired Sharp as a bouncer. If a man got out of line, he could literally pick him up and throw him out the door. Once, four robbers held up Asher at his Black Cat Cafe, and he came out from behind the horseshoe-shaped counter firing his .45. When Sharp heard the shots, he was next door at the Avalon Court with one of Rone's waitresses. He came running down the gravel drive-way wearing only his candy-striped shorts, and as each would-be robber backed out of the cafe, Elmer hit him in the head. When the police got there all four were lined up against the building.

In the melee Rone was shot in the stomach and hustled off to the hospital. Then the police turned their attention to the crime scene. To their astonishment, the four subdued men had no wallets, watches, or rings. "Elmer had robbed the robbers and stashed the stuff in a nearby shrub."[7]

George Wilderspin told of the time burglars broke into Sharp's home. Elmer's wife wanted him to chase them away before they got anything, but business had been slow and Elmer had a better idea. "Just lay quiet, Maydell," he said. "Lay quiet. Let them get inside, maybe they got some money on them."[8]

Someone once said of Elmer, "if his brains wuz castor oil, he couldn't physic a red ant." But he knew how to make money. He bought a carload of cheap suits from an outlet store for $5.00 each. After removing the labels he went around to pool halls and honky-tonks peddling "stolen imported suits" for up to $25.00.

Elmer wasn't the only tough guy on the highway. One night at the Black Cat a gambler-veterinarian who always carried two pairs of brass knuckles, was shooting dice after hours. Everybody got pretty drunk and the bouncer tried to throw them out. The bouncer reached into his back pocket like he was going to pull a pistol, and the veterinarian hit him with the brass knuckles. The bouncer slid across the floor into the cigarette machine. The machine fell on him and his coat sleeve got caught under the machine and torn off. The next day the bouncer's wife called complaining to the bartender. Her side of the conversation was, "He just got the sleeve tangled up in the cigarette machine and when they got the machine off of him, the sleeve tore." He listened to the caller. "Well, what do you want me to do?" He paused. "Okay, a new suit. Do you want me to find the damn sleeve?" Evidently her answer was yes. "Was there an arm in it?"[9]

At one Jacksboro Highway beer joint a half dozen bare bulb

lights were strung from the telephone pole to the front of the building. Several patrons, after a few beers, started betting who could shoot the most bulbs. They took out their pistols and began firing from the front door. After a couple of bulbs had been hit, one marksman accidently hit the electric wire and all the lights went out. He declared himself the winner.

Such were the stories and characters of Thunder Road. The police called it the Jax Beer Highway. It finally got such a bad name that even patrons of the classier clubs were hesitant to go there. Musician Bill Luttrell summed up the demise, "The bands wouldn't play there unless they lost work and didn't have anywhere else to go."[10]

By the 1960s the Big Band sound was a pleasant memory. Rock and roll assaulted the ears of all but the younger generation. The folks who danced under the stars at the Rocket Club stayed home to watch *I Love Lucy* on black and white television sets. Auto junkyards and used furniture stores sprang up where once there was glitz and glitter. Many of the club owners had gone to that Big Honky-Tonk in the Sky (or elsewhere), and the buildings were run-down eyesores.

The final nail in the coffin came in the form of a Caterpillar tractor. A six-lane parkway, complete with grassy median strips, covered what remained.

Chapter 3

Search Begins for
"Hidden Gambling"

As gambling became more and more open, church leaders and some city council members called for a cleanup of places on the Jacksboro Highway and elsewhere. Spurred by public outcry or the need to look vigilant, city and county lawmen made periodic raids and arrests. Their efforts ranged from ineffective to outright comical.

A three-inch newspaper clipping dating back to 1934 hailed the arrest of five men charged with gambling. In what seemed to be the rule rather than the exception, they were no-billed for lack of evidence. Thus Claud Green escaped prosecution for alleged gambling at the Ringside Club. Tony Loicano and others were charged with keeping premises for gambling in the 1000 block of Main Street. They also walked. The grand jury deemed there was insufficient evidence to warrant a trial. This was not the last time the Ringside Club and the Loicano family would come to the attention of law officers.

Just three years later city councilman W. J. Hammond demanded that gambling be shut down; law officers promised they would if they could find any. Looking at dozens of places along the Jacksboro Highway would have been a good start. The East Side Club, Turf Club, the Top O' Hill Terrace, and numerous country clubs kept slot machines. Downtown hotels such as the Blackstone, Seibold, and

Westbrook always had dice games. Tiffin Hall leased the entire second floor of the downtown Commercial Hotel for his games.

City Manager George Fairtrace was quoted as saying that if gambling could be found, ". . . of course we'll wipe it out. But we honestly don't know of any going on now."[1]

One councilman suggested taxing the gambling equipment the police were unable to find. Another nixed the idea for fear that taxing the marble boards and other gambling devices would give the phantom machines legal status. This scenario made the newspapers for a few days, then died from lack of interest.

As the city geared up for the Texas Centennial, gambling became even more open and widespread. In August 1937 vice squad officers arrested seven men in the downtown Insurance Building. Another five were arrested in a building at Fifth and Main. Police raided the Petroleum Building and netted nine more. The operator of the game in the Petroleum Building fired his lookout. "You sit there and look for a man in a white hat and two six-shooters and let these city cops walk right by you,"[2] he snarled.

Six months later, one floor up in the same building, nineteen were arrested. Officers confiscated over $1,200, an improvised dice table, and nine chairs. Raids continued, fines were collected, and the gamblers took a few days off before setting up shop in the same or nearby locations.

E'gildo Lanzarotti left his native Italy after World War I seeking a better living for himself and his family. He settled in Fort Worth and for a while worked at a macaroni factory. By the late 1930s Mac, as he came to be known, opened a pool hall on E. Broadway and ran a poker game in the back. His son recalled the time a black and white squad car pulled up to the pool hall. The uniformed policeman said, "God dang, Mac, you got to put up a partition across that damn poker table back there. Hell, anybody walking down the street can look over that painted window and tell what you're doing. Hell, that's real embarrassing."[3] He meant embarrassing to the police, not to Mac.

Another push in 1944 made the front pages. "Gamblers Are Rounded Up by Rangers in 8 Raids,"[4] was one of the headlines. Lawmen arrested a total of 107 persons. While gambling might have been an equal opportunity activity, arrests were not. The November 4 *Fort Worth Star-Telegram* noted, "All the men Rangers arrested were white men."[5] The local cops arrested the Negroes, the reporter noted.

Blacks and whites paid $10.00 fines and were released. Prominent businessmen, such as "Frank Freshair" were released on appearance bonds.

Lanzarotti's son said that in 1944 or 1945 some company, he didn't know the name of it, put a slot machine in his father's downtown pool hall, the Fort Worth Recreation Club. It was located at Twelfth and Main, across the street from the Gusher Cafe and only blocks from the police station. In the summers he worked at the pool hall. One night the phone rang and the fifteen-year-old picked up the receiver.

"Pool hall."

"Who's speaking?"

"This is Louie."

"Are you Mac's boy?"

Lanzarotti's son answered in the affirmative, and was told that in about thirty minutes two uniformed policemen would be there. "It's nothing to get excited about. They're just going to look around." The caller told him to go back and pull the door over the slot machine. He did as he was told and within the hour two policemen came in, walked around, and left.

He said he never knew who the caller was, but he assumed it was someone from the slot machine company.[6] When asked if his father paid off the police, he said he had seen such payoffs but he didn't know how much money was involved. It just seemed a natural part of doing business.

A few years later Lanzarotti operated a cafe in River Oaks. He ran a poker game upstairs, had a pinball machine that paid off in cash, and had punch boards. The son remembered a truck driver who stopped in for lunch. He dropped $60.00 playing the punch board—more money than most working people made in a week. One River Oaks police chief questioned what was going on when there were more cars in the parking lot than customers in the cafe, but nothing came of it.

R. E. Dysart became Fort Worth chief of police in May 1945. Under his direction, arrests for gambling went from 138 in the first five months of the year to 2,246 the next five months. Business was brisk at Corporation Court, as nearly $7,000 in bonds was forfeited. To the gamblers involved, this was merely overhead expense. Dysart held as tight a rein on his men as the mayor and city council allowed him. Apparently it wasn't tight enough.

By 1949 gambling had become so brazen that another public relations attempt was made. A grand jury spent the month of May hearing from gamblers and law officers. This followed a request by a city councilman for an investigation into possible gambling graft within the city. Chief Dysart, Sheriff Sully Montgomery, Lake Worth Constable Paul Meador, and other officials appeared before the panel.

Dysart, Montgomery, and Meador were joined by several club and tavern owners. All swore innocence. When asked the reason for their appearance, District Attorney Hellman refused to comment.

Among those questioned was a club owner who told of paying $500 a month to the district attorney's office for protection. Yet another paid a similar amount to an attorney who served as a go-between.

Meanwhile, Police Lt. George Hawkins reported arresting twenty Negroes for gaming in a back room on E. Ninth Street. They posted $10 cash bonds and were released. Hawkins said his men found no other evidence of gambling. He failed to mention that when the vice squad planned a raid, at least a dozen people knew when and where the raids would occur.

Carl Freund and another reporter from an afternoon paper complained to Sheriff Sully Montgomery about the timing of raids. "When you raid before midnight, the morning paper reporters get the scoop. Give us a break. Stage a raid at 2:00 A.M. and that way we'll be the first to report it." Montgomery's response was, "I've been fair with you. Why not raid early and go home and get some sleep? I'm giving you a break. I'm telling you I'm going to raid the 3939 Club tonight at 11:40."[7]

One beer joint owner told about his warning system. He stationed an employee in the parking lot in a car that had a rope tied to a bell inside. He was instructed to pull the rope if law enforcement officers approached. Texas Rangers got wise to the setup and slipped in behind the man. "Don't touch that rope," he was ordered. The owner paid a fine and was out of jail the same day.

Even when a club didn't get a tip on an impending raid, things could go wrong. One vice officer investigating a game in the 800 block of Main Street walked in and found six men gambling. They scattered in all directions, and he grumbled, "Too many doors in that place."

There was a gambling operation near the old Southwest International Airport so open that even Governor Price Daniel got complaints about it. He ordered the Rangers to shut it down. They said they were having trouble getting sufficient evidence. Daniel then turned the matter over to the Department of Public Safety's intelligence unit.

Two Houston agents came to Fort Worth, posing as oilmen. They checked into a well-known hotel and asked a bellman to direct them to "the action." An hour later they were playing at the targeted club. They made their cases and wanted to handle the arrests themselves. Director Homer Garrison vetoed the idea as being a slap in the face to the Rangers. Instead, he told them not to involve the Rangers until the last minute to prevent a tip-off.

They followed orders, and with a Texas Ranger headed out to make the arrests. On the way the Ranger who was driving said he needed to stop and buy gasoline. While in the service station he was observed making a phone call. They arrived at the club, and burst in shouting "This is a raid." About a minute later the club's telephone rang. A DPS man answered and heard, "They're getting ready to bust you. You better shut down." He replied, "Sorry, you're a couple of minutes too late." The caller was heard to mutter a disgusted, "Oh hell."[8]

Even with a slightly tainted white-hat reputation, the Texas Rangers were more successful at finding hidden gambling than city and county officers. The day after Hawkins claimed the city was clean, Rangers filed five complaints for slot machine operations and five complaints for a card game. The operator paid $63 for the card game and $14 for each of the slot machine citations, then it was back to business as usual.

At the same time of this raid, Hawkins said he checked "about 50 places," and found only one slot machine. It was a 5-cent variety, confiscated from a place on the Weatherford Highway. More for show than an attempt to stamp out gambling, fifteen men and women were arrested at 1510 Houston Street. This action took place only five blocks from the police station.

In 1949 Chief Dysart promised to investigate Councilman M. M. McKnight's concern about graft. He threatened that if he found any evidence of payoffs in the department, "[he would] see that the public knows about it."[9] His men on the take made sure he didn't find any evidence.

A *Fort Worth Press* reporter checked county records and discovered more than twelve months had passed since a charge of operating a gambling house had been filed. The last case filed, and still on the books, had never been tried. This proved the lack of serious effort on law enforcement's part, the reporter maintained.

Rev. Karl Bracker, president of the local General Ministers Association, was also skeptical of police efforts. He told the City Council, "For the past year, we have been investigating vice conditions. . . . Prostitution, slot machines and pinball machines and obscene literature can be found in all sections of our city."[10] He went on to question how these conditions could exist short of widespread payoffs.

Reverend Bracker said he had received dozens of anonymous tips concerning the locations of slot machines and marble boards. The callers would not give their names because they feared retaliation, he explained. The minister gave authorities a list of places where he or his congregation had observed gambling devices in operation.

Pressure from church and civic groups escalated. Bowing to the pressure, District Attorney Stewart Hellman announced his office had been working on the problem for a week or ten days. Casting doubt on the information supplied by Rev. Bracker, the district attorney stressed the need to get provable facts, not rumor or hearsay. Hellman did not indicate he planned to subpoena any witnesses.

Assistant district attorney A. L. Wardlaw, who was in charge of the grand jury, issued an invitation to citizens to tell what they knew about the situation. A special session was scheduled, and the jury waited almost two hours.

Not a single witness appeared. Perhaps they didn't have row boats. This was May 16, 1949, the day of the worst flood in Fort Worth's history. The Clear Fork of the Trinity River covered almost all of the lowlands in the area. Montgomery Ward, on West Seventh Street, suffered water damage on the second floor of its eight-story retail and catalog building.

Satisfied there was no gambling, Wardlaw led the jurors to another matter. He turned their attention to the case of Norman D. Bailey. The former Dallas policeman was charged with attempting to bribe City Councilman McKnight. He claimed a New York syndicate would pay $500 a month if allowed to run gambling in the city. The fifty-two-year-old Dallasite was no-billed. Upon further examination of the hapless man, it was found he had been confined to a Waco veterans' hospital mental ward.

Grand jury deliberations continued throughout the summer. In August, bookmaking charges were brought against Tom Daly,

Clyde Neal, and Robert Kemper. They were arrested in raids led by Chief Dysart on two downtown locations. The cost of gambling had gone up. They were required to post $1,000 bonds.

On page one of the *Dallas Morning News*, October 8, 1950, reporter Harry McCormick wrote of his recent excursions into Tarrant County. "Wide open gambling—dice, horse race bookmaking, slot machines or roulette—has been running unmolested in Fort Worth and Tarrant County."[11]

Making no effort to hide his identity, McCormick played blackjack at a downtown club in the heart of the business district. Going to a bar with a sports theme, he noted loud speakers hawking odds, and positions of the horses. Results from tracks in New York and New Jersey were posted on big scoreboards hanging on the walls. The reporter lost $6.30. Next he moved on to an East Side club where he won $58 at a dice table. He recognized many Dallas citizens among the customers at all the clubs he visited.

Ironically, McCormick found Jacksboro Highway to be well policed. On the three trips he made for his story, he saw two Texas Highway Patrolmen, two motorcycle police officers, and two policemen in a squad car. Cadillacs on the parking lots of the more upscale clubs were as common as bicycles at an elementary school. Many of the high-priced autos sported Dallas County numbers.

"Impossible!" said Tarrant County lawmen. Privately they wished the troublemaker would stay on his side of the Trinity. They certainly didn't want him to appear before the grand jury. They feared he might divulge names and addresses of those involved.

Sheriff Montgomery and Assistant Police Chief R. R. Howerton assured the public they arrested gamblers when they found them. They claimed there simply wasn't much gambling going on in Tarrant County. Chief Hawkins, who replaced Dysart in late 1949, called the report of widespread gambling "bunk."

The minister of St. John's Evangelical Church was unimpressed with Hawkins' and Montgomery's assurances. In a scathing sermon, he likened their efforts to heroic raiding of minnow tanks.

The day after the *Dallas Morning News* story, the *Fort Worth Star-Telegram* quoted District Attorney Hellman as saying: "Tarrant County has been singularly blessed by being free of violence that has marked gambling activity in Dallas."[12] He didn't deny the existence of gambling, just violent gambling. However, attitudes changed with the bombing death of Nelson Harris six weeks later.

Chapter 4

The Killing Begins

The November 22, 1950, car bomb deaths of Nelson Harris and his twenty-five-year-old wife, Juanita, sent shock waves throughout the community. Eight blocks away from the scene of the crime, the blast rattled windows at West Van Zandt Elementary School. Three miles south, a housewife hanging out diapers on her backyard clothesline wondered what caused the explosion.

Neighbors and civic leaders angrily denounced the cowardly action. It was one thing to kill a gambler, they argued, but quite another to kill a young woman in her eighth month of pregnancy.

* * *

In the late 1930s Harris, still in his teens, worked as a bouncer in bars and clubs on the Jacksboro Highway and downtown. He came to the attention of the courts when he was convicted of being a delivery man for the notorious, nationwide Green Dragon Dope Syndicate. Only twenty years old, Nelson was known as "the Kid." In July 1940 he was lectured by the presiding judge on the evils of the drug traffic and given a two year sentence.[1] The federal penitentiary at Levenworth, Kansas, became the learning ground for his later exploits.

The car bombing of Nelson Harris and his wife blew the lid off crime and corruption in Fort Worth.
—Photo courtesy of Henry H. Wright

In the spring of 1945, Harris was fined $1,000 and his license was suspended for thirty days for serving mixed drinks at his club, Nelson's Place, 2238 Jacksboro Highway. He was enjoined from operating a place selling alcohol, including beer, without a bond.

From that time until his death five years later, he divorced one woman and married Juanita Bean of Cisco. She had been a waitress at his Jacksboro Highway place. Harris and Juanita lived in several Texas towns, including Eastland, Midland, and Odessa, operating cafes and taverns. At times he worked in the oil fields and at construction sites. Also, according to law officers, he gambled and ran petty rackets.

Returning to Fort Worth around 1948, he was employed at different clubs. At one time he and Tom Daly ran the Ringside Club. Later Harris served as a "yardman" at the Four Deuces, where he screened incoming customers. If he knew them and they had the right connections, they were allowed entrance. If they were curiosity seekers or people without proper references, they were turned away. It was his responsibility to step on a hidden buzzer if lawmen approached the premises. This warning gave Pappy Kirkwood time to get illegal gambling equipment out of sight.

At the time of his death he was believed to be associated with the 2929 Club, on Crockett Street on Fort Worth's West Side. Nelson's first wife, Jessie, told police he gave her his card, "2929," and told her to call him there if she ever needed him in an emergency. But the manager of the club refuted that contention, saying "Harris never owned one bit of this place. He never was in here except a couple of times, and then just to pass the time of day."[2] The 2929 Club was licensed as the West Side Recreation Club in Marion Hopper's name, so perhaps the manager was telling the truth.

Harris also reportedly had Houston connections. He asked a friend to drive him to Houston and back one night. Harris explained he was exhausted from lack of sleep, but it was imperative that he see someone in the channel city. The friend turned him down because his own wife was expecting a baby at any time and he didn't want to leave her alone. This was just days before Harris was killed.

After the bombing, his mother-in-law told police she thought he worked for an oil refinery. "He never said anything about gambling. Juanita never talked about his business either," she added.[3]

The bombing itself was the work of a professional. Jack Nesbit, a known "nitro man," was suspected, but never charged. The explosion outside Harris' duplex apartment shattered the quiet in the peaceful residential neighborhood.

Detonated when he turned on his car's ignition switch, the nitroglycerin bomb killed him instantly. The force of the blast almost decapitated him. His eyes were blown out, and his body was embedded into the car's upholstery. Mrs. Harris, face blackened and her body pierced with metal fragments, was rushed to the hospital. She died forty minutes later, and her unborn child was declared dead.

A crowd of 1,000 people jammed nearby streets and craned their necks trying to see the carnage. Windows in neighboring apartments were broken, and debris littered the street and front yards three houses away. The car battery was blown through a window, spraying acid on a baby lying in his crib. Kitchens in two adjoining apartments received severe damage and a piece of metal from the car was blown through the frame wall of a neighbor's house.

Battery acid also covered the door leading into the Harris' apartment. Mack Williams, a *Fort Worth Star-Telegram* reporter, just out of the service and wearing a new civilian suit, was careful not to touch the door with his bare hand. He was not so careful with his sleeve. The acid made quick work of the fabric and he was left with a one-sleeved suit coat.

As if the sensational bombing wasn't enough to occupy newsmen, the same day a B36 bomber crashed in Johnson County. Reporters were calling in the latest details on both the bomber and the bombing. Reporters at the *Fort Worth Press* and *Fort Worth Star-Telegram* were scrambling to keep the stories separate and straight.

Inside the Harris apartment, an autographed picture of Sheriff Sully Montgomery was the first thing that caught reporter Williams' eye. The inscription read, "To my good friends, Nelson and Juanita." Montgomery admitted knowing Harris for about twenty years, but insisted they weren't close. "He used to come into the office sometimes to visit, but we didn't run around together or anything like that,"[4] he said.

In an unpublished story, a police reporter told of a telephone call to Harris' unlisted number shortly after the blast. He picked up the phone and heard a gruff voice warn, "Tell the S.O.B.'s friends they'll get the same."[5]

※ ※ ※

The very nature of the game requires successful gamblers to be con artists. They must convince clients that the next roll of the dice will be a winner. They are friendly, outgoing, and good company. Nelson Harris was one of the most personable of the bunch.

Most who knew him described Harris as a nice, ordinary fellow who always wore a suit and tie. Few saw him as a major player in the Fort Worth crime scene. Nevertheless, the underworld grapevine ordered everyone to "clam up." Police Detective Captain Howard

Grant was quoted as saying Harris was a "likable clean-cut man of many friends and acquaintances."[6]

Evidently he had at least one enemy, and the police had a major crime to solve. In the days immediately following the murders, detectives combed the city trying to look busy.

As failure is an orphan, a fallen comrade is a former friend. "I didn't know him very well." "Haven't seen ol' Nelson in years." "I ain't got nothin' to say," were typical responses around town. W. C. Kirkwood denied Harris was a regular employee. He said the slain man parked cars for tips. "I finally had to let him go because I had evidence he was operating a call girl service—some sort of white slave racket—on the side."[7]

Under pressure from the media and city manager to do something, lawmen quizzed notorious badman LeRoy (Tincy) Eggleston and Dallas gambler Herbert Noble. Neither cast any light on the bombing.

United States Senator Estes Kefauver's crime investigating committee looked into the possibility of an organized crime connection. The police chief, sheriff, and district attorney assured the committee it was a local matter. However, they were having a harder time hewing to their previous avowal that there was no gambling in the county.

Mrs. J. G. Bean, Juanita's mother, had been staying with the couple as they awaited the imminent birth of their first child. She told investigators Harris was in good spirits and never spoke of threats or trouble in his business. The white-haired widow said the three of them visited a carpenter friend of Nelson's the night before the bombing. They returned to the Wingate duplex about 10:00 P.M. and went to bed.

Other sources revealed a darker scenario. "'He had been bucking floating crap games with Noble's money,' one gambler told the *Star-Telegram*, 'and somebody got tired of it.'"[8] Harris was also wanted for questioning in a West Texas burglary at the time of his death.

Fort Worth attorneys Doss and Ross Hardin revealed Harris placed three calls to them the night before his death, and one that morning. He indicated he needed to see them on a matter of "life and death." Harris had recently been seen with narcotics dealers, but the Hardins indicated they didn't know what the calls were about.

Nelson and Juanita Harris were buried side by side in DeLeon,

Texas, where Harris was born. The ninety-seat chapel was full to overflowing as two families tearfully bade farewell to their loved ones. Among the mourners was Jesse Harris, Nelson's first wife.

Police found leads hard to come by, but a local newspaper received information linking Harris to a gambling deal gone sour in Odessa. The unnamed source, known only as a night club owner, said Harris wanted to operate games in the club. The owner stressed he wanted no part of Harris or gambling in his place. He also mentioned gambler Jim Thomas as a partner in the scheme.

Two weeks later police brought in a dozen local gamblers and associates for a full day of questioning. The twelve were picked up at unnamed gambling spots in the same county where a week before officials had declared there was no gambling.

The men brought in for questioning—James (Jim) Thomas, Carl Tiffin Hall, Howard Stripling, John Reynolds, George Wilderspin, A. R. (Bob) Floyd, Elmer Sharp, Grady Whitehead, Robert Whitehead, Ernest Hayes, Dick Crownover, and Tincy Eggleston—made the front page of the newspapers. But that was about all that was accomplished. Chief George Hawkins said, "We didn't find anyone who seemed to be mad at anyone else. . . ."[9] Raiding officers reportedly searched the gamblers' homes and businesses, but found nothing. Police dismissed the men without charges.

At the court house the investigation developed a life of its own. The grand jury went beyond probing the bombing, and delved into matters that caused discomfort to more than one elected official. Spurred by a Dallas newspaper's October 8 front page exposé of gambling in Tarrant County, the grand jurors began to ask embarrassing questions like, why did Nelson Harris have a card in his wallet identifying him as a special deputy sheriff? Why would an ex-con and known gambler have two personally autographed pictures of Sheriff Sully Montgomery? The good sheriff claimed ignorance concerning the card. He had been on vacation at the time of the bombing, but he would "do a little checking."

The January 1951 grand jury, headed by Ray Finney, became interested in one of Nelson's notes. A memo, written on the back of a cafe business card, listed several Fort Worth police officers and payoff amounts. "Capt. Durd (*sic*) 30.00; Howard 50.00; Burk 30.00; Lt. Etel (*sic*) 25.00. . . Vice 125.00. . . ."[10] City council members demanded an explanation. Chief Hawkins assured his boss, City Manager W. O. Jones, that everything possible would be done to uncover possible graft or payoffs. He said this with a straight face which must have brought snickers to every gambler in town. Carl Freund reported, "Police Chief George Hawkins told *The Press* he had complete confidence in the men named and planned to take no action at this time."[11]

Capts. Karl Howard, R. H. Burks and J. B. Derden, and Lts. Ed Lee and D. W. Bevil, and Sgt. V. O. Cox denied having any dealings with Harris. Attorney Ross Hardin claimed he made the names of these men public to hasten the discovery of the murderer.

Within a week the mayor posted a $1,000 reward for information leading to the arrest and conviction of any cop on the take. Councilmen also passed a resolution asking the grand jury to broaden its scope to include alleged payoffs.

The *Fort Worth Star-Telegram* obtained bank records of a former police vice squad officer who deposited $3,880.94 in his account during a two-month period. In another document, he listed a "$35 to $40" checking account. This same officer wrote four checks, totaling $90 which were deposited by coin machine companies. These actions were clearly suspicious, but Chief Hawkins announced the day after that the man had been selling some cattle he owned. The money had come from doing legitimate business, he explained.

The actual murder investigation of Nelson Harris took a back seat to the revelations about widespread gambling and corruption at both the city and county levels of law enforcement. On February 23, 1951, Austin Harris was summoned to appear before the grand jury and bring thirteen record and ledger books belonging to his late brother. The books purportedly contained information on dice games and payoffs.

In one of the notebooks passed to the grand jury, Harris listed financial records, telephones numbers, and personal reminders. Among the jottings in the newspaper article were, "One page of the book showed 'raid numbers' and listed the home and office telephone numbers of numerous law enforcement officers.... Another entry said, 'Check—about special deputy cards for the boys.' ... A two-line entry . . . apparently referred to crooked dice said, 'Get 6-ace flats and fade-a-ways (pass outs)'"[12]

A confidence man, whose IQ was about the size of his hat band, decided to cash in on the search for Harris' killer. In a downtown tavern he boasted he knew who did it and had a suitcase of evidence he would sell to a reporter for $4. Passing on the opportunity to surely win a Pulitzer prize, the doubtful reporter called police. An investigation revealed the man was wanted in Montague County for swindling. He was jailed and later handed over to those authorities.

Four and a half months after the bombing, Chief of Detectives H. Clay Bishop announced progress was being made on finding the Harrises' killer. Police had narrowed the suspects down to two, he said. He didn't name them.

One theory, not espoused by the police, held that Tincy Eggleston killed Harris and planted a bomb in his own car to throw off suspicion. An informant told of the two quarreling over money gained in a divorce scam. It seemed they agreed to accept property from an unnamed oil man who wanted to cheat his soon-to-be ex-wife out of part of their community property. He deeded mineral rights and other valuable assets to Eggleston and Harris for the duration of the divorce proceedings.

After the divorce, they deeded the property back to the original owner and pocketed a tidy fee for their services. But greed reared its ugly head. Tincy supposedly didn't like the split. He and Harris argued. It wasn't long before Harris' fragmented body made the front page of the newspapers.

Another theory held that "the Syndicate," a nationwide crime organization, was behind the bombing. Apparently Harris had mouthed off to the wrong people when the Syndicate tried to take over Tarrant County crime. In testimony to a grand jury, Jay Harris named Tiffin Hall as the kingpin of organized gambling. He said his brother refused to work for the man, ". . . he (Nelson) thought Hall was a lieutenant in the gambling empire of Nevada rackateer Benny Binion."[13]

Yet another possibility was that Jack Nesbit, a former inmate of Kansas and Oklahoma prisons, planted the bomb. This theory was based on Nesbit's disappearance the day of the bombing.

Austin Harris vented his frustration at the lack of progress in the case. "I just want to see the killers of my brother caught. It doesn't seem like some of the officers do,"[14] he told *Fort Worth Press* reporter Carl Freund.

Despite Bishop's claim that the identity of the killer was at hand, no one went to trial for the bombing. Most people believed a gangster did it. The case is still open.

Chapter 5

Enter the Grand Jury

The Nelson Harris bombing led to the most far-reaching grand jury probe in the county's history. Traditionally, after three-month terms, the panel of jurors changed. But new juries kept hearing stories of gambling and payoffs. In early 1951 Ray Finney was elected foreman of the sitting grand jury. Finney, a long-time North Side resident, school board representative, and member of the Methodist Church, took his duties seriously.

Criminal District Court No. 2 Judge Dave McGee deplored the lack of respect for law in the county. He left no doubt he wanted this grand jury to do a better job than past juries. The judge offered legal assistance beyond that provided by the district attorney's office. He also wanted a through investigation of the November bombing deaths of Nelson and Juanita Harris.

The temperature dropped to zero degrees on the last day of January. Inside the courtroom, the inquiry into the deaths of Mr. and Mrs. Harris generated enough heat to singe the hides of several city and county officials.

Attorneys Doss and Ross Hardin dropped a bombshell when they released Harris' personal papers listing law enforcement personnel and amounts of money. The Hardins also revealed that someone had ransacked their law office in an attempt to get the documents, but the search was in vain. They wisely had secreted the records in multiple places for safekeeping.

Among Harris' notations was "Howard 50.00." Police Capt. Karl Howard challenged the disclosure, saying "I don't know anything about it. I've never had any dealing with Harris. And I've never taken payoffs from anybody."[1]

Jay Harris, a Midland barber and Nelson's brother, was brought before the grand jury. He had been in hiding since receiving threats against his life. He brought with him a trunk full of Nelson's private papers. Harris said "he would give them anything [the grand jury] may want," and testified for two hours in an unusual night session.

On Friday, February 16, the jury heard from a Baptist preacher and a vice squad sergeant, among other witnesses. The entire vice squad had been summoned, but only R. E. Pinkard testified. This was the same group that a traffic patrolman, now retired, described as "a joke."

Six weeks into the term there was talk of asking witnesses to voluntarily take lie detector tests. Referring to Nelson Harris' "little black books," Finney commented, "When bribes are made and payoffs consummated there are usually only two persons present, the one making the payoff and the one receiving the payoff."[2] Harris was dead, so obviously the foreman was referring to law enforcement officials.

Jay Harris recalled his brother complaining about cops always coming around for money. Protection was one of the biggest expenses in running games, he asserted. Approving the idea of the lie detector test, Harris noted, "They should pull in all the big time gamblers here and ask them to take it, because they've all been paying the cops."[3]

This brought howls of protest from William C. Kirkwood, owner of the 2222 Club since 1934. "Old Man Deen (the Mayor) knows we've never paid off anyone. . . . We've had no occasion to make payoffs. There may have been gambling at the club in 1944-45, when Bert Wakefield had it, but there hasn't been any since I've had it."[4] This statement was made the same day the *Fort Worth Press* published a story about the Senate Crime Investigating Committee. "A Chicago manufacturer of gambling equipment has told . . . names of his customers in Fort Worth and other Texas cities."[5] Among those was the 2222 Club. There was no indication Kirkwood volunteered to take a lie detector test.

Within a week of Kirkwood's denial, a member of the grand jury visited the club and observed a dice game. Four days later Chief George Hawkins admitted he had not checked the 2222 Club since becoming head of the police department. "But my men have and they've found no gambling there recently," he said."[6]

Pat Kirkwood laughed about the raids, saying they were always forewarned. When the police arrived, all the gambling equipment was out of sight. The scene looked like a cocktail party. When the vice squad left, the equipment was rolled out and the "cocktail party" reverted to the serious business of gambling.[7]

Jay Harris also pointed to gambler Tiffin Hall as the one who "knew plenty" about payoffs. He labeled Hall as the kingpin of gambling in Fort Worth. True, Hall's gambling had been a factor in the city since 1920, but Kirkwood, Fred Browning or Bert Wakefield could legitimately claim that infamous crown as well.

Harris concluded his attack on Hall by telling the grand jurors that Nelson refused to associate with the restaurant and hotel owner because he was believed to be a lieutenant in the Nevada syndicate headed by racketeer Benny Binion. Hall denied both allegations.

The payoff accusations led to an offer of help by an attorney from a neighboring county. "I know nothing about the local situation and know nothing about the grand jury and have no ax to grind," he said.[8] State Attorney General Daniel promised to assist if requested to do so. Finney admitted the jury would consider the offers. This was the first public indication of discord in the investigation.

Meanwhile, Jessie Harris, Nelson's ex-wife, revealed her life had been threatened. She claimed to have been told to deny that the lists of names and amounts produced by Jay Harris were Nelson's handwriting. Frightened, she packed and was ready to leave town. "I'm not foolish enough to stay around here after disputing certain people's word," she said.[9]

Mrs. Harris told the jurors, despite the threats against her life, that the lists of names of Fort Worth police officers were in Nelson Harris' handwriting. However, she doubted the dice game record recently introduced to the grand jury was in her ex-husband's hand. She said she had no idea who wrote the record in question.

After testifying, Jesse Harris went into hiding. Later, another witness suggested the record of the dice game might have been written by Juanita Harris, who kept the family books.

A man identified as a former friend of Nelson Harris gave the *Fort Worth Star-Telegram* a notebook he said he picked up at the site of the fatal bombing. Notations included financial data and telephone numbers of several city and county law enforcement officials. The telephone list was titled "Raid Nos."

Mrs. Georgia Fisher, a former waitress at a Camp Bowie Blvd. nightclub, related to newsmen how she had observed Chief Hawkins and Sheriff Montgomery separately talking with Nelson Harris. "They would sit in a booth with Nelson and talk over a cup of coffee for 10 or 15 minutes. (Then) they would get up and leave. I don't remember how many times each of them was there, but it was quite often."[10] She said these meetings usually took place before a new game started. Mrs. Fisher heard Harris say he paid off all of the little guys that patrolled the area, as well as "some pretty big names."

Another woman, also a former waitress at the club, was closeted with the jurors for thirty-five minutes. Described as a "mystery" witness, the short, stout, dark-haired woman ordered reporters to leave her alone as she left the courthouse.

On February 21 Police Chief George Hawkins, the sheriff, and ten secret witnesses were heard. When asked to comment on reports that jurors themselves had seen gambling in progress around town, the chief maintained his department was vigilant in shutting down vice whenever they found it. Sheriff Montgomery disavowed any knowledge of big-time gambling or payoffs in the county.

* * *

The investigation was being felt all the way to Austin. State Representative H. A. (Salty) Hull introduced a bill extending the term of the jury for as long as it would take to finish its work.

The case mounted against those sworn to uphold the law. Fear was palpable in the hearing room. Some witnesses, including Jay Harris, refused to testify if the district attorney or his assistants were in the room.

Judge Dave McGee met with grand jurors for more than an hour to find a solution to the problem. A compromise was reached—the district attorney could be present to consider the Harris slayings and other cases, but must remove himself when witnesses testified about gambling and payoffs. Veteran court reporter Lee

Henry was replaced. The judge refused to confirm rumors of a replacement for Mr. Hellman.

After a weekend recess, testimony resumed. District Attorney Hellman objected to the ouster, but agreed to leave the room when jurors requested him to.

Austin Harris, another brother of the slain gambler, appeared before the investigative body. He volunteered his testimony and expressed frustration at the lack of progress in solving the crime. "I just want to see the killers of my brother caught. It doesn't seem like some of the officers do," he said.[11] Like his brother Jay, he refused to talk in the presence of the district attorney, declaring he "didn't trust nobody." Following his testimony, he continued hiding in West Texas.

Finney and his fellow grand jurors then heard from Houston City Councilman Louis Welch. Volunteering to appear before the grand jury, the embarassed Sunday school teacher said he knew of nothing concrete. He said he had casually mentioned to a Fort Worth city employee that he certainly wasn't surprised that gambling was going on in Tarrant County and Fort Worth. He told the grand jury of visits where he observed slot machines, punch boards, and marble boards and "heard of" other forms of gambling. "To me that is evidence in itself of collusion between gamblers and law enforcement officers," he said.[12]

Gambler Benny Binion, a native of Grayson County, was not so willing to testify, at least not in Fort Worth. Binion believed the invitation to appear before the grand jury was a thinly disguised ploy to get him back to Texas where he could be charged with operating a $1,000,000 numbers racket in Dallas. If the twelve jurors wanted to visit him in Las Vegas, he'd cooperate. He denied any knowledge of the Harris bombing and the attempts to kill notorious Dallas gambler Herbert "The Cat" Noble.

Even without Binion's testimony, the grand jury felt it was making progress. Ray Finney was determined to sort fact from fiction concerning gambling and possible corruption in Fort Worth.

For the rest of February the grand jurors heard scores of witnesses. From Arlington pool hall operator Albert D. Austin to Judge Robert B. Young, people from all walks of life were sworn in. Some testified willingly, some by subpoena, some secretly. On February 27 jurors listened as a secret witness told of personally

Special prosecuter John Honts (left) and grand jury foreman Ray Finney leaving the Tarrant County courthouse.
—Courtesy of *Fort Worth Star-Telegram* Photograph Collection,
The University of Texas at Arlington Libraries.

seeing payoffs. When pressed by reporters, Finney would not identify the witness or divulge any details of the testimony.

Vice squad raids increased under the glare of daily newspaper
reports of open gambling. Slot machines and marble boards were
"discovered" and their owners charged. Lee Moore, Benny
McDonald, Carl Wynn, Ray Moore, and Leslie Frankrich posted
bonds of $1,000 each when their marble boards were confiscated.

Charges were filed against cafe and drug store owners for permitting gambling on their property. Conspicuously absent, however, were raids on the plush clubs that catered to prominent citizens.

At the court house, as the revelations became more and more
tangled, changes took place in the proceedings. Normally, an assistant district attorney acted as legal council to the grand jury, but
Stewart Hellman had felt it important that he, rather than an assistant, meet with the jurors. Now the grand jury itself, rather than the
district attorney, issued subpoenas.

Another change took place in late February. Eleven of the
twelve jurors wanted to hire a special prosecutor. When the lone
holdout agreed, they exercised their legal right and replaced Stewart
Hellman with special prosecutor John B. Honts. Hellman did not
go willingly. The story was that when the grand jury decided to
name a special prosecutor Hellman said, "I'm the district attorney
and I intend to stay in this grand jury room." Ray Finney, a tall,
muscular refinery worker, answered, "Mr. Hellman, the question
about you staying in this room is, are you going to walk out that
door or am I going to throw you through that damned door?"[13]

Publicly, the district attorney questioned the legality of the
move, saying ". . . let the chips fall where they may."[14] In a terse,
three-paragraph statement, Hellman denied obstructing the investigation. He reiterated it was his sworn duty to serve as legal council to the grand jury, but that, in the interest of harmony, he would
step aside.

Chapter 6

Meet John B. Honts, the New Prosecutor

A t the invitation of the grand jury, and with the approval of Judge Dave McGee, John B. Honts took over questioning for the county. Honts, a former district attorney in Dalhart, Texas, took the oath of office March 1 from Criminal District Court No. 2 Judge McGee. Grand jury foreman Ray Finney, Court Reporter J. C. Gross, and newspaper reporters and photographers witnessed the swearing in.

Honts, a forty-four-year-old Fort Worth lawyer, was also a well-known speaker at civic events, and he wrote poetry on the side. His book of poems, *Life Silhouettes: Lines Inspired for Everyone*, was a local best seller. In it he presented his down-to-earth humor. His strong spiritual underpinnings radiated through his words and in his Sunday School lessons at Arlington Heights Methodist Church. Neighbors frequently saw him puttering around in his yard, snipping a shrub here, planting a rose bush there. To those with whom he worked, the Virginia native was seen as a totally honest man.

On his first day with the grand jury, Honts emphasized he was not out to persecute anyone. His job would be to clear the names of the innocent and bring charges against the guilty. Finney welcomed the new advisor and noted he believed the jury's progress would be enhanced.

A week into the job, after studying transcripts of previous testimony and hearing witnesses, Honts told the *Fort Worth Star-Telegram*, "we know who knows." He also admitted that getting the facts was becoming more difficult because of threats made to witnesses.

In addition to gambling at clubs and hotels, the grand jurors probed the operation of slot machines and marble boards. Clarence Cleere, who said he no longer owned marble boards, testified on three consecutive days.

During the first week of March, the grand jury subpoenaed thirty persons charged with owning slots and marble tables found in late February raids. Before the subpoenas could be served, that investigation was put on indefinite hold.

Honts wanted to get to the bottom of bribery accusations, but an underworld "iron curtain" had dropped. Bailiffs searched for four known gamblers, but the bashful quartet was nowhere to be found. "They might as well come on in," Finney warned,[1] implying that the jury would wait them out, even if it took all year.

Prior to Honts' appointment, the grand jury had requested bank records of eleven police officers and elected officials. Now they had questions for certain officers. They wanted to know how these public servants could afford luxury cars, expensive homes, and other valuable property on their city and county pay. The answers lacked credibility.

H. H. Monroe was the first black man to serve on a Tarrant County grand jury. The retired Pullman car porter was a quiet, refined man who did more listening than talking. Once, in an effort to draw the man out, Finney asked about the concerns of the colored community. "Mr. Monroe, you are as much a part of this jury as anyone. Do you have any questions about the grand jury?" The man thought for a moment and said, "Well, yes sir, I do. Why is it when a colored man kills another colored man he either has to stand trial or pay a $500 fine to the grand jury?" Finney explained that the grand jury did not assess fines. Finney also realized the assistant district attorney assigned to the grand jury was pocketing the money and dropping the cases.[2]

The grand jury handed down their first indictments on March 31, 1951. A record shattering sixty true bills named both the big fish and the little ones in the Tarrant County gambling sea. Club owners Fred Browning of Top o' the Hill, between Fort Worth and Arlington; Bert Wakefield, Phil Long, and Les Hutt of 3939 Club,

Jacksboro Highway; W. C. Kirkwood of 2222 Club, Jacksboro Highway; George Wilderspin of East Side Club, Haltom City; and W. D. Satterwhite of the Skyliner Club, Jacksboro Highway were among those indicted.

For a few days President Harry S. Truman's feud with General Douglas MacArthur pushed grand jury news off the front page. The general wanted to bomb China to halt Chinese involvement in the Korean battle, but Truman feared such action would bring Communist China and Russia into the war. Truman won.

Back at the courthouse, the grand jury indicted Tiffin Hall, H. D. "Red" Oden, Frank Cates, and eighteen other gamblers before its term ended. Most were cited with two or more counts of keeping and exhibiting gaming equipment or permitting gambling on property they controlled. Slot machine cases were filed against Jack Frankrich, Bennie McDonald, Lee Moore, and Ray Moore.

Defense lawyers Leo Brewster, M. Hendricks Brown, Jesse Martin, Byron Matthews, Clifford Mays, and Dave Miller scurried to post bonds for their clients. These attorneys were no strangers to the workings of the criminal justice system. One was a former district attorney, and four were assistant district attorneys at one time or another. The bonds, at $1,000 each, came to a total of $32,000. It was also reported that, "The jury also returned three indictments against Chief Sheriff's Deputy A. B. Carter, charging him with demanding illegal fees in connection with transfer of lunacy patients to state hospitals."[3]

Other officers escaped indictments, but were not spared the wrath of the jury. In his report to Judge Dave McGee, Ray Finney declared, "the relationship of pay-off to near open vice did and does exist in Tarrant County."[4] He characterized officers as being grossly derelict in their sworn duty to uphold the law. Particularly telling was the fact that offenses had been committed since officials declared they found no gambling in the county. In a secret finding, the jurors prepared to indict thirty-four top-ranking Fort Worth policemen. The mayor, city manager, and grand jury worked out a compromise. No lawmen would be indicted if George Hawkins was demoted, and a squeaky-clean chief named to conduct a massive cleanup of the department. The man for the job turned out to be R. R. Howerton, and the document was never made public.

Foreman Finney promised that in their extended term the

jurors would ferret out proof of other failings and act accordingly. He was quick to praise the majority of law officers who were doing their jobs, and he felt they were hindered by the few who put personal gain before duty.

Chief George Hawkins publicly maintained his previous stance. "I don't think any member of the Police Department has been neglectful of duty,"[5] he commented. District Attorney Stewart Hellman refused to make a statement.

Following the embarrassment of the grand jury report, the police and county officers stepped up their enforcement of anti-gambling laws. Suddenly raiders were confiscating slots and marble boards in all parts of the county. A locksmith was called in. On the first day, $1,468 was taken from twenty-five machines. By the second day, $3,111.37 was turned over to a bank for use by the grand jury to defray its expenses.

Perhaps the reason they found the machines was because there were so many of them. State Attorney General Price Daniel revealed taxes had been paid on 1,547 slot and marble machines in 1951. This placed Tarrant County second out of the 254 counties in Texas, only 32 machines behind Dallas County.

Defense attorney Clifford Mays' defense centered around the contention that the machines had been in open operation for years. Payoff money was part of the deal. Everyone—the district attorney, the police, the sheriff—knew about the gambling. They had watched players in bowling alleys, country clubs, drug stores, and taverns.

Hellman began poring over grand jury transcripts as he and his staff prepared cases for prosecution. Three weeks later he shocked the community and angered the grand jury by making a deal. Regarding the operation of slot machines, the district attorney and defense lawyers Mays and Hendricks Brown agreed to reduce the felony cases to misdemeanor charges in exchange for guilty pleas. The felony charges could have led to prison terms of two to four years; the misdemeanor charges involved court fines and costs. Hellman noted the number of misdemeanors would correspond to the number of felony indictments. Seventeen slot and marble table owners paid fines of $100.00 per charge, and gave up claim to the machines.

One owner paid a top fine of $461.60. Most paid an average of $240.00 Payments were made by attorney Mays. None of the owners were required to appear in court. "Those boys (the defendants) are all local boys with good reputations," Mays said.[6] Others who were less charitable in their assessment pointed out several of "those boys" had arrest records going back many years.

The question being whispered in the halls of the courthouse and argued in the coffee shops was, "Did . . . Hellman agree to permit slot machine and marble board owners to plead guilty to minor charges because he feared their trials might bring out facts to embarrass his administration?"[7]

The district attorney pledged to bring to trial those indicted for running dice and card games before the summer recess. Six weeks before the recess, he was still studying testimony and evidence. Free on bond were such big-time gamblers as Fred Browning, Tiffin Hall, W. C. Kirkwood, Bert Wakefield, and George Wilderspin. They and others listed in the March 31 charges were in no hurry.

A well-known lawyer once said, "The job of a defense attorney is to keep his client out of jail." To do this he should use every means available short of outright breaking the law himself. Actual guilt or innocence was secondary to convincing a judge or jury the client should not go to jail. The lawyers for those indicted by the grand jury were well-schooled in this philosophy.

After much delay, Hellman seemed ready for trial. In an adroit move, the gamblers asked for and got a pre-trial hearing. Never in the proceedings was guilt considered. Instead, lead attorney Leo Brewster attacked the grand jury. First he questioned the legality of John Honts' appointment. "We want to emphasize now that nothing personal is involved," Brewster stressed, claiming Honts was a friend.[8]

In a timely *Dear Abby* newspaper column was this humorous exchange between a lawyer and a defendant:

> Q: Now, Mrs. Johnson, how was your first marriage terminated?
> A: By death.
> Q: And by whose death was it terminated?[9]

To the lay person, such technicalities are ludicrous. To an attorney, these sorts of questions could lead to an acquittal.

One charge against Fred Browning read:

IN THE NAME AND BY THE AUTHORITY OF THE
STATE OF TEXAS THE GRAND JURORS OF THE STATE
OF TEXAS, duly elected, tried, impaneled, sworn and charged to
inquire of offenses committed in Tarrant County, in the State of
Texas, upon their oaths do present in and to the Criminal District
Court Number Two of said County that one FRED BROWN-
ING hereinafter styled defendant, in the County of Tarrant and
State aforesaid, on or about the 1st day of January, in the year of
our Lord One Thousand Nine Hundred Fifty-One did keep and
exhibit a gaming table and bank for the purpose of gaming,
AGAINST THE PEACE AND DIGNITY OF THE STATE.[10]

The legal document ordering Sully Montgomery to arrest
Browning read:

To Any Sheriff of the State of Texas, Greetings:
You are hereby commanded to take the body of Fred
Browning, and him safely keep, so that you have him before the
Honorable, the Criminal District Court No.2 in and for the
County aforesaid, at the Court House thereof, in the City of Fort
Worth, instanter, then and there to answer the State of Texas on a
charge by indictment, with offense of Keeping and Exhibiting
Gaming Table and Bank, Keeping a Gambling House, Permitting
Place Owned to be Used for Gaming, Permitting Place Under
Control to be used for Gaming, Permitting Place to be Used for
Gaming, Exhibiting a gaming device for gaming, a felony.[11]

Browning's lawyer moved for a dismissal because the indictment
did not specify the dimensions or description of the "the aforesaid
gaming table." He was overruled.

The second defense argument rejected the legal status of the
jury panel. Browning's attorney subpoenaed every member of the
grand jury as hostile witnesses.

Civil pretrial hearings are common. But in this rare criminal
pretrial hearing, the question before the judge was the validity of
the indictments. Attempting to prove they were not, Brewster
scored a telling blow. He established that Mrs. Lewis Wall, Jr., district clerk, and Dick Williams, deputy criminal district clerk, had
not taken the required oath when the special grand jury panel was
drawn. This oath enforced secrecy of the panel names until released

by the judge. Both Wall and Williams were familiar with the ordinance and testified they had not broken the secrecy rule even without the oath. Williams swore the names were sealed when he got them, and still sealed when he gave them to Judge McGee. It was to no avail. The defense won the point.

Regarding Honts' appointment, the gamblers' lawyer called the district attorney to the stand. "Hellman testified he was 'ready, willing and able at all times to perform all the duties of district attorney, including working with the grand jury on all matters.'"[12] He further stated that despite his protests, he was excluded from the grand jury room.

Brewster asked Hellman, "You had nothing to do with these particular cases?"

"I had not. Except that the grand jury borrowed my court reporter, Lee Henry."[13]

Hellman's response brought a quick, but polite reaction from Honts. Upon questioning by the special prosecutor, the district attorney admitted he had sat in the room on occasion. In the peculiar workings of admissibility, the reason the grand jury felt the need to replace Hellman was never entered into the record.

Honts, too, was called to testify. He was a less compliant witness for the defense. Jesse Martin, another attorney for the gamblers, attempted to discredit Honts' motive:

> Martin: "You told the grand jury you would take the job as a public service, didn't you?"
> Honts: "How did you find out I told the grand jury that?"
> Martin: "You make an investigation and find out if you want to know," he snapped back.[14]

Honts contended he did not seek publicity for his work with the grand jury. He testified to having two telephone conversations with Ray Finney. He also discussed with Judge Bob Young and county legal advisor Jesse Brown the appropriateness of his serving. Martin's questioning of Honts' motivation died for lack of credibility.

Failing that argument, Martin next pounced on Honts' participation in the jury room. The special prosecutor declared his aim was to "educate the grand jury on the law, because they were needing help."[15] He added that he interrogated witnesses, advised jurors of how certain testimony stood related to law, and helped in drawing the multiple-count charges. Honts said some counts were inserted in the indictments for "protection."

When Martin asked who would be protected, Honts responded, "The state's." Honts elaborated that, "Some of those counts were to keep a man from finding a loophole when his case comes to trial."[16]

Martin's questioning of foreman Ray Finney followed the same course as that of the special prosecutor. For an hour and a half the defense hammered at the weaknesses of the grand jury without once mentioning the defendants.

The trouble began when Hellman made no objection to Martin's caustic questioning of Honts and Finney. It exploded into hot anger during Honts' cross-examination of the jury foreman. Defense attorney M. Hendricks Brown aggressively objected to Honts' right to question any witness. The judge overruled the objection.

Hellman rose to his feet. He made it clear he had not delegated any authority to Mr. Honts, or considered him to have the legal standing as an assistant to the district attorney. "Then why don't you get over there with those fellows?" Honts snapped, gesturing toward the defense attorneys.[17]

Spectators gasped at the acrimonious exchange. Judge McGee gavelled the courtroom to order, and Honts continued his questioning of Finney.

Brown again objected to Honts' participation, but said he would recognize Charles Matthews from the state attorney general's office as a legal cross-examiner. Before the judge could rule, Martin told the packed courtroom Matthews had been thrust upon the local district attorney. "After the attorney general had already said he was sending the gentleman here. . .(there was) nothing to do but accept him."[18]

Judge McGee glared at Martin and stated he had requested assistance from the attorney general. Matthews offered to ask the same questions Honts asked, but McGee ruled that would not be necessary.

Perhaps only two people in the court room knew how the trial would end. Prior to its opening, one of the indicted men reminded Hellman of what he said when he made the first monthly payment to operate gambling at his club, "If I go down, you go down."[19]

"The district attorney's office declined to draw the true bills and the jury acquiesced in that decision, since it would be an empty and expensive gesture. . . (to pursue the matter),"[20] Finney concluded in his report.

The gamblers won in court, yet they lost in the long run. The new police chief greatly curtailed local gambling. Slot machines were destroyed or dumped into Lake Worth.

Sheriff Montgomery resigned to fight an income tax evasion charge. District Attorney Stewart Hellman was defeated in the next election.

Ray Finney went back to work at the refinery. John Honts continued his law practice. But for those indicted, things were never quite the same following the work of the 1951 grand jury.

Chapter 7

Stopping the
Rolls of the Dice

No gambler wants to roll two one-spots, called snake eyes, but it happens. To Fort Worth gamblers, the 1951 grand jury was snake eyes. Of the thirty-two men named in the grand jury indictments, many were employed as dealers, shills, or in some cases bouncers. Ivy Miller, Jerry Rosenberg, Oscar Donley, and L. J. "Chili" McWillie, identified as associates of Fred Browning, fit in this mold.

In like manner Mack Taylor and Pete Ford, who worked for W. C. Kirkwood, were small fish in a big pond. Tiffin Hall's "associates" included Bob Floyd, Dewey Inman, and Red Oden. Floyd was a money dealer. He had the ability to quickly collect and distribute cash. The amounts ranged from hundreds to thousands of dollars per roll of the dice.

Some who were indicted owned the property where gambling took place, but were not necessarily gamblers themselves. After the crackdown, those not closely tied to the local scene drifted off to other cities like Las Vegas.

For many gamblers snake eyes bounced in the form of a federal income tax evasion conviction. That's what brought down Benny Binion. In the thirty years prior to his 1952 conviction, he went from being a pal of small-time hoodlums and racketeers to being a Las Vegas casino kingpin.

Binion was involved in the 1932 Dallas shooting death of California gambler and real estate promoter B. W. Freiden. A retired police captain recalled the murder, saying Freiden ran several policy wheels and was making a lot of money. "On September 12, 1936, Binion and his top gun, Buddy Malone, blasted Frieden. They emptied their .45 automatics into Frieden, who was unarmed." Then Binion shot himself in the shoulder, inflicting a superficial wound. He turned himself in to the sheriff, claiming self-defense.[1]

He beat the rap and continued to control the policy games until Sam Murray paid more protection money and became the top dog. Two years later Binion got word Murray was at a certain address without his bodyguards, one of whom was Herbert "The Cat" Noble. Binion and Ivy Miller went looking for Murray. When he stepped out on the street, Miller fired before Murray got his gun out of its shoulder holster. The outgoing Dallas County district attorney's last official action was to dismiss charges against Miller due to "insufficient evidence."

Binion was in control again until the 1946 cleanup by District Attorney Will Wilson. Finding the desert climate more to his liking, Binion moved to Nevada.

In applying for a gaming license he swore he was not engaged in gambling in any state where gambling was illegal. The Nevada Tax Commission noted, "Our investigation of his activities in Dallas . . . has disclosed there is not concrete evidence that Binion in any way was involved in the [Herbert] Noble slaying."[2] (By this time Noble had been assassinated.) Character witness Nevada State Senator E. L. Noles characterized Binion, known in Vegas as "Cowboy," as an affable, dynamic, and generous man. Longtime associate George Wilderspin of Haltom City simply referred to him as "a nice guy." Had the commissioners spoken to Dallas authorities they would have gotten a different side of the man from Texas.

In his testimony before the Commission, Noles continued, "Charitable organizations hail him as a philanthropist, and unfortunate individuals look upon him as a sweet Prince of 'Touch.'"[3] The good senator failed to mention Binion's generosity to him, which came in the form of a Hudson Hornet. The car became known in underworld circles as the "Binion Bullet."

In answer to charges by the 1951 Tarrant County grand jury probe, Ben Lester Binion claimed he owned no property in the county, and had no influence there. The first assertion perhaps was true. Binion had been a Dallas gambler, but he undeniably had an influence on local gamblers. He loaned money to them and some said he co-owned several gambling spots. Fred Browning, Top o' the Hill Terrace owner, died owing Benny $70,000.

Binion's refusal to return to testify was based on his belief that if he ever set foot in the Lone Star State he would be charged with policy gambling. His Dallas partner, Harry R. Urban, Sr., had just been sentenced to four years in prison. Authorities in Dallas wanted him for running a $1 million a year operation with Urban. Binion invited the grand jury to Nevada, telling reporters he would talk under oath about anything. "I've been lied about, misquoted, cussed and discussed. Maybe I deserve some of this, but I'm not near as bad as I have heard I am."[4] In his fight against extradition, Benny told Judge Edward P. Murphy he feared for his life if he were forced to return to Dallas.

The transplanted Texan prospered, and at the time of his arrest for income tax evasion, he owned the Horseshoe Casino in Las Vegas, four Cadillacs, and a 229,000-acre ranch, complete with 2,000 Herefords and 800 horses.

He pleaded *nolo contendre* to underpaying his 1949 income tax and was jailed in Nevada. Out on bond, his tax troubles were not over. The following year he was in federal custody in San Antonio and fined $20,000. This was a mere pittance compared to the $638,000 in fines and back taxes he paid for filing false returns during the 1945 to 1949 period. The millionaire gambler, speaking earnestly to Federal District Judge Ben H. Rice said, "I didn't intend to cheat the government. I'm kinda ignorant. I got to gambling and all, you know."[5] His plea that his wife and four children needed him, and his promise to retire to his Montana ranch fell on deaf ears. The judge sentenced him to prison for five years on each of four counts.

* * *

Bert Wakefield was one of the gamblers who moved to Las Vegas. The former operator of the plush 3939 Club on the Jacksboro Highway had been a friend of Benny Binion for years. When things got too hot in Texas, Wakefield migrated to Nevada, where gaming was cool.

The physically slight man, now in his fifties and bothered by heart trouble, was described by a defense attorney as "a scholar and a gentleman." Certainly Wakefield did not consort with the likes of notorious gangsters such as Edell Evans, Tincy Eggleston, or Cecil Green. He was a businessman; his business was running a gambling house that catered to other businessmen.

A native of Denton, Texas, Bert lived in Fort Worth some forty years before he moved to Nevada. He claimed he received only a few traffic tickets prior to the grand jury indictments, and swore he had never been arrested either in Texas or his newly adopted state.

For weeks, Harry Claiborne, his Las Vegas attorney who specialized in fighting extradition attempts, jockeyed through the Nevada court system trying to prevent Sheriff Sully Montgomery from getting his hands on the gambler. Following the request by Texas Governor Allen Shivers that Nevada surrender Wakefield, Claiborne persuaded Governor Charles Russell to set a hearing on the matter. This delaying tactic preceded several filings of writs of *habeas corpus* to forestall any action. But the lawyer was tripped up by one judge who refused to allow a writ of *habeas corpus*, because Wakefield was not yet in custody. While the attorney was arguing against this mere technicality, Wakefield walked into the courtroom. Montgomery nabbed him on the spot.

The actual arrest was a tug-of-war. The sheriff had one of Wakefield's arms, and Claiborne grabbed the other. Montgomery, a former professional football player and ex-ranked boxer, won the war and hustled the Texan into a waiting car.

Dressed in a tailor-made suit and white silk sport shirt, Wakefield appeared tired as reporters questioned him upon his arrival at Dallas' Love Field. He denied connections with Las Vegas operations. "All I know is Fort Worth gambling, he said."[6] Fort Worth attorney Arthur Lee Moore posted $5,000 bond, and Wakefield was free. Like the others indicted by the 1951 grand jury, his felony indictment was reduced to a misdemeanor and fine. He returned to Las Vegas.

※ ※ ※

Lester Hutt, an associate of Wakefield's in the operation of the 3939 Club, was not as smooth an operator as Wakefield. Hutt built his combination home and gambling establishment on the Jacksboro Highway. The house itself was set back off the road.

Only wealthy, known customers got in. To reach it, guests passed two guards at the entrance, then drove up a curving driveway past two more guards. In the basement, Hutt's gambling area resembled a movie set of a Las Vegas casino.

Hutt, too, was charged by the grand jury with gambling and paid his fine. But only weeks later he was in trouble again. In August 1951 police charged him with assaulting a Carswell airman. The fight took place at Hutt's Skyline Drive Motel. Sergeant Marcus Clemmer said he was talking to a Negro porter at the motel, "When a man drove up, started an argument, drew a pistol, ordered him off the premises and then hit him."[7] District Attorney Stewart Hellman later dismissed the charge.

Hutt's next encounter with the law involved the federal authorities. He and his wife Helen were slapped with a $33,533.35 tax lien for the years 1943, 1944, and 1948 through 1950. Following the close of that suit, Hutt reportedly moved to San Antonio.

* * *

One of the most colorful characters to populate the Jacksboro Highway was Asher Rone. His rap sheet extended at least as far back as the 1930s. In 1937 he was charged with keeping a South Side gambling house, the Eighth Avenue Klub. This club had been well known for its risqué pictures painted on the walls. A new man on the police force, dressed in street clothes, watched a dice game in progress for fifteen minutes before the vice squad arrived. He grabbed the dice and $139 as evidence as his colleagues arrested the seven men and two women players. All posted bond and that was the end of it.

Rone bought the Avalon Courts, and opened the Avalon Night Club at 2243 Jacksboro Highway. He was a neighbor of W. C. Kirkwood, but the two had little in common. Kirkwood's 2222 was like a country club compared to the joint at 2243. At one time Rone was hauled into court on charges of operating a public nuisance. The Health Department threatened to close him down unless he cleaned up the toilets.

Filthy bathrooms weren't his only problem. During World War II Rone was named in the first suit filed under the Office of Price Administration's price ceiling. The Feds accused Rone of overpricing beer at his Avalon Club. "The complaint alleges that on July 26

Asher Rone once owned the Avalon Motel.

—Photo by author

(1943) Rone sold one customer three 12-ounce bottles of beer at 21 cents a bottle; on July 27, one 32-ounce bottle to a customer at 36 cents, and on July 28, five 12-ounce bottles at 21 cents each, in each instance the price exceeding the ceiling."[8] The legal price was eleven cents, later raised to twelve cents.

Rone's Avalon Courts adjoined Nelson Harris' ill-fated club. One fateful day Rone made the mistake of visiting his neighbor just as Harris was trying to break up a fight. Four customers, unhappy over the slow service, threatened to "take over the place." With weapon in hand, Harris objected. He pistol whipped one man, then accidently shot Rone. The bullet entered his left side and exited out his back. He was taken to St. Joseph's Hospital where it was determined no vital organs had been hit. Harris suffered head lacerations, but did not require hospitalization. One of the customers fled and the other three became guests of the sheriff. They made bond and were treated for minor injuries.

In late 1945, when Rone drove to his place of business, a robber met him with a gun. Later he told police two men bound his hands with adhesive tape and bailing wire. They took $2,100 from the office safe, two pistols, ten cartons of cigarettes, and $20 from Rone's wallet.

In 1952 Rone was robbed a second time at his South Side Hemphill Courts at 2:00 A.M. December 13. He lost $160 to a nervous young gunman in that crime. He shrugged and went back to bed.

Rone was among the thirty-two gamblers charged by the grand jury in 1951. He paid his fine, and considered it part of the cost of doing business. Soon after, he and his wife Grace Riggs Rone, got into trouble with the Federal Bureau of Internal Revenue, which claimed the Rones owed $1,059.93 on their 1946 earnings.

With the closing of gambling, and the advent of national motel chains taking over old-style tourist courts, Rone sold his Fort Worth holdings. The site of the Eighth Avenue Klub is now a shopping strip. He moved to Roosevelt, Oklahoma, where he operated a liquor store until his retirement. Asher Rone, known as one of the toughest of the Jacksboro Highway toughs, died peacefully at the age of eighty-seven. His body was returned to Fort Worth and interred in Greenwood Cemetery.

✻ ✻ ✻

"TIFFIN HALL BRANDED KINGPIN OF GAMBLING HERE BY HARRIS," the *Fort Worth Press* headline read February 15, 1951. Jay Harris, brother of slain gambler Nelson, named Hall as the "Big shot at the head of gambling here."[9] Hall denied it. Most observers doubted Hall's prominence, but none questioned his involvement in the gambling scene.

The short man's most striking feature was his cold blue Alaskan Husky-like eyes. He spoke in a high-pitched, squeaky voice. Hall listed his businesses as cafe and hotel ownerships. The 1996 Mexican Inn menu included a biographical sketch of its founder:

> In 1920, when Fort Worth was still young, a colorful and free-spirited man came to the city and brought with him a special brand of pride and independence. . . . Only 20 years old, he was already a skilled gambler. Soon Tiffin established gambling halls in secluded corners throughout his new hometown. . . . In 1936, Tiffin the gambler entered the world of legitimate business when his first Mexican Inn Cafe opened its doors at 5th and Commerce

Streets in a downtown building already 50 years old. . . . On a good day in the 1930's, restaurant receipts might total only $25.00, but rumor spoke of much greater amounts accumulated each night when gamblers gathered in the second floor rooms above the Mexican Inn. Wary of traditional advertising, Tiffin commissioned a family pet burro named Star to generate interest in the new cafe. Star would be dressed in a banner reading, "MEXICAN INN CAFE . . . MEXICAN FOOD EXCLUSIVELY . . . FOLLOW ME TO MEXICAN INN," and turned loose somewhere downtown. He would find his way back to the side door of the restaurant and beg for tortillas. The police would be compelled to 'arrest' him for being on the street without a permit. Again and again, the exploits of Star amused the citizenry and frustrated authorities.[10]

Gambler Tiffin Hall once owned this popular eating place. It is now owned by Chris Carroll.

—Photo taken by Ann Arnold.

At the time of his indictment by the grand jury, Carl Tiffin Hall owned the Madoc Hotel, 1313 Main, the Commerce Street Mexican Inn, and another restaurant at 612 N. Henderson, at the southernmost end of the Jacksboro Highway. He also banked games on the second floor of the Commercial Hotel at 505 Main. Desk clerk Jack Everett told his bride to "never go on the second floor." He didn't want to know what went on there.

Hall was one of the dozen gamblers rounded up for questioning after the death of Nelson Harris. Like the others, he swore no knowledge of the bombing and was released. Arrest was nothing new for him. Fort Worth police records showed Hall had been arrested sixteen times since he came to town as a "colorful and free-spirited man." Most of the charges were for vagrancy, meaning pimping, or gambling.

Tiffin was well liked by his employees. He stood up for them and even unofficially adopted a Mexican youth. A retired reporter told of Hall's concern for an employee who told his boss he had killed a woman: "Tiffin called me and asked what he should do. I told him to call the police. 'But what if he was drunk and just thought he killed someone, I'd be the laughing stock of the department,' was Hall's response." The reporter agreed to ask a friend in homicide to go discreetly to the address given. If they found nothing, no one would be the wiser. If something was found, the reporter was to get exclusive coverage.

He and the detective searched the house, and, finding nothing, were ready to leave. The reporter later recalled, "The detective opened what he thought was a back door. It was a closet door and out plopped a body." Needless to say, he got his story and the employee was charged with murder.[11]

Tiffin Hall was terrified of being robbed. Unwilling to declare his assets, and thus unable to bank all his gambling money, his hotel suite was equipped with numerous electronic devices. He was never more than a few feet away from a switch with which to summon help. He was not so fortunate regarding his Cadillac. When the vehicle was stolen from Shepherd's Parking Garage, Tiffin sued and won almost $600 to pay for damages to the late-model car.

In 1966 Hall suffered a stroke and was permanently disabled. He died in 1973 at the age of seventy-three. One source said he died of syphilis. Whatever the cause, he was one of the few midcentury characters who died in bed. His second wife Helen, and trusted employees continued to operate the Mexican Inns until the Spring Creek Restaurant chain bought them in 1980.

* * *

George Wilderspin dabbled in several businesses, but he considered himself a cattleman. Wilderspin, who once took 1,557 Mexican cattle to Montana in railroad cattle cars, would have a been a soulmate to Larry McMurtry's fictional drovers in *Lonesome Dove*. Now in his eighties, Wilderspin can reminisce about his first-hand experiences with many of the people who did business on the Jacksboro Highway. Most of them he describes as "nice fellows."

As a young man Wilderspin traveled all over the country performing at rodeos, and he held a calf roping title for many years. In 1936 he and Howard Westfall loaded their horses and tack into his six cylinder Chevrolet pick-up and headed for California. They teamed up with James Kinney. The three rodeoed and hired on as ranch hands to make their expenses. Later, Kinney wrote a book about their adventures, and Wilderspin divulged that sleeping on a bedroll in the Nevada desert was not as romantic as the songwriter would have us believe: "Nothin' up there but rocks. That feller that wrote *Home on the Range*, he ain't never slept out on the ground."[12]

On another trip he and rodeo performer-turned gambler Louis Tindall camped in Yellowstone National Park. Wilderspin, to prove he could, roped a bear. Unfortunately for him, a park ranger saw it and he was arrested. He recalled, "They put me in jail for thirty days and that so-and-so (Tindall) ran off and left me."[13]

Wilderspin was a friend and colleague of Benny Binion both before and after Binion moved to Las Vegas. According to Wilderspin, Binion at one point offered him a partnership, but he didn't specify in what business.

In Fort Worth Binion bought 300 head of cattle from Wilderspin, and the two transported them by train to Whitewright, near the Texas-Oklahoma border. The plan was to put the cattle on Binion's father's land. The only problem was that there were no fences. Benny rode ahead of the herd and George brought up the rear. By the time they got to the elder Binion's place they were 125 head short. It took Wilderspin three months to round up the strays.

Wilderspin said Binion wanted him to go elk hunting with him in Montana. "'Get you a rifle,' he said. What he wanted was for me to ride on the train with him and if anybody gave him any trouble, shoot him."[14]

For many years Wilderspin was associated with the Fort Worth Stockyards, leasing or owning land and cattle around the state. He got into the gambling business that would result in an indictment when he bought a cafe on E. Belknap. The owner insisted Wilderspin buy his wife's beauty shop in the same building.

George was never a fancy dresser. Levis, scuffed boots, and a sweat-stained cowboy hat were his uniform. He looked like he didn't have next month's rent money. When the seller asked how he was going to pay for the purchase, Wilderspin peeled out $25,000 in cash. Later he bought the motel next door as well.

Wilderspin recalled his entry into the gambling world: "Two boys from Dallas, who had been partners with Benny in Las Vegas, asked if they could open up gambling. . . . I said 'I don't know. I'll go to town and see.'" The club was in Haltom City, so he went to county officials and worked out a deal. "I didn't talk to Hellman. I talked to Wardlaw, Hellman's head man." He said Sully held up his end of the deal. "That little old Hellman, he called me up there in his office one day and he said, 'Now I'm going to tell you something. I'm running this.' And he said you're gonna pay me $500 a month. I said 'fine. I'm gonna pay you, but if I go to the penitentiary, you're going with me.'"[15]

He was indicted by the 1951 grand jury for running a gambling room at the East Side Club. Through his attorney, Wilderspin got word that Hellman was going to prosecute him because he was the only gambler who could beat it. Wilderspin paid a visit to the district attorney.

A short time later, A. L. Wardlaw showed up at Wilderspin's house, saying, "You scared my bossman to death. What did you tell him?" Bluffing, George told the assistant district attorney, "I said the IRS is fooling with me. They said I could make all the money I wanted to for the next five years if I'd tell them I gave him some damn money."[16] Two days later the district attorney reduced the indictments from felonies to misdemeanors.

After the grand jury publicity, Wilderspin closed the East Side Club and sold his E. Belknap property to Buddie Markum. It became the site of Buddie's Super Market. Wilderspin continued in the cattle business, sometimes flying his own plane to look at property or livestock. "Cattle," he said, "is the only way I ever made any money."

Chapter 8

Evans Livestock Company: "Heifers for Sale"

Edell Evans' name wasn't listed in the telephone directory. To reach the pudgy, elegantly dressed pimp and gambler, hotel porters and others knew to call the Evans Livestock Company. His "heifers for sale" were shapely blondes, brunettes, and redheads.

In addition to running a call girl operation and hosting a "few friends" at a dice table, Evans raised and raced greyhounds. The balding "Mr. Five by Five" kept the animals in his backyard kennels. He trained them and entered them in races throughout the South. When he wasn't home, he was driving to or from a race with a trailer attached to the back of his Cadillac.

The dogs didn't bother the neighbors, but the girls did. On one occasion a scantily clad woman ran from door to door seeking help. She claimed Edell was after her. That was one of the few times he had any trouble with his girls. He was considered to be sneaky, but not mean.

People living in his North Richland Hills neighborhood noted girls arriving and leaving the $50,000 Evans house at all hours of the day and night. Typically, a cab would honk and a well-dressed young woman was driven to a destination only guessed at by the annoyed residents. At times Dorothy Jean Evans, Edell's wife, would provide transportation in her own Cadillac. It was assumed she knew the procedure, having been arrested forty-five times for vagrancy herself.

One source, when asked about Edell Evans, replied, "He weighed about 300 pounds and had about that many girls."[1] Generally he was not well liked. Other gamblers rarely had a good word when it came to Edell. They considered pimps only a cut above child molesters on the criminal social scale.

In 1941 Clifton Edell Evans was twenty-five years old when he was arrested for theft of a penny cigarette machine. By 1950 he was an ex-convict, having served a term for violating the white slave law. He was charged with the rape of a twenty-two-year-old waitress. The woman reported being threatened after filing the charge. Evans was released on $8,000 bond; $5,000 for the rape, $3,000 for the threat.

He stayed out of the limelight for the next three years. That intervening period must have been good financially, for in 1953 when he reported to the sheriff he had been robbed, he listed the loss of a diamond ring. The ring was described by a reporter as having a stone big enough to break a toe should it fall out of its mounting. The armed robbers also took a diamond stickpin, watch, and $5,250 in cash.

In February 1955, Henry Rogers, a Dallas insurance man, complained to police he was assaulted at a dice game in Evans' home. He told of losing $500 in a crooked game at Evans' fashionable residence on Hardisty Street. Rogers, age sixty-five, revealed he and another man were taken to the game by two women whom they met in Dallas. The women were later identified as Dorothy Jean Evans and Mrs. Johnnie Cresap. (Mrs. Cresap was the estranged wife of a man accused but not convicted of being involved with a plot to rob Cuban gun merchants.)

Authorities from the sheriff's office and the district attorney's office joined suburban Police Chief Ross Stowe in a raid of the house. They found an estimated 4,000 pairs of dice, cartons of poker chips, decks of playing cards, and other gambling equipment.

Assistant District Attorney Randell Riley filed a simple gambling complaint, citing lack of evidence to secure a felony charge. Evans admitted to "having a few men over" for a friendly game and at times using crooked dice. He laughingly paid a $25.00 gambling fine plus $17.50 in court costs. He denied hitting Rogers. When asked who hit Rogers, Evans replied, "Don't ask me about nobody but myself. . . I'm no stool pigeon."[2] Police later charged Leroy "Tincy" Eggleston with the assault.

A grand juror disagreed with Riley's assessment of the case against Evans. He believed there was ample evidence to convict him. Moreover, the juror argued a $25.00 fine "didn't mean a thing" to Evans.

After studying the law, Riley filed a felony charge against Evans for possession of gambling equipment. Attorneys Jack Ray and Foy Curry posted the $1,000 bond and Evans was out of jail for the second time that week.

Fort Worth police were under orders to arrest Evans and his wife as "undesirables" anytime they were seen within the city limits. A mere three weeks later, Evans was arrested at the Parrish Inn, 3920 E. Belknap. Officers found a loaded high-powered automatic rifle in his black Cadillac in the tavern parking lot.

After a night in the Fort Worth jail, Evans still looked dapper

Gambler Edell Evans posting bond
—Courtesy of *Fort Worth Star-Telegram* Photograph Collection,
The University of Texas at Arlington Libraries.

in a well-tailored suit and snap-brim hat. His disposition did not match his appearance, however. Refusing to talk to reporters, he yelled for the turnkey to "lock him up" rather than answer their questions.

After this incident, Evans' luck grew worse when he was thrown out of George Wilderspin's club for being a pimp. Some weeks later a police detective alerted Wilderspin that Evans had hired a man to shoot him. Fate, in the probable form of Tincy Eggleston, intervened and it was Evans who got shot.

Meanwhile, Evans kept rolling snake eyes. Just a week after his overnight stay in the Fort Worth jail, he was picked up by the Dallas police. In addition to $1,500 cash, he was carrying a loaded shotgun. An interesting item found in the car was a bill of sale from an Oklahoma City firm. Evans, known to run fixed games, had purchased one pair of special electric dice and a pair of squares (untampered dice) to match.

He had also been given a ticket for running a red light two days before his arrest. Dallas officers charged him with vagrancy, despite his claim to be a legitimate business man. He was released on a habeas corpus writ.

Back in Fort Worth, Evans' attorney worked out a deal on the February complaint. Due to a faulty warrant, part of which had not been filled in, the Tarrant County district attorney's office felt they did not have a strong case. Evans pleaded guilty to permitting his home to be used for a "policy" game, a fancy way to say cards and dice playing. He peeled off $250 worth of bills from a fat wad and walked out a free man.

Attempting to polish his public image, Evans told reporters he had "no girls at all" in his home. Ray said of his client, "Edell has made some mistakes. . . . He intends to live as a respectable citizen in his community."[3] Skeptics muttered, "When pigs fly."

Evans bought a new dark blue four-door Cadillac on Saturday, April 4, 1955. The new car smell mingled with the odor of blood when police found it two days later. The car was located 200 yards off Valley View Rd. in northwest Dallas County. A sheriff's patrol discovered the locked automobile about 3:30 P.M. Monday, keys still in the ignition. Evans' blood was in pools on the royal blue upholstery and a portable ice chest on the back floorboard.

Her hair piled stylishly atop her head, Dorothy Evans told Sheriff Bill Decker she thought her husband was killed fighting off

Edell Evans reputedly rose from his shallow grave and bit the ankle of one of his killers.
—Photo courtesy of Henry H. Wright

a robber who wanted his diamond ring and his money. She didn't know of any enemies who might have wanted Evans out of the way, she declared.

Mrs. Evans told authorities her husband left home about 11:00 P.M. Sunday, but she was away at the time and did not know where he went or who he went to see.

A maid said Evans told her he was going to a Jacksboro Highway tavern "to meet Cecil."[4] The meeting was to take place at the Pandora Club, just north of the 28th Street intersection.

To Mrs. Evans, why her husband did not take his seventy-five-pound German shepherd was a puzzle. The dog, described as "very vicious," usually went with her husband when he thought he might be in any danger. It was later discovered the dog had been boarded at a veterinary clinic the previous Thursday.

Evans always carried a shotgun under the front seat of his car. This weapon was found when officers searched the vehicle. Unwilling to state who the victim was, and lacking a body, Dallas County Sheriff Bill Decker and Tarrant County Sheriff Harlon Wright theorized that "someone" had been struck by a blow or hit by a gunshot blast while seated in the driver's position. The victim either fell or was pushed to the passenger side of the front seat. Investigators found evidence of blood running down the right-hand side of the front seat, onto the floorboard and between the crack of the closed door. No blood was found on the ground where the car was abandoned. This led to speculation that the attack took place elsewhere and the auto then driven to the Valley View area. Tests proved the blood to be human. Everyone thought it was Evans', but where was the body?

Nine police characters, including three from Fort Worth, were questioned by Dallas deputies and released. No one, including Dorothy Jean Evans, could shed light on who might have been out to get Evans. An anonymous tip, which proved to be false, had Evans and a friend badly beaten up and hiding in a cabin on Eagle Mountain Lake.

It didn't take long before the rumors began to buzz. In Fort Worth, people speculated that the Richland Hills gambler was on the hit list of a local gangster for wife theft. A woman Evans used as a shill reportedly left her husband for him.

In Dallas, underworld sources said local and Oklahoma gamblers were after Evans because of shady dice games. This was related to the February incident in which Evans admitted to playing with crooked dice. It was reported locally that, "Four experienced Fort Worth gamblers dropped $38,000 to Evans, and then became incensed when newspaper reports of a raid at Evans' home stated the set-up was rigged for crooked games."[5] Police later found out Evans kept a stooge in the attic. He watched the game through a peephole and activated a magnet which caused the dice to fall to Evans' advantage.

More than six months after Evans' car was found, police received a telephone tip from a woman who said the gambler could be found in a shallow grave at the north end of Lake Worth. The body was put there, she said, by Cecil Green and Tincy Eggleston. By this time both Green and Eggleston had themselves been victims of gangland slayings.

Who was the woman who tipped the officers off to the body? A *Fort Worth Press* reporter quoted a source "that [had] been reliable in the past." The source, Evelyn Robertson, Eggleston's girlfriend who shared an apartment with him, supposedly told a friend Evans was "tortured horribly" by Green and Eggleston. Pressed by detectives who reminded her of her anguish in the days following Eggleston's disappearance, they urged her to tell what she knew: "Think of Dorothy Jean. . . . Months have passed and she still doesn't know what happened to her husband."[6]

Robertson claimed to have overheard Green and Eggleston talking at a drinking party. They bragged about their own "private graveyard" where they had buried Evans. The only clue to Robertson as to the whereabouts of the grave was Green's comment that he "almost turned Edell's car over in a big dip in the road while driving away from the grave."[7] For three weeks deputies searched every pasture near a dip.

Finally on November 1 their labors paid off. In the area between Scenic Drive and the northwest shore line, a piece of bloodstained cloth was found. Digging in the soft soil at the edge of a lane that circled a field, police officers uncovered a bony elbow. The press later reported, "The corpse was on its right side, a silky sports shirt pulled over the face."[8] Although badly decomposed, part of the face was intact. Sheriff Wright and Police Chief Cato Hightower were certain it was Evans.

Found in the shallow four-foot grave was a blue-steel .38-caliber Smith & Wesson revolver. Several spent shells were nearby, leading officers to surmise he was killed with his own gun. Also recovered was a sports jacket, with a dirt-caked .25-caliber pistol in one pocket.

Evans was dressed in trousers, underwear, and socks. His specially made shoes, with built-up heels to give the gambler another inch of height, bore the mark, "Made especially for Washer Brothers." The sports coat's label read, "Exclusively Stardust hand tailored." Evans was wearing a leather belt with a holster fitted on the left side.

Edell's remains were taken to Lucas Funeral Home for positive identification. At first the pathologist was mystified as to the cause of death. Later he divulged Evans died from a .25-caliber slug that coursed up a nostril before lodging behind his sinus. "He probably threw his head back at the moment the trigger was pulled and the

Officers uncover the body of Edell Evans.
—Courtesy of *Fort Worth Star-Telegram* Photograph Collection,
The University of Texas at Arlington Libraries.

bullet went up his nostril,"[9] Sheriff Wright said. The freak wound accounted for the huge amount of blood found in the Cadillac.

Dorothy Jean Evans and her attorney, Jack Rey, identified the body. The distraught woman, who had married Evans when she was sixteen, felt some relief that the uncertainty was over.

Speculation that Evans was not dead when dumped into the makeshift grave led to some wild stories. "There was speculation that Eggleston and his underworld running mate, Cecil Green, tortured Evans—using methods similar to those employed by Chinese Communists—in a futile attempt to make him reveal where he had hidden money."[10] Another version of the story had his killers slitting his veins and leaving him to bleed to death.

Clifton Edell Evans was buried in Everman Cemetery. A Baptist minister, Rev. Jim Meriweather, officiated. Relatives and a few friends attended the grave side service. Evans' twenty-year-old son by a former marriage, Clarence (Sonny) Evans, did not attend the funeral. He was in the federal reformatory in El Reno, Oklahoma.

Jack Rey said that, to his knowledge, Evans did not leave a will. The estate would be divided among the widow, two sons, and Dorothy Jean's one-year-old daughter, he indicated.

The widow Evans was not yet out of the spotlight. Driving her pink Cadillac, Dorothy Jean caused heads to turn in her hometown of Cleburne. She attempted to buy a house with a large dining room "so friends could play games." But an uproar by neighbors squelched the deal.

A year after the death of her husband, she was dating Fort Worth oilman Hobart Upham. He was a generous suitor. The federal government filed a tax lien of $84,134 against her for gifts from him estimated at a value of $500,000.

Evans' sister filed suit against her, claiming she had appropriated Evans' sons' inheritance. Mrs. P. E. Jones, guardian of the boys, Sonny and Dennis, said the estate consisted of the Richland Hills house, several automobiles, a stable of race horses and dogs, and an undetermined amount of money in several bank accounts.

Jack Rey said Dorothy Jean "hocked the family jewels" to pay the government. In the summer of 1958 she reportedly married a Santa Fe railway company electrician.

Chapter 9

Deuces Were Wild

The battered mailbox at 2222 Jacksboro Highway reads "Kirkwood." Today weeds grow between the cracks in the narrow asphalt lane leading to what was one of the plushest gambling establishments in Fort Worth. Except for the lane and jagged remains of the concrete foundation, the three-acre plot has returned to the natural growth of a vacant lot. It was not always so.

* * *

Pappy Kirkwood was born and reared in Water Valley, Mississippi. After the eleven-year-old boy's father died in the state prison for killing a man, William C. Kirkwood fended for himself. His first job, at fifty cents a week, was sweeping the railroad station in the small town. He learned telegraphy, but his new occupation did not pay enough to meet the family expenses. With time on his hands, he learned the tricks of gambling from trainmen waiting for their connections. The money he made helped at home, but the thrill of rolling the dice was his greatest reward. Soon he was a better gambler than the men who had taught him. He left the small Mississippi town and headed west.

For a while he worked for the railroad in Tulsa, Oklahoma. It was the 1920s and Tulsa was awash with oil money and gamblers. He began to make more money at dice tables than at the telegraph key. Then he ran into trouble with some important people and decided to move on.

When W. C. Kirkwood first came to Fort Worth, he lived at the old Metropolitan Hotel on Main Street. He gambled, made some money, and married Faye Leberman, the daughter of an Olney rancher. After the birth of their son, W. C. "Pappy" Kirkwood bought land just outside the city limits in 1932. His house was one of the few built that Depression year.

At that time it was not illegal to have gambling in one's home. Kirkwood and others took advantage of this technicality.

He built a white stucco Spanish Colonial-style house. It sat perched on a hill overlooking the main strip between downtown Fort Worth and Lake Worth. The house originally had 2,500 square feet; Kirkwood enlarged it as the need arose until it measured 5,000 square feet. It featured a large living room complete with a bar. High ceilings lent an open atmosphere in keeping with the posh western furnishings.

The front door had a peephole to screen visitors. 2222 Jacksboro Highway was home to Pappy, his rodeo performing wife, Faye, and their son Pat. "I lived here, in a back room,"[1] Pat told a reporter in

High rollers once drove up this driveway to the 2222 Club.
—Photo by Ann Arnold.

1995. Except for two years during World War II, when the government used the property for Bachelor Officers' Quarters, the Kirkwoods lived there for fifty years.

In addition to the main house, there were apartments for employees. At one corner of the property was a stable for Mrs. Kirkwood's horses. Her most famous horse, the dancing Crown Jewel, and other animals were exercised in the stable yard. Storage buildings and ample parking completed the acreage.

The 2222 Club attracted some of the richest and most powerful men in the state. Kirkwood, a diminutive man with delicate hands, had no use for the penny-ante games of drifters and grifters. From its beginning the Four Deuces catered to up-scale gamblers and wheeler-dealers. A yardman (not the kind who mows lawns) guarded the entrance to the grounds. Admittance was by invitation or recommendation only. It was easier to get into the leading country club than to get into the Four Deuces.

Kirkwood was an amiable host. Without charge he served his guests thick, juicy sirloin steaks and only the best booze. He followed it up with expensive cigars. These he considered part of the cost of doing business.

Another aspect of doing business was his generosity at Christmas. Son Pat told of his school holidays spent in giving out hams, steaks, turkeys, and whiskey to their forty employees, as well as many city and county lawmen.

Pappy made his money at the gambling tables. In the '40s and '50s as much as $200,000 to $300,000 might change hands in a single night. Such notables as Gene Autry, a friend of Mrs. Kirkwood, and Dick Kleberg of the King Ranch were regular visitors.

Numerous local movers and shakers frequented the club. According to Pat, on Sunday afternoons his father would close the house to everyone except Mrs. Amon Carter, the wife of the owner of the city's leading newspaper. She and her lady friends loved to play roulette. Kirkwood instructed his dealers to overpay when Mrs. Carter won. "Do you think Pop wanted Mrs. Amon Carter to leave a loser?"[2] Pat asked.

Frank "Bring Em Back Alive" Buck was a regular guest when he was in Texas. He wasn't a gambler, but enjoyed the food, drink, and camaraderie.

Perhaps Kirkwood's most notable guest was Texan Speaker of the House Sam Rayburn. The Speaker was a bachelor and a Baptist who lived with his teetotaler sister in Bonham. Nevertheless, he enjoyed the company of Pappy Kirkwood and Jack Daniels. Pat Kirkwood recalled, "Pop would close the place and they'd drink and eat and talk all night."[3]

It was an open secret that the Four Deuces was a gambling site. Pappy allowed only those rich enough to lose money without hurting their families to gamble. From time to time law enforcement officers carried out symbolic raids to appease the church crowd and city council. These raids of course were conducted when no church people or councilmen were customers. Always forewarned, the gambling equipment was shoved behind false walls, and the gamblers turned into guests quietly drinking and chatting at a private cocktail party.

The key to Kirkwood's long success was his even-handed dealing with everyone, including those on both sides of the law. "Fifteen of the 17 hoodlums who died in the hoodlum wars were my breakfast companions," Pat related to a newspaper reporter.[4] The elder Kirkwood would go deer hunting with them, but wouldn't let them gamble at his club. He also forbade his employees to gamble for money on the premises.

Despite his influential clientele and lack of rowdiness, Kirkwood was subject to visits by the authorities. Pressed by the outcry of citizens and ministers against gambling, District Attorney Stewart Hellman visited four clubs on the Jacksboro Highway in February, 1951. One was located at 2222. Hellman and his aide were given a tour of the upstairs living quarters by Pappy himself. Downstairs, Pete Peeples, manager of the on-site restaurant, conducted the tour. Two outbuildings on the grounds were inspected. To the surprise of no one, not a hint of illegal gambling was found.

A month later Kirkwood did not fare so well with the grand jury, which returned sixty gambling indictments on March 30. Included in the list of top Fort Worth gamblers was the name W. C. Kirkwood. Pappy protested vigorously and claimed innocence, but to no avail. He was charged with two counts: running a gambling house and permitting betting on dice and card games on August 12, 1950 and February 3, 1951. The Four Deuces was also on a list of gambling places submitted to the Senate Crime Investigating Committee by a manufacturer of gaming equipment.

Defense attorneys immediately set out to question the validity of the indictments. Their arguments, plus the absence of many of the prosecution's key witnesses, finally resulted in the postponement and eventual dismissal of the charges.

However, the grand jury did have an impact on the club. Law enforcement became tighter. The city council ordered a crackdown on all forms of vice. The big spenders could hop a plane, or fly their corporate jets to Las Vegas where gambling was legal. Things would never be the same at 2222 Jacksboro Highway.

Kirkwood also dabbled in oil and real estate. He found they lacked the excitement of gambling. By 1972 his eyesight was failing and age was taking its toll. Cataract surgery did not restore his sight, and he slowly accepted the fact that his gambling days were over. He closed the Four Deuces, but continued to live there.

William C. Kirkwood died in 1983 at the age of ninety-three. He lived a colorful life and the legend lives on. Pat Kirkwood declared gambling was his father's whole life, and it was a good life. "Fundamentally, I really and truly think he just liked to play," he said.[5]

After the estate was probated, Pat Kirkwood offered the historic landmark to anyone who would take it for the flip of a coin. There were no takers. The Historic and Cultural Landmark Commission wanted to save the building, but was unsuccessful. Next Kirkwood tried to auction the property, and again there were no takers. Unwilling to spend the money needed to satisfy the city code inspectors, he reluctantly bulldozed the building where millions of dollars had once changed hands. Quenton McGown, speaking for the commission, noted, "It was a terrible loss because architecturally it was a great spot. It was heartbreaking because of the folklore attached to it."[6]

The glory days of the once famous 2222 Club are long past.
—Photo by Ann Arnold.

Chapter 10

Murder,
Made for the Movies

The murder of William P. Clark had all the ingredients of a movie script. He was a wealthy oil man found dead in his twenty-two room mansion in an exclusive residential area. When Clark filed to have his marriage to a younger woman annulled and cut her out of his will, she supposedly hired a hit man to kill her husband.

At first Clark's death was ruled a suicide. The decomposing body of the sixty-year-old Texas and New Mexico oil man was found on May 22, 1953. Neighbors had noted Clark's car in the front driveway and newspapers stacked up on the porch and Peace Justice Dick Callaway was called in to investigate. He broke into the locked house and discovered the body. It was lying face down on a thick plush carpet in a dressing room of the elegantly furnished home. A .25-20 pump rifle lay on a chair in an adjoining bedroom.

The body was fully clothed, but the trouser pockets were turned out. Further investigation led officers to conclude that two large diamond rings and a significant amount of cash were missing.

From the beginning, Clark's brother, Phillip, discounted suicide as the cause of death. He told authorities William never left his car overnight in the front drive. Moreover, if his brother intended to shoot himself, he would have used his pistol, not a shotgun. He also questioned why a freshly lit cigar was thrown into a flower bed next to the front door.

After an autopsy and discussions with homicide detectives, Callaway changed his ruling to murder. Pathologist Dr. John Andujar reported Clark died of a gunshot entering his right cheek and fracturing the entire left side of his skull. He declared death to be instantaneous, and the absence of powder burns led him to believe the weapon was too far away to cause accidental death or suicide. Blood clot patterns on the carpet eliminated the possibility of suicide.

Investigators, in a further search of the crime scene, found a hollow-nosed .25-20 bullet lodged in the thick carpet. It had been overlooked because it was covered by dried blood. The position of the bullet gave rise to speculation that the killer shot Clark behind the left ear. The bullet passed through his head and exited just below the right cheek.

Now that they had a high profile murder on their hands, city detectives, aided by investigators from the district attorney's office and Texas Rangers, set out to solve the crime. First questioned was a Negro yardman who trimmed the grass three days before the discovery of the body. Police believed he may have been the last person to see the victim alive.

The yardman told of a woman visitor the afternoon of the murder, but he didn't know who she was. Clark supposedly greeted the woman, who said to him, "Hello, Bill. How in the world are you?"[1]

The tall, dark-haired "mystery woman" turned out to be a middle-aged church worker. Identified as Mrs. Kathleen Paylor, she often visited the members of First Presbyterian Church, of which Clark was one. Mrs. Paylor could shed no light on the crime.

Leo Brewster, the dead man's attorney, revealed that his client had reported two death threats just days before the slaying. While authorities sought the killer, Brewster sought to prevent Mary Clark, the widow, from gaining control of the $750,000 estate.

The divorce battle had begun six months earlier when Clark went to court asking that his third wife and her parents, Mr. and Mrs. R. H. Bates, be evicted from the Winton Terrace home. Married less than two years, Clark alleged Mrs. Clark had made false representations and lured him into matrimony for his money. He contended the house was not part of community property. Judge Bob Young granted his request, but ordered the oil man to pay Mary Clark $300 a month pending settlement of the divorce or annulment.

Following his brother's death, Phillip Clark of Hobbs, New Mexico, was named administrator of the estate. In a probation hearing, Phillip asserted his brother wanted to leave the bulk of his estate to four charities. According to the will, Mary Clark was to receive $10.00.

Mrs. Clark's attorneys argued the will drawn up in Hobbs was invalid because the name of a recipient was incorrect. The will stated one-fourth of the estate should go to "Shriner's Crippled Children's Home in Fort Worth." There was no such place. Clark was a regular contributor to the Shrine Hospital for Crippled Children through the Fort Worth Moslah Temple, but neither hospital nor home was in Fort Worth. Under New Mexico law any reference to a non-existent institution automatically left the entire estate to the widow, her lawyer argued.

Brewster pleaded for the intent of the will: "Under all of these facts it would be inconscionable (*sic*) and inequitable to recognize a claim by Mary Clark based upon a technicality that there was a mistake in the exact name of the beneficiary, and thereby take away from an institution dedicated to public good a sizable bequent (*sic*) and give it to the last person in the world that William P. Clark would have wanted to receive it."[2]

Months later the lawyers were still wrangling over the estate. Brewster requested permission to continue with the annulment suit filed a few weeks before Clark was murdered. He said similar cases had been heard and he had legal ground to go ahead with the suit. Judge Young took the matter under advisement.

Two years later, after the trail of the murderer had grown cold, the police received a bit of good luck. Harry Huggins, a five-time loser charged with burglary, told police that, "about $10,000" and some jewelry had been offered to kill Clark and fake a robbery. Confessing to his part in the crime, the forty-eight-year-old Denton man filled in details police had been unable to uncover.

Huggins said he, Tincy Eggleston, and Cecil Green went to the Clark home where he posed as a Western Union messenger. When the unsuspecting victim met him at the door, one of the men knocked a cigar out of his mouth and they barged into the house.

The men ordered him upstairs and made him lie down in the dressing room. Huggins stated that Clark was shot when he was out of the room. Upon hearing the shot, he returned and asked, "What did you shoot him for?"[3] His companion answered that it was part of the deal.

Accompanied by detectives, Huggins re-enacted the crime at the Clark home. Convinced of the accuracy of the ex-convict's account, police arrested Mary Clark and Tincy Eggleston on April 7, 1955. Cecil Green and his attorney, Jack Love, walked into police headquarters the next day. Detectives questioned Clark, Eggleston, and Green at length. All steadfastly denied guilt.

A forty-six-year-old blond, Mrs. Clark was arrested at 8:30 A.M. at her dry cleaning establishment on W. Magnolia Street. Wearing a silk jersey dress, white stole, and white shoes, she listed her address as 1462 W. Jessamine when she was booked. The accused woman covered her face with the stole and refused to answer reporters' questions other than to say, "I don't know what it's all about."[4] After eighteen hours of intermittent questioning, Clark still denied knowing Eggleston, Green, or Huggins. Arthur Lee Moore, Mrs. Clark's attorney, noted the police had questioned his client five separate times since the murder and had never found anything, thereby proving she was innocent.

Tincy Eggleston was not only in trouble with the law, but also in trouble at home. At 5 A.M., police arrested him at the apartment of Evelyn Robertson, his shapely blonde girlfriend. He was wearing shorts; she was clad in light blue pajamas. A .45 caliber automatic pistol was taken from a dresser drawer.

At police headquarters his attorneys Truman Power and George Cochran, argued for Tincy's freedom: "Every time there's a murder in this town they pick up my client."[5]

Green, though not a stylish dresser, nevertheless was neatly attired when he arrived at headquarters. He proclaimed his innocence, but refused to answer reporters' questions concerning his relationship with Eggleston and Huggins. On attorney Love's advice, he kept quiet about his recent activities and whereabouts.

In protective custody, Huggins was asked his motivation behind incriminating himself and his friends. He admitted he, Eggleston, and Green had a falling out, but he refused to say why. As for snitching on the Clark case, he claimed his conscience hurt him over the death. He was not an angel, but he wasn't a killer, either. Police Chief Cato Hightower assured the public Huggins had not been promised immunity for his information.

Jack Love sneered at the suggestion that Huggins' conscience figured into the situation: "It's impossible for me to believe that an ex-convict who already has served time for murder would let his conscience bother him in a matter such as this."[6] He suggested Huggins had been "encouraged" by the police.

As helpful as Huggins' information was, investigators needed more. As a suspect in the case, Huggins' statement could not be used against one of the principals in the crime unless there was physical evidence to corroborate it. The rifle found with the body was the gun used in the shooting. But another rifle, one stolen from the home that night, had been tossed into the river, according to Huggins. Police dragged the Trinity River near Greenwood Cemetery looking for the second rifle, hoping it would link the three to the scene of the crime. They did not find it.

Mary Clark, Eggleston, Green, and Huggins remained in county jail awaiting an examining trial to determine if there was enough evidence to hold them. Clark would be charged with being an accomplice to murder, while the others would be charged with murder.

The hearings took place in Criminal District Court No. 2. Eggleston, wearing blue-and-white striped coveralls and a stubble of dark beard, was calm and deliberate as the judge ruled he should remain in jail. Mrs. Eggleston, angry over discovery of the "other woman," still defended him. Admitting he was not a model husband, she maintained his crimes did not include murder.

Mary Clark's case was heard next. She peeked through the white stole she had used for the past two days to shield her face from cameras and prying eyes. Sobbing as the judge ruled that she, too, should be returned to jail, she meekly followed the deputy sheriff out of the courtroom.

Green, dressed in the same manner as Eggleston, sat silently as the judge ordered him back to jail. He casually walked out without acknowledging reporters or onlookers.

All were indicted by the grand jury and were soon out on bond. Green and Huggins were quickly released to their lawyers after posting bonds of $15,000 each. Mrs. Clark's bond of $25,000 was easily met and she was let go. Eggleston's attorney, Truman Power, took longer to round up $50,000 for his bond. The amount was reduced to $20,000, and a smiling, clean-shaven Eggleston walked out of jail.

By the time of the trial both Eggleston and Green had been

killed. Mary Clark alone faced a jury. Her trial made headlines for being the longest and costliest trial in the county and taxpayers forked over $3,499 in expenses. Five days were consumed seating a jury in the sensational case.

It also had the largest number of exhibits, more than 150. Among the exhibits were torrid love letters the defendant wrote to a New York playboy shortly before she married William Clark.

In his charge to the jury, Judge Willis McGregor defined murder, accomplice, malice aforethought, conspiracy, co-conspirators, and circumstantial evidence. He told the jury they must find that Eggleston murdered William Clark, "and that before he did so, Mrs. Clark 'advised, commanded or persuaded' him to do so."[7] The jury deliberated eight hours before finding Mary Clark not guilty.

Upon hearing the verdict, she took a deep gulp of air. When the full realization hit her she fell onto the shoulder of her attorney and wept. She was helped from the courtroom and taken to a waiting automobile. "I knew when I had my case presented to an unbiased and unprejudiced jury," she told a reporter, "I'd get justice."[8] The Winton Terrace home was declared community property and Mary Clark remained there after the trial.

With both Cecil Green and Leroy Eggleston the victims of gangland slayings, only Huggins was left to serve time. He was sentenced to eight years in prison.

Chapter 11

Blood Made Him Sick, But He Killed Anyway

ecil Green was a chief suspect in the slayings of Mr. and Mrs. Herbert Noble and Mr. and Mrs. Nelson Harris, two couples killed by bomb blasts. Cecil, considered one of the most notorious hoodlums of his day, had a serious weakness for someone in his line of work—the sight of blood made him sick.

Crime was a family tradition for Green. Big brother Hollis DeLois "Lois" Green broke into the big time when he robbed the Renfro Wholesale Drug Company of $17,000—a lot of money in 1943. He might have gotten away if two children playing nearby had not suspected something was wrong and scratched the license number of the getaway car into the sidewalk. Six years later Lois was blasted by two bullets in a Dallas nightclub parking lot.

A retired Dallas officer attributed twenty-two murders to Cecil's big brother, adding, "For my money he was the most desperate, the most depraved thug that ever operated in this section."[1] Lois was only thirty-four when he was killed, but he had taught his little brother the finer points of hijacking, burglary, and safe cracking. According to those who knew him, Cecil was a follower, not a leader like Lois. A retired Fort Worth police chief recalled that both "were really bad actors."

By the time the younger Green was thirty years old he had served time in prison and was known to law officers in Kansas,

Oklahoma, and Texas. Cecil, a sidekick of Tincy Eggleston, was charged with assault, burglary, robbery, safe cracking, and murder during his reign as one of three leading hoodlums in the Metroplex.

He and Eggleston were arrested in Oklahoma City and returned to Texas to face charges of armed robbery of a poker game in Austin late in 1953. The two were accused of robbing over $2,000 in cash and $1,850 worth of jewelry from a game in a private home. The eleven players failed to identify the suspects. The district attorney was forced to release them. At the time of his arrest, Green was out on bond while his lawyer was appealing a five-year sentence for armed robbery in Sayre, Oklahoma.

Austin police believed Sid Foley and Green's girlfriend Rita Davis were involved in the robbery, but did not have enough evidence to hold them.

Back in Fort Worth, the four were arrested after a gun battle erupted between them. Detective A. C. Howerton said Foley told him, "It all started when Eggleston and Green 'conned him out of his wife.'"[2] The deserted husband found the men in a car on the Jacksboro Highway with the woman. Foley fired two pistol shots into the vehicle, but was unable to get his shotgun into action before they burned rubber and escaped. Two days later Foley spotted Mrs. Foley and Rita Davis in a parked car on Central Avenue near North Main. Foley attempted to pull his wife out of the vehicle, but Davis jumped into the fray and chased him away with a loaded shotgun. He fled on foot, but not before neighbors called the cops.

Davis telephoned Green to come to their rescue. She and Green were arrested for disturbing the peace and taken to the police station. Eggleston and Foley voluntarily appeared the next day. They were told to "get out of town" or be arrested as vagrants.

Green's take on the murder of Edell Evans sounded like pulp fiction. Supposedly he told it like it was. Evans hired Eggleston and Green to kill a minor competitor in the prostitution business. They abducted the intended victim and explained they had a contract out on him. They assured him they had nothing personal against him, and promised to make the death quick and painless. The quick-thinking man asked who wanted him out of the way. "It can't hurt to tell me, I'll be dead anyway." That made sense to Green and he revealed Evans' name. In the exchange that followed, Evans quickly became the target:

"How much is he paying you?"

"Fifteen thousand up front and another fifteen thousand when the job is finished."

"What if I pay you $20,000 to kill Edell instead of me? You already have the $15,000, so you would come out ahead."

Green admitted he never was very good at math but it sounded like a better deal to him. Eggleston said he didn't care who got killed. A job was a job.

Green, Eggleston, and Evans then went in Evans' car to view the "body." Tincy, who was in the back seat, put a gun to Edell's head and fired, rendering him unconscious. They lugged him to an already prepared shallow grave. Cecil went to get a shovel from his car, and to recover from his queasiness caused by the bloody scene. Evans, so the narrative goes, came to, raised up and bit Eggleston on the ankle. As one reporter later noted, "Tincy let out a scream you could hear in twenty counties."[3] So they shot him again, covered him up, and high-tailed it out of there.

Cecil was killed, Tincy escaped. Was he set up?
—Photo courtesy of Henry H. Wright

Green had been out on bond for the William Clark murder only two weeks when he was mortally wounded. An anonymous call sent an ambulance to the By-Way Drive-In, 5605 Jacksboro Highway at 11:45 P.M. May 2, 1955. The ambulance drivers found Green lying on the ground beside his Cadillac, recognized the gangster, and radioed police.

The victim had been shot in the upper right chest, the right side of his head, and in the right arm. Police counted seven bullet wounds. The medics rushed him to St. Joseph's Hospital. Green, in true gangland fashion, refused to talk about the shooting. When questioned, he merely shrugged and smiled faintly.

Officers found rifle shells at the site of the ambush, but other clues were hard to come by. An unconfirmed report said a Cadillac was seen racing from the drive-in. Another said someone was seen in a pasture behind the building.

Police pieced together a sketch of the assault. Tincy Eggleston had been in the car with Green. "We were parked out there and saw this other car nearby. Just before the shooting started the lights of another car hit us and then the shooting started,"[4] he told investigators. He emptied his pistol in the direction of the shooters as he ran for cover.

They agreed it was the work of a professional killer, probably from out of town. Underworld rumors buzzed about Kansas City killers having a $20,000 minimum contract to hit the notorious pair. A police informer said Eggleston, Green, and a well-known Fort Worth defense attorney were planning to set up a protection racket. Supposedly that was the reason someone hired the out-of-state hitmen.

The attorney, a big, somewhat cowardly man, begged a reporter to keep his name out of print in connection with the shooting. Lack of sufficient documentation kept the story out of the newspapers. The badly shaken attorney went back to defending, rather than partnering with his clients.

To add another twist, rumor had it that when the Kansas City people didn't get to Fort Worth at the appointed time, the source implied the cops took care of the matter.

The police would only speculate that badman Gene Paul Norris was their number one suspect as the shooter. Norris was fingered because the ambush took place in front of a tavern run by Gene Paul's sister. Those who knew the truth of the matter are dead or aren't talking. The only indisputable fact was that Green died from the ambush.

Dr. J. H. Marr, a chiropractor, reported witnessing the shoot-out. He said he was across the highway and saw a Cadillac, presumed to be Green's, drive up beside a car parked at the front of the darkened tavern. That car drove away, and within seconds gunfire erupted from the side of the building.

"If Green ever knew who or what was behind the lethal hail of lead, he never said before lapsing into a death coma."[5] Detective A. C. Howerton recalled that the ex-convict expected a violent death, adding that he hoped he got it in the head. He didn't get his wish. Green lingered sixteen hours before breathing his last.

Private services were held for the thirty-nine-year-old police character. Green's friends provided a showy casket banked by pink, red, and white floral arrangements. Rev. Erwin F. Bohmfalk, Methodist district superintendent, conducted the rites. "There is so much bad in the best of us / And so much good in the worst of us / That it does not behoove any of us / To talk about the rest of us,"[6] he said.

Joan Green and her two small daughters came from Dallas for the funeral. Because she had car trouble on the way over, the service was forty-five minutes late in starting. Not everyone signed the guest register. Among those who did sign was Leroy Eggleston. Rita Davis' name was not listed.

Green had $1.56 in his pocket when he arrived at the hospital that fatal night. The funeral cost about $1,700. The hat was passed before the service began. The cost was only partly covered.

Chapter 12

Little Gambling House on the Hill

Fred Browning, a friend of Benny Binion, could have taught the Las Vegas operator a thing or two. Browning created the most lavish gambling establishment in Texas when Vegas was just sand and sage.

Being a plumber in his father's business lacked the excitement Browning craved. In 1921 he purchased a tea room located between Arlington and Handley, Texas, and the sedate tea room, run by two sisters, became Top o' the Hill Terrace—and Handley became East Fort Worth.

From the first, Top o' the Hill catered to the rich and adventurous. One almost expected to see the Great Gatsby drinking fine whiskey, eating aged sirloin steaks, and playing roulette. The whiskey was not always legal.

Even minor surgery did not keep Browning from a court hearing because of the whiskey. "Fred Browning, owner of Top o' the Hill Terrace near Arlington, late Wednesday afternoon from his bed in a hospital pleaded not guilty to federal charges that he purchased stolen, nontax-paid whiskey."[1] United States Commissioner Lois Newam conducted the unusual proceeding, assisted by a federal marshal. Attorney Arthur Lee Moore represented the patient.

The three-count indictment stated that Browning and two others removed forty-five gallons of distilled whiskey from a warehouse in Bowling Green, Kentucky. They transported the spirits across state lines in leather-covered copper containers disguised as luggage. In a plea bargain, Browning paid the obligatory fine and the charges were dropped.

Over a period of more than two decades Fred and Mary Browning hosted thousands. In addition to running the club, both loved horses. Arlington Downs, which operated as a pari-mutuel track from 1934 to 1937, was a favorite spot to watch their prize animals. They started their stable with Royal Ford. Later they raced nationwide, owning stakes-winner Pharamar and a string of more than fifty horses.

Pat Kirkwood, son of the Browning's rival, W. C. Kirkwood, commented on Mrs. Browning's knowledge of horses: "You could ask her what a horse named 'Dog Bone' did in California in 1938 and she would just rattle it off to you."[2]

Fred Browning was also interested in professional boxing. He sponsored Lew Jenkins, an unknown Texas fighter. "A star was born, almost overnight, not so many hours ago in Madison Square Garden's ring,"[3] enthused AP sports editor Dillon Graham. He described Jenkins as "the cruelest, most murderous little puncher to come along in years." The "Sweet Swatter" from Sweetwater was crowned lightweight champion in May 1940. Unfortunately, drinking and the inability to handle pressures of the big-time led to his quick fall from grace. He and Browning lost touch, and twenty years later he was arrested for grand larceny. The forty-seven-year-old ex-champ was apologetic. "I didn't mean to do this, but I'm flat broke and I'm hungry."[4]

A carefully planned raid of Top o' the Hill in the summer of 1947 resulted in the confiscation of $25,000 in equipment. Fifty patrons and eight employees were arrested. The *Star-Telegram*, following Amon Carter's edict of not printing names of prominent citizens, didn't print the whole story. Fifty years later a retired reporter told of the incident.

Top o' the Hill had a narrow escape tunnel leading from the gaming room to an open spot down the hill. One very influential citizen who happened to have his broken leg in a cast, was there the night of the raid. Somehow in the excitement he got his cast stuck in the tunnel. The people behind him could not escape. Arrested and fined, they resolved never again to gamble with anyone whose leg was in a cast.[5]

For Browning, hard times fell on the hill after the 1951 grand jury exposé. With his health failing, the once flamboyant sportsman sold the club. It first became the Arlington Country Club, then the Arlington Bible College.

Jack Gordon, dean of Tarrant County entertainment writers, recalled his visit to the infamous site after it was converted to the country club. He observed children playing in the big living room where some of the nation's "fattest of the fat cats" once played. A milk bar, with the bartender standing in a trench in order to be on eye-level with his customers, was doing big business.

Taken on a tour by manager Ben Dobson, Gordon noted a heavy, barrel-like safe. Browning had preferred to do his own banking, and huge sums of money must have reposed in the safe at one time.

Fred Browning, "one of the four most important gamblers in the metroplex,"[7] died of heart failure in 1953. Despite the millions of dollars that changed hands at the Top o' the Hill, he died a relatively poor man. Born and reared in Tarrant County, Browning was buried in East Fort Worth's Rose Hill Cemetery. As Jack Gordon said at the time, "Old crapshooters may never die, but they sure do fade away—and fade they have from the big house atop the hill near Arlington."[6]

He had borrowed heavily from Las Vegas gambler Benny Binion, and from local oil man Sid Richardson. The Browning estate was sold in order to partially pay off his debts. In lieu of repayment, Richardson received forty-six horses. He was represented in the transaction by his attorney, John Connally. Asked what Richardson planned to do with the horses, Connally, who would go on to become governor of Texas, replied, "I don't have the faintest idea."[8]

In 1969 University of Texas student Gloria Van Zandt wrote a term paper titled "Top o' the Hill Terrace set many a fortune spinning" for a Texas History course. She captured the flavor of the place and the period:

> Two miles west of Arlington just off Highway 80 lies a most serene and inspiring acreage belonging to the Baptist Bible Seminary. Many of the expected 450 fall students will come seeking their bachelor's degree in religious education, divinity, sacred music or perhaps their master's of theology.
>
> The students will be most impressed with the newest structure on campus which will contain the administrative offices and

student dining hall. Without doubt, they will be astonished to learn that less than 25 years ago the foundation of that very building was once the casino area of one of United States' most notorious and luxurious gambling palaces—Top Of The Hill Terrace.

Sermons and hymns now ring across the terraced hills which once hummed with the playing of slot machines, roulette wheels and an occasional shout of "Craps" from the dice tables.

In an attempt to trace the origin of this once famous establishment, the earliest account is from a man who claims he hauled lumber there in 1924 or 1925. The structure built on the 1,000 foot peak of the 46.4 acres was reportedly the home of two elderly spinster ladies who ran a home-style restaurant with fried chicken as their speciality.

During the '20s, a middle-aged Fort Worth plumber named Fred C. Browning decided to change occupations. He left his plumbing business to operate a few small gambling houses in the area. He was operating in the Texas Hotel, then he and some of his friends decided to have their own establishment.

On Nov. 30, 1921, Mr. Browning bought the front tract of land where the spinsters' restaurant stood, which included the house. On Sept. 28, 1935, he acquired the adjoining back tract of land. These two land purchases compiled the 46 acres on which the Top Of The Hill casino operated.

The entrance and guardhouse of the Top of the Hill Club.
—Photo by author

Immediately upon acquisition of the acreage, extensive remodeling of the house began. The new owner first had the house moved aside so that the basement could be built; then, the house was replaced on top of the new basement. The main floor was the only visible structure above the ground. The inner floor and the basement were much larger than the house and were built expressly for casino operations.

The Browning's house (which faced Division) was not visible from the highway. In order to reach the house, it was necessary to enter the large iron gates of the stone entrance and ascend the winding paved road. The exact date that the casino opened is not certain; but it is known to have been in operation during the early months of 1933.

There were usually two guards stationed at the gate. One stayed in the gatehouse to telephone the house and gain permission to allow the patrons to enter the grounds. The other watchman opened the gates.

Top Of The Hill was officially billed as a dining resort; but, "the only thing money could buy there was chips." In reality, food and drinks were served free to the patrons. "Most patrons came with at least $500 to spend."

The casino was open from 8 P.M. until 2 A.M. every week night; but on weekends it was not unusual for it to still be open when the sun came up. They served the best meat money could buy and had their own 8 by 12 meat lockers in the kitchen. (It might be noted here that this was during the Depression years when beef was not plentiful even when one could afford it.)

The ground (*sic*) surrounding the Browning's home were quite beautifully landscaped. Ardie Harrison was the caretaker and had four other full-time employees working for him. He worked for Mr. Browning from the time the property was bought until Mr. Harrison's recent retirement as keeper of the ground for the Baptist Seminary. The estate had many acres of formal gardens containing fountains and small fish ponds. A large greenhouse was kept filled with lovely plants and supplied fresh flowers daily to the house and dining room. Mr. Harrison said he worked in the daytime and didn't know what went on at night.

Mr. Harrison further stated that he was a Christian man and didn't gamble—"all those people been awfully good to me, and I don't think I ought to talk about them. You know, Mr. Browning's gone now and I sure wouldn't want to talk about him."

When the seminary bought the estate, one of the conditions

under which Mr. Harrison stayed as caretaker was that he didn't have to tell anyone anything.

One story Mr. Harrison has been known to tell was how Mr. Browning once trusted him to bring back $90,000 from a bank in Fort Worth.

From all accounts, the grounds were truly palatial. Driving to the parking lot in back of the house afforded a view of the 50 by 25 foot tiled swimming pool (which has been drained since the early 1950s) and patio area which had a connecting cabana.

Walking from the parking lot, one could wander through the beautiful tea garden which surrounded a gazebo, and gaze down at the gracious swans on the mirror-like pond. The tea garden was built on a raised plateau and is believed by many to have a false bottom. The students at the seminary claim that the water doesn't drain off of it like it does elsewhere on the grounds and that there must be a secret tunnel leading to a room under it.

From the tea garden one would have to walk to the terrace to reach the back door of the house. The back door was the main entrance for the patrons of the Top Of The Hill. There were five doors through which one passed to finally reach the casino. The first door was one with a two-way mirror which lead (*sic*) into an entrance hall. From the entrance hall, one passed through another door which had a peep hole. Behind this door was the hat check girl and cloak room.

"Park your revolver here" was a sign that hung over the doorway. After checking belongings, one still had another door to pass through before gaining entrance to the lounge and restaurant area. This third door had a small trap door and after being correctly identified, one would most likely be greeted by Mrs. Browning, who served as official hostess. She would always offer free drinks and dinner and would later show patrons to the game room.

The meals were prepared by a Negro woman named Gussy who lived on the premises with her family in a nice house located through the archway behind the parking lot. Everybody like (*sic*) and said she was a marvelous cook. She kept a spotless kitchen and served gourmet meals using linens, china, silver and crystal.

One of the best known stories told was of a quite famous meal undoubtedly Gussy must have served—"Browning's $120,000 breakfast." The story goes that a group of West Texas oil men flew in for a little fun and games, and by 6 A.M. they had lost $80,000 to Browning. Browning stood up and said that he wasn't one to stop when he was the winner, but he suggested that they take a short break, wash up and eat, then return to the table. So they had breakfast and shortly after daybreak returned to the casino.

Three hours later, the oil men had won the $80,000 back and $40,000 more.

Mr. Browning had planned his home with much foresight for its use as a gambling casino. Even with the possibility of unannounced raids, there was not much cause for concern since his fortress was considered virtually raid proof. The building was so ingeniously constructed for its functional purpose, that it remains a wonder that a raid was ever effected.

The grounds of the estate were surrounded by a wired alarm system. "The only way one could possibly get in was through the front gates." The house was mostly glass windows with steel shutters. The front door of the house was kept heavily bolted. As mentioned before, patrons generally entered through the back door.

On the ground floor of the house were located the lounge, restaurant, the Browning's living quarters and guest rooms. The inner floor of Mr. Browning's bedroom led down to a secret inner floor which was directly over his office in the casino. The inner floor was partitioned into passageways and secret rooms.

Another trap door from upstairs led into a second secret room on the inner floor which was connected to a third but smaller room. The third room was above the casino, and here there were two-way mirrors through which the gamblers and casino could be watched. The ladder down to the room was carpeted so the viewer would not be heard entering or leaving his perch.

When permitted to enter the casino in the basement, one gazed upon three pool tables with low swinging lights above each, two roulette wheels, two black jack tables and two craps tables. There were nineteen paid dealers operating the tables. One of these dealers was a good friend of the Brownings and stayed in the house in one of the bedrooms upstairs. Out-of-town guests were frequent in the Browning's home and nice accommodations were available.

At the base of the stairs leading into the casino one could turn left and would be in front of Mr. Browning's office, which was well hidden behind a very large wooden door. His office was carpeted in black and had dark walnut paneling throughout. In his office was a large safe which kept the average bank roll needed for each evening of $200,000. The safe had a time lock and opened each evening at 8 P.M.

An average "take" for the casino was an estimated $50,000 to $100,000 nightly, and on the weekends this amount was more than doubled. Figuring on these tabulations, it is a low estimate to say the $50 million was made at Top Of The Hill during its 22 years of operation.

Because of the large amount of money on the premises, Mr. Browning hired a man to patrol the back of the hill with a 30-30 rifle. "Nobody knew of his being there, and in the event of robbers, he had plenty of ammo."

There were three known trap doors in the walls of the basement casino which were opened by turning a key in the wall. These trap doors led to smaller rooms behind false walls and were used to conceal the gambling equipment. One such false door was camouflaged by a frame holding cue sticks.

Another of these trap doors led to a little room containing a vast network of switches. Above this concealed room was a hidden loft where I found some old newspapers dating back to 1933. If one were to walk straight through the door from the casino into the switchboard room and continue straight to the far side of the room, one would uncover another secret door. This door led to the notorious secret tunnel. This 50-foot long tunnel was about four feet wide and ten feet tall. It led to the west side of the wooded hill and was densely concealed with shrubbery.

The caretaker said the tunnel was constructed for a fire exit from the casino. However, it did appear to the writer to be quite conveniently located should the gamblers desire to make a hurried exit. There are rumors that other tunnels led from the casino to other rooms, but if this was true they have long been sealed off. No proof exists of another casino.

The bar was also located in the basement and was a beautiful, round, twelve-foot bar with a wall of mirrors behind it. "Hogan" was employed as barkeeper and kept the casino clean. He was well liked and since there was no charge for drinks, Hogan no doubt retired a rich man from his tips.

At this point, it would be pertinent to explain the sentiment regarding the attitudes toward gambling in those days and the social trends which allowed such a casino to exist.

During part of The Top Of The Hill's grand era (1933-45), horse racing and certified betting were legal in Texas. Arlington had one of the largest and most famous tracks in the south. The participators from Arlington Downs also contributed greatly to the success of the Top Of The Hill.

Police Chief A. B. (Ott) Cribbs, now retired, remembers "gambling was pretty much wide open then, and slot machines were not uncommon to be found most any public place." One gambler said he didn't really care to gamble that much but that it was a nice place to go and he could be assured of meeting some influential people who would help him in his line of business.

Another referred to the Top Of The Hill as "Vegas—before Vegas was," and said, "it was nothing for gamblers to fly in to shoot dice and bring their bodyguards with them." The Top Of The Hill was referred to as "the biggest gambling house in the United States." Rich people came from all over to gamble, because it was a straight house.

Gambling was considered more or less legal by the citizens and was rather accepted prior to 1947. One of the ladies in the seminary office commented that some years ago a prominent banker paid them a visit to try to establish their account with his bank. He commented that things sure had changed since he had last been there.

It must also be considered that this was during the prohibition period and there was a lot of black market money floating around. Bootlegged whiskey and big name dance bands were all a part of the action at the Top Of The Hill.

Also, the people of that period were without television and did not have the great resources available for recreation and entertainment that we do today. They were heavily burdened with hardships connected with the war. The Depression years were traumatic and brought much cause for worry about the future. These reasons and others contributed to the quest for fun and excitement—which was exactly what the Top Of The Hill had to offer.[9]

Chapter 13

"Tincy": Meaner Than a Junkyard Dog

To some he might seem meaner than the proverbial junkyard dog, but to others Leroy "Tincy" Eggleston was a dapper, even-tempered man who happened to be a gangster. A newspaper reporter who wrote reams about Tincy's criminal activities remembers him as a sociable guy who could tell a good story. A former employee said a person couldn't ask for a more considerate boss. A friend who had known Tincy since both were high school students described him as the "kind of guy who would give you the shirt off his back."

Another boyhood friend declared Cecil Green's influence turned Tincy into a killer. Was Cecil the leader and Tincy the follower, or the other way around?

As a youth on Fort Worth's North Side, Tincy was a familiar sight making deliveries for local drug stores. His first recorded arrest was on April 12, 1926. By the time of his death almost thirty years later, Eggleston's police folder had grown to be one of the thickest in the department's files.

Tincy was born in the Central Texas town of Belton. The family moved to Fort Worth when he was six. He attended public schools and had a seemingly ordinary childhood. His criminal exploits, which ranged from burglary to suspected gangland slayings, were a puzzle to his family. His older brother, J. W. Eggleston, noted the two had little in common and had not been close for years. J. W. was interested in machinery, and Tincy was interested in horses and livestock.

Eggleston's interests continued into adulthood when, as a teenager, Al "Cotton" Farmer, who made a name for himself in stock car racing circles, exercised horses for Eggleston. As one reporter pointed out, "Tincy's family listed his occupation as 'cattleman' on the funeral records. . . ."[1]

His first arrest in 1926 was for burglary. He was released, and two years later he was charged with burglarizing a dry cleaning shop. By 1929 the arrests were frequent, and in December he was sentenced to two years in the penitentiary for bootlegging. Three years later he was back in court for violation of liquor laws.

The end of Prohibition necessitated his going into a new line of work. In January 1934 he was handed a thirteen-year prison sentence for robbery. He escaped, was recaptured, and served the remainder of the sentence, less good time allowance.

Back on the outside, soon he was in trouble again. Now thirty-four years old, he had picked up the nickname "Little Oscar." Charged with hijacking a load of liquor and $90 cash from Ivan Stanley of Pampa, he was held in the Wheeler County jail. While in custody he got into an altercation with another inmate, which required eight stitches in his tongue. Attorney Clyde Mays posted bond, but could not keep Eggleston from being convicted. In June 1941 he was again sentenced to thirteen years for robbery.

Tincy's next run-in with the law occurred in August 1947, when he and three others were arrested for keeping a gambling house on the 1000 block of Main in Fort Worth. Like a Mafia command post, the house had an electric lock on the front door and a lookout stationed nearby. The first lookout signaled to a second one, positioned on the second-floor landing. The police showed a search warrant and entered the house. They found twenty-three gamblers and a "large, round oil-cloth-covered dining table, with a section cut large enough to admit a chair and a man. . . ."[2]—a gambling table. Among the group, a known safe cracker was held for questioning. A man repairing an air conditioner was released. The police found no cards, dice, or money. They had no choice but to leave without the suspected gamblers in tow.

Just hours after gambler and ex-convict Nelson Harris and his wife Juanita were blown to bits by a car bomb, a similar bomb was found under the hood of Tincy Eggleston's car. Two stories have emerged concerning those bombs. One came from Tincy's report to the police. He said he received a telephone call informing him of the bombing of his friend Harris' car. Checking his own vehicle, Tincy noticed the hood of the 1950 coach was slightly ajar, and called a mechanic.

"*Whoosh!* I shook that thing in there,"[3] related S. D. Dickerson to police and Carswell Air Force Base demolition experts. Dickerson's auto repair shop on Highway 81 was a short distance from Eggleston's two-story cinder block house south of Burleson. The nervous man watched as the experts carefully removed the quart jar of "jelly" to an open field. The jar, filled with an apple butter-like substance with black specks in it, was wrapped in heavy duct tape. Two wires led to the automobile's ignition system. The experts agreed that it was made by someone who knew how to make bombs.

Eggleston had no comment as he looked at the four-foot-wide, three-foot-deep hole made by the exploding device. He stuck to his story; he didn't know of anyone who wanted him or Harris dead. He noted that his nine-year-old daughter heard the dogs barking during the night. A Burleson youth reported seeing a car late the night before on a side road about 200 yards from Eggleston's rural home. The mystery of who planted the bomb was never officially solved.

Years later another theory was proposed by someone who knew both Harris and Eggleston. This man contended the two had a falling out over money. In his account, Tincy first put the bomb in Harris' car, then put one in his own automobile. After the Harrises were killed, he "discovered" his car had been tampered with.

Lending support to the theory that Eggleston rigged his own car was a story from a longtime acquaintance. Shortly after the Harris bombing, he and another man went out to Tincy's house to plant several pecan trees. Before they could get to the house they were attacked by what he described as "some really bad dogs." He and his friend had to get on top of their car. They threw their shoes and boots at the dogs and waited several hours until Tincy came home and called off the dogs. "It would have been impossible, impossible for anybody to get in there and mess with Tincy's car."[4]

Whichever account is true, Nelson Harris was dead and Tincy Eggleston had a few more years to live.

In the days before college boys on athletic scholarships also got cars and money, two college roommates worked as weekend bartenders at a club in which Tincy had a financial interest. The gambler would come around in the afternoons, always friendly and soft-spoken. At the students request, Tincy showed them the .45 semi-automatic he always carried.

"Late one afternoon my roommate showed up at the dining hall on the campus driving Tincy's car. After dinner he asked several of us if we wanted a ride back to the dormitory," one student recalled. Knowing the owner's reputation and what happened to his friend Harris, the guys declined, "In fact, we all ran when my roommate got in to start the engine."[5]

A mere four months after the Harris bombing, Tincy was arrested and charged with assault with intent to murder following a brawl in the Do or Don't Lounge, 1100 Main Street. A witness said two airmen, twin brothers, were drinking beer and minding their own business when Tincy came to their booth, pulled a gun on them, and threatened to blow their brains out. Tincy claimed he merely asked them to tone down their profanity, as ladies were present. He also claimed he didn't have a gun. From that point on, the argument became "did, too/did not."

The twins were treated at Carswell Base Hospital for cuts and bruises and released. Assistant District Attorney Truman Power, who later would serve as defense attorney for Tincy, filed charges against him. Attorney Clifford Mays bailed his client out of jail. Again.

After three postponements, a jury was seated to hear the case one year to the day after the "did too/did not" fracas. The state's case fizzled when Mrs. Velma Hudgins, wife of the lounge owner, testified that she asked Tincy to intervene because the twins were making obscene comments to her and a woman friend. Her testimony was bolstered by that of Double-O Malone, a songwriter. He told the court he heard a whole lot of cussin' goin' on.

Eggleston pled guilty to a reduced charge of aggravated assault and paid a $500 fine. The irony was that he had agreed earlier to a $1,000 fine and the state turned him down. He could have received a maximum fifteen-year sentence had the two witnesses not come to his defense. Surely only a cynic would wonder how much the witnesses cost him.

While out on bond Eggleston got into more trouble. In July

1951 he was indicted by the grand jury for keeping a gambling table and bank. "Keeping a bank" meant he provided the money to pay off a winner, but kept the losers' money. He was also charged with exhibiting a slot machine.

Clifford Mays again came to the rescue, and a $1,000 bond was posted. The offenses allegedly took place at the Skyliner and Annex Clubs in May 1949. The trial was set for October, but postponed due to missing witnesses. Tincy calmly played solitaire in an ante-room while the legal maneuvers were going on. Upon hearing of the postponement, he gathered up his cards and went home.

Another trial was scheduled for December. Essie Graham, one of the missing witnesses in the previous trial, was found and forced to testify. She admitted to working as a shill in the Annex for several months during the time in question. She remembered seeing Eggleston at the club from time to time, but she claimed Nelson Harris, now conveniently dead, hired her and ran the club. Out of the presence of the jury she was questioned by District Attorney Stewart Hellman:

> "Did you testify before the grand jury that you were paid by Tincy?"
> "I did testify but I just don't remember what I told them."
> "Did Tincy employ you?"
> "No, he didn't."
> "Did you testify that Nelson Harris and Tincy Eggleston were mere associates with Mr. Satterwhite (W. D. Satterwhite, operator of the Skyliner) in the game?"
> "I don't think I did."
> "Did you testify that Tincy met people when they came in?"
> "I don't remember. If I did I was mistaken."
> "Did you testify Tincy Eggleston was the manager of the game?"
> "I don't remember."[6]

Hellman, realizing the case was lost, rested for the state. Judge Dave McGee instructed the jury to find Tincy not guilty.

Graham's hazy memory was typical of witnesses against Tincy. The defendant, dressed in a two-tone sports outfit, was the picture of composure. Perhaps he knew ahead of time how the case would turn out. Only when a television cameraman tried to get footage of him did he respond in anger.

Depending on the people one talked to, and the situation, Tincy's behavior showed a complexity common to many gamblers and con men. Most of the time he was pleasant and polite. His darker side was shown only to victims of his crimes. He was both charming and vicious, but cunning at all times. Eggleston told a reporter one time, "If you're ever robbed, you better hope it's by a pro like me. Why should I turn up the heat by killing you just to take your money? Only young punks do that. Now, if someone offers me $25,000 to kill you, that's another matter."[7]

A retired secretary related a story about a visit Tincy made to her school. His reputation as a killer was already well known when he went to pick up his eighth grade daughter Carole. He walked into the office, identified himself, and asked that Carole be called from her class. A student helper went to fetch the girl and the secretary motioned Tincy to a chair. He sat down and, putting a cigarette in his ever-present black holder, lit up. It has ever been the rule that nobody, not even the superintendent or God, smokes in a school office. The secretary wasn't about to tell the city's most infamous gangster not to smoke. Carole left with her father, and the secretary opened the windows to get rid of the smoke and breathed a sigh of relief.

After hearing this story a retired law officer, who knew Tincy from his many arrests, said, "If asked, Tincy would have graciously extinguished his cigarette."[8]

While fortune smiled on Eggleston when he appeared in court, he was not immune from further arrests. In late June of 1952 he was charged with burglary of a 650-pound safe. Officers contended Tincy and an accomplice stole the safe from a Breckenridge ranch home. They removed an estimated $130,000 in cash and valuables, then dumped it into the Trinity River just south of the Benbrook Dam spillway. The safe was discovered by two teenagers on their way to church.

Lawmen theorized that Paul Tomlin, Eggleston's partner in crime, had surveyed the ranch house two months earlier. He and Eggleston visited rancher Henry Compton on the pretext of buying a horse. Tomlin asked for a drink of water and was allowed to go into the house. He emerged a short time later. He decided not to buy the horse, and the two left.

Knowing of Tincy's expertise in burglary, investigators didn't question his means or methods, but they had one burning question about the crime. How did he get a 650-pound safe out of the house without leaving even a minute scratch on the floor? Eggleston wasn't talking, and it will be up to the television producers of "How Did He Do That?" to solve the mystery.

Stephens County Sheriff Tom Offield and Texas Ranger John Cope produced warrants for the arrest of Eggleston and Tomlin. Claiming he was at the Audie Murphy Rodeo in Euless at the time of the burglary, Tincy surrendered to Fort Worth detectives John Dunwoody and Grady Haire. He was taken to the Breckenridge jail.

Tomlin had served time in the Eastland County jail for cattle theft. He had also been in Huntsville for forgery, and in El Reno, Oklahoma, for income tax fraud. Now he was nowhere to be found.

Tincy, meanwhile, was cooling his heels as a guest of the sheriff. Walterine Eggleston tried to make bond for her husband, but the papers were not properly notarized. Clifford Mays indicated he was turning the matter over to someone else. Then came Spencer Shropshire and Robert L. Wright; bond was made and Tincy was out of jail. The Stephens County grand jury failed to take action on the case. It was left open and Tincy walked again.

Leroy Eggleston couldn't seem to stay out of trouble. In November the United States Bureau of Internal Revenue filed tax liens of almost $3,000 against Tincy and his wife. They paid Uncle Sam his due and the case was dismissed. Where did the money come from to pay the taxes? Tincy didn't say. Perhaps it was just coincidence that the money taken in the Breckenridge burglary was never recovered.

His next brush with the law came in Dallas late in December 1952. He and ex-convicts Willard Hubler and Boyd Penn were caught unloading burglary tools from a pick-up truck to a late-model Cadillac. Penn also had fifty narcotic tablets in his possession. By this time many believed Tincy was dabbling in drugs.

Eggleston must have enjoyed traveling because he got around a lot at the height of his "career." He was arrested in Oklahoma City for a robbery in Austin. It seemed three masked men robbed a poker game of $11,000 and jewelry in the state capital. Tincy and Cecil Green, also wanted for that crime, at first refused to leave Oklahoma. Unable to avoid extradition, they were placed in the Austin city jail. The charges were dropped when none of the poker players could, or would, identify the pair. It wasn't mentioned if anyone saw "Tincy" tattooed on the first joint of the robber's left forefinger.

Back in Fort Worth, Police Chief Cato Hightower declared enough was enough. Eggleston, Cecil Green, Sid Foley, and Green's girlfriend Rita Davis were paraded before city and county officials. "We can't force them to leave town," Hightower said, "but we can make it undesirable for them to stay, even if we have to pick them up every 15 minutes."[9]

Two uniformed policemen in a squad car tried to carry out the chief's directive. They spotted Tincy and three other men in a car on a downtown street. They pulled the vehicle over and, with guns drawn, ordered the occupants out. Unknowingly, the patrolmen were about to arrest two deputy sheriffs and a reporter taking Tincy to be questioned by Dallas authorities. "How were we supposed to know when you guys were in plainclothes and driving an unmarked car?"[10] they sputtered.

It was a whole month before Eggleston was the focus of law enforcement efforts again. Johnson County officials, armed with a warrant, searched Tincy's south Fort Worth home for loot taken in a Cleburne grocery burglary. He wasn't there and his wife said she didn't know where he was. The search failed to turn up anything.

According to one source, Tincy was using more and more narcotics by 1954 and becoming careless. Burglary and crooked gambling were necessary to support his habit. That could account for his next arrest. In early 1955 he was charged with assaulting a player in a poker game at the home of gambler and pimp Edell Evans. Attorneys Jack Love and Truman Power got him released on $1,000 bond.

As previously noted, Eggleston, along with sidekick Cecil Green were implicated by Harry Huggins in the spring 1953 murder of wealthy oil man William P. Clark. The police report noted, "Huggins believed Tincy had been paid $10,000 as part of the deal."[11]

Again Eggleston found himself in jail, but he was not without friends. Two drunk Dallas residents came to Fort Worth to see their old buddy, and "One of the men told Deputy Sheriff Jim Floyd he had known 'old Tincy' when they were both serving 'a little time' in the pen."[12] The deputy turned the men over to city detectives, who planned to question the two after they sobered up.

A hearing was held in Criminal District Judge Willis McGregor's court on April 12, 1955. Eggleston, Green, and Huggins were indicted for murder. At first District Attorney Howard Fender recommended Tincy be held without bail. To do that, however, he would have to tip his hand to the defense. "In order to continue to deny bond it would be necessary for the state to make a full disclosure of its cases,"[13] Fender said. Speculation that the state's case was not airtight arose when a $50,000 bond for Eggleston, and lesser amounts for the other principals, was recommended the next day.

While Tincy was still in jail, his wife Walterine was trying to locate his car and find out more about that blonde named Evelyn Robertson. The car, a 1953 Oldsmobile, was still parked outside Robertson's apartment on W. Pulaski. Walterine claimed not to know her husband had been seeing Robertson, but the police had known about the liaison for over a year. Only sixteen when she married, Tincy's wife admitted he wasn't an ideal husband. She added he hadn't been at home much the past year.

Jack Love, Eggleston's lawyer, appealed for and won a reduction in bond. Tincy was released on $20,000 bond into the waiting arms of his wife who undoubtedly had a question or two about a certain blonde.

Two weeks after he was released from jail, Tincy narrowly missed being assassinated. Cecil Green was not so fortunate. Green took seven bullets, and died the next day. "The rain of bullets apparently also were aimed at Green's crony, Tincy Eggleston, who reportedly shot his way out of one of the tightest spots into which his dangerous career ever has taken him,"[14] wrote Bill Haworth. Eggleston's only injury was a cut in his upper left arm caused by flying automobile window glass.

Jack Love said after his all night investigation of the shooting: "Tincy believes hired out-of-town killers did the job. It was a professional job, with a pattern of cross fire laid down very smoothly. Tincy got a look at the men and said he had never seen them around here."[15]

Eggleston assured police he would not try to settle the score, since he couldn't go gunning for someone he didn't know. Instead, he went into hiding. After two months Walterine Eggleston, still smarting from the discovery of her husband's girlfriend, attempted to file desertion charges. District Attorney Fender advised against such action since Tincy sent her money periodically from his unknown whereabouts.

Would Tincy come out of hiding for his assault trial? Truman Power assured the court his client would be there. However, the case was never heard. A mix-up in notifying Henry Rogers, the victim, plus missing witnesses, caused a delay. Edell Evans was to be a witness, but he was missing, and only his blood-soaked Cadillac had been found. The case was set for the fall session of the court. It was cancelled when Tincy's body was found in early September.

By late summer Tincy had come out of hiding and returned home. Things seemed back to normal. Mrs. Eggleston told officers that the day he disappeared he mowed the lawn and didn't act worried about anything.

One source claimed Eggleston became increasingly reckless as his drug habit made greater demands on his pocketbook. His legal bills were mounting. He resorted to extortion of his friends in the underworld. According to one man who knew him, "Tincy would demand a 'loan' of several thousand dollars with no intention of paying it back."[16] Also, he knew the workings of the criminal element in the county. When a robbery of a gambling game or the burglary of a business netted a substantial haul, Tincy demanded a cut, threatening to take it all.

Tincy's stature in the underworld changed when he was indicted for the murder of oilman William Clark. If the police could knock Eggleston down a peg or two, why couldn't they, the victims wondered. Tincy was losing his touch.

Reporter Harley Pershing quoted a source who said Tincy contacted one of his intended victims and demanded $5,000. The man replied he could only come up with $1,000, and "Eggleston warned that it was $5,000 or the man was in plenty of trouble."[17]

Thursday, August 25, 1955, Eggleston received a telephone call supposedly from the extortion victim, setting up a meeting to turn over the money. Eggleston told his wife he was going to the North Side to meet a man and probably wouldn't be home until morning. Instead of meeting one man, two were at the rendezvous site. According to Pershing's source, Tincy knew both and did not perceive himself to be in any danger: "Tincy asked for the $5,000 and for an answer he got a gun barrel poked into his side."[18] The three drove to a secluded spot outside the city limits, and Tincy was ordered out of the car. He was shot in the back of the head. Slumping against the car seat, the man who lived by the gun died by the gun.

The two men dumped the body into an abandoned well, and drove Eggleston's automobile to a grocery store parking lot. The blood-smeared vehicle was discovered the next day. Vandals had stripped it of hub caps and fender skirts.

Tincy Eggleston lived in this modest Southside home at the time of his death.
—Photo by Ann Arnold.

Underworld scuttlebutt questioned how Eggleston escaped with minor cuts and Green got seven bullets, when both were in the same car. They surmised Tincy set Cecil up. Why didn't Tincy donate blood to his good friend, they asked themselves? This lack of concern added to their suspicions. Perhaps some friends of Cecil's revenged his death by killing Tincy.

A variation of that theory was told by an underworld tipster. He said when the shooting started that night in May, Tincy grabbed Cecil and used him for a shield. This time he didn't have a shield.

Tincy was long overdue, detectives theorized. Who did it? "Figuring out 'who got Tincy,' said one man in the underworld circles . . . 'is just like trying to guess which tooth of a buzz saw cut a man. There were too many people who wanted Tincy.'"[19]

Days before they found the body, an anonymous tip to the district attorney's office led officers to Buddie's Super Market, 3230 N. Main. In the parking lot they found Eggleston's vehicle with blood on the right front seat and floorboard. Some blood had started to seep under the right front door. Inside the 1952 Oldsmobile, police found a Panama hat, a jacket with a cleaner's tag "EGG," and an empty .12-gauge shotgun shell. The gangster's Belgian automatic pistol was still over a sun visor.

Investigators found a shovel, spading fork, and pick in the trunk of the car. Puzzled, they speculated that Tincy had been forced to dig his own grave. This was put to rest when Mrs. Eggleston explained she and her husband had recently used the tools beautifying her parents' graves in a Cleburne cemetery.

A tug of war developed over the Oldsmobile. Police discovered it was registered to Clinton Earl Hudspeth, a safe cracker who was a cohort of Eggleston and the late Cecil Green, but the car actually belonged to Tincy. Hudspeth claimed it. Police said Mrs. Eggleston should get it. In stepped the finance company who contended payments were past due, and the car should go to them. Eggleston's failure to make the payments clearly emphasized how desperate he was for money at the time of his death.

While city and county officers searched for Tincy, his wife and daughter kept a sad vigil at their Southside home. Waiting by the phone, Mrs. Eggleston told a reporter, "This isn't the first time—but it's never easy."[20] She recalled Tincy's last day at home. Two men from Dallas, whose names she couldn't remember, visited her husband for about two hours. They left, and soon he left. She suspected he was going to see his blonde girlfriend. She was right, but the woman told police he stayed only a few minutes. She insisted she had no idea where he was going when he left her apartment.

Young couples parking and sparking on a country lane was a common occurrence at mid-century. What was uncommon for one such pair was the sound of

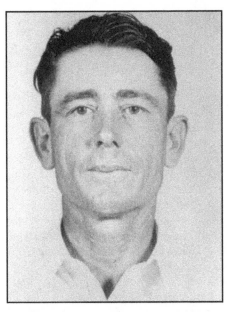

Police belive that Leroy "Tincy" Eggleston's extortion of "friends" led to his winding up in an abandoned well.
—Photo courtesy of Henry H. Wright

nearby gunfire. About 7:00 P.M. almost a week later, a man reported to Sheriff Harlon Wright he heard shots and gave the location. Wright and Deputy Vernon Johnson combed the area north of Saginaw-Watauga Road. They searched an old vacant house, but found nothing. About 100 yards from the three-room structure, they discovered an abandoned well. Closer examination revealed bloodstains and strands of hair on the outer rim of the rock-lined shaft. A .12-gauge shotgun shell lay eight feet away. Peering into the well, they only could see broken bottles, cans, and trash floating in the murky water.

Darkness had fallen, but a portable power unit from the White Settlement Fire Department provided enough light for the officers to continue their search. A grappling hook brought the badly decomposed body to the surface of the water, and at 10:00 P.M. what was left of Leroy Eggleston was pulled from his watery grave. Late into the night firemen were still probing for missing chunks of flesh.

Peace Justice Whit Boyd made an informal pronouncement of murder. He would later state the cause of death was three blasts of buckshot. Wright speculated Eggleston was shot at close range once before being dumped, and then again in the well. Double O buckshot was recovered from his head, liver, and lungs. One shot blew away the back of his skull. The abdominal wound "performed a gall bladder operation," scattering gall stones inside the body.[21]

Lawmen scoured the area, including two other wells on the property, looking for Edell Evans. They didn't find the missing gambler, but they found three pairs of lady's stockings in one of the wells.

A wallet containing $7 and pictures believed to be the victim's wife and daughter were found on the body. The wallet also contained a tire company credit card issued to "Mr. T. Eggleston, Rt. 2, Box 20, Burleson," Tincy's former address.

There was no doubt in anyone's mind that the body on hand was that of the missing gangster. However, Deputy W. M. Young's task was to fingerprint and make positive identification.

Tincy's body had been in the well six scorching August days when it was recovered. Rolling the bloated fingers on the inkpad, Young performed his gruesome chore with professional detachment and went home. That night Mrs. Young prepared her husband's favorite meal—baked chicken, golden brown, meat so tender it was falling off the bone—but, "He took one look at that chicken, and bolted from the table, declaring he guessed he wasn't hungry after all."[22]

Thirteen-year-old Carole Ann Eggleston talked to reporters as she comforted her mother at their Southside home. Neighbors brought food. School friends stopped by to offer their sympathy. Walterine Eggleston, now a thirty-one-year-old widow, looked at the dress she would wear to the funeral. Carole slipped an arm around her mother and said, "It won't be too bad, we'll be together."[23]

At Shannon Memorial Chapel about forty people joined Eggleston's wife and daughter for a final farewell. *Fort Worth Press* reporter Carl Freund was among them. Because of the summer heat he had worn a sport shirt to work, but thinking this inappropriate attire for a funeral, he went home and put on a suit and tie. He shouldn't have bothered. Except for him and the minister, most of the other men wore short sleeved sport shirts.

Rev. Arthur W. Franklin, substituting for Carole's pastor, told the mourners, "Mr. Eggleston lived his own life and died as he lived."[24] Fifteen floral arrangements added color to the simple cypress coffin of the man who once terrorized the North Texas area. Of the handful of mourners, many did not sign the guest book.

In contrast to the showy funeral of Cecil Green, Tincy's was short and simple. Another difference was the fact that forty-six-year-old Leroy Eggleston's funeral was paid for. Ray Crowder Funeral Home is still waiting to be paid the $850 owed for Green's funeral.

Walterine Eggleston was melancholy following her husband's death. Six months after his murder, she attempted suicide. Saying she was tired, she shot herself in the stomach. She recovered from the wound, and tried to make a new life for herself and her daughter. She never remarried. Thirty years later she died and was buried next to Tincy in the Cleburne cemetery.

Chapter 14

No Chamber of Commerce Type Gambling Machines

Following the 1849 gold rush, California was the "anything goes" state. It seemed only natural that Charles Fey's invention, the slot machine, was an instant success in San Francisco. He sold more than a million three-reel Liberty Bell model machines over a thirty-year span. San Francisco's newspaper, *Morning Call*, in 1909 proclaimed, "The slot machines have been particularly popular in San Francisco and at all points in California, where small coins are not held in particular respect and where the spirit of the public is fun loving and prone to take chances."[1]

The slot machine industry proliferated. By 1932 Mills Novelty of Chicago employed 1,000 people and sold 40,000 machines in a variety of styles.

Soon after the bombing of Pearl Harbor, the manufacturers ceased production and converted to war contracts. After the war, the 1951 Johnson Act prohibited interstate shipment of slot machines except to those states where they were already legal.

They were not legal in Texas. That prohibition, plus the 1951 grand jury investigations, spelled the death knell for slot machines in Fort Worth.

Closely akin to the slot machine was the marble table. At the beginning of the Depression, a young businessman named Raymond T. Moloney, after hours of stubborn argument, persuaded his senior partners to join him in a bold venture. He invented a simple cabinet, eighteen by twenty-four by eight inches, containing an eleven-hole bagatelle board incorporating seven glass marbles held under glass, a spring-tensioned plunger and a coin slide. He named it after a popular satirical journal, *Ballyhoo*. Within a year upstart Bally Manufacturing began its surge to the top of the amusement machine business. Improvements were made on the original model. Steel balls replaced glass marbles.

Other manufacturers jumped on the bandwagon. The Keystone Novelty and Manufacturing Company of Philadelphia marketed the "Goofy" machine. Chicagoan Sam Gensberg's electric-powered machine featured twelve colored lights. Other manufacturers, whose own machines used naked glass bulbs, hounded Sam to learn his secret. He never told them he covered his lights with colored gelatin capsules used for horses, which he bought at a veterinary pharmacy.

The original cabinets evolved into free-standing devices. Players used plungers and hard rubber levers to propel balls through an obstacle course. After the ball was shot out, it rolled down the sloping surface, bouncing off colored bumpers. Each bumper hit added to the score until finally the ball fell into the opening at the end of the playing field. The skilled player could win free games or cash. The advantage of marble tables (also called marble boards and pinball machines) was that they could arguably be called amusement, rather than gambling, machines.

Slot machines and marble boards were to the Chevy crowd what roulette and blackjack tables were to the Cadillac crowd. Just as Prohibition spawned the bootlegging industry, so the Depression paved the sidewalk for pinball machines. Men were looking for an escape from the destitution that surrounded them. They flocked to the penny arcades, hoping desperately for a quick win.

In the 1940s almost every bowling alley, beer joint, cafe, and drug store had marble boards, punch boards, slots, or a combination of the gambling devices. In 1951 state legislation outlawed the ownership, display or use of slot machines. A 1956 ruling effectively did away with marble boards. But prior to those measures, there were numerous half-hearted attempts by city and county officials to eliminate the machines.

The heat was on as early as 1935. Police were ordered to pick up "all marble machines and similar mechanisms for the operation of games of chance and skill. . . ."[2] The following year there was controversy over the collection of taxes on the machines. County Commissioners Court ordered the collection despite the possibility such taxation might become a moot point. Should a case before the Court of Criminal Appeals be ruled in favor of the owners, saying the machines were legal, the tax would hold. If the court ruled the machines were illegal, they would be confiscated, ruling out taxation. Collect it anyway, said the commissioners.

In January 1937 owners were again pitching their claim that marble boards were not gambling machines. The appeals court ruling favored the state. Directives went out that all machines in the county were to be destroyed.

But like spring weeds, the machines made a comeback. Coin machine owners from time to time petitioned city councils to allow operation of their machines without harassment.

The Frankrich family, Ernest Harris, the Loicano brothers, and Benny McDonald owned most of the machines in Tarrant County. Tony Loicano had been in business longer, but the Frankriches were important players among the owners. When an effort was made to increase the number of machines in 1941, the Frankrich and Loicano families proposed a plan whereby 750 marble boards would be worked jointly by fifteen owners. Each operator would control fifty machines.

Tony Loicano said the pool would be headed by Sammy Frankrich. The members would share the profits equally. Frankrich told a *Star-Telegram* reporter they had a loosely formed organization to share revenues and legal expenses. Member Jack Maloney, owner of Panther Novelty Company, explained, "Actually, the idea is just for a cooperative to divide average receipts and keep the boys from trying to cut each other's throats. Nobody's going to be excluded."[3]

Well, not exactly. At first Leslie Frankrich, Sammy's brother, said he would have nothing to do with Tony Loicano. The disagreement stemmed from a difference in estimates of the weekly take. Loicano said the machines would take in $10.00 a week; Leslie said they would be lucky to get half that. Evidently they worked out their differences because Loicano declared, "I'm in on that pool and they can't put me out."[4]

The group was unanimous in reminding city council their machines and boards helped the economy by providing small business owners additional income. One tavern owner said that "His machines paid all his overhead. What he made from the bar was all profit."[5]

Frankrich and others reminded the council it was elected on a platform of helping small businesses, and the coin machine owners were willing to do their part. The marble board proprietors argued their machines were for entertainment, not gambling. They cited numbers of people employed because of coin machine revenue and told of instances where businesses failed without them.

Sammy Frankrich noted he had spoken privately with every council member to garner their support. He said Fort Worth was the only big city in the state that didn't allow the boards. City attorney R. E. Rouer advised against the move, but like those weeds in the spring, the machines popped up all over the city. The pool disappeared. Instead of cooperation, the owners competed, sometimes ethically, sometimes not.

By 1944 there was another push to rid the city of slots and marble boards. The smashing of slot machines in the basement of city hall made the front pages of the local newspapers. Up until the time of the 1951 grand jury indictments, there was an on-again off-again battle to appease the citizens. The police claimed they picked up the machines whenever they saw them. The owners grumbled about the high cost of payoffs to keep operating.

Kalman and Annie Frankrich started in the grocery business in the 1920s. The store, located at 219 Burnett, was a family enterprise when the three sons and two daughters were growing up. After their father's death, the sons closed the store and concentrated on the coin machine business.

The Frank-Rich Distributing Company was located at 102 W. 11th Street, according to the 1937 Fort Worth city directory. J. A. Frankrich was listed as the owner. Leslie was one of five men charged in February 1951 with keeping and exhibiting a gaming table. The case was referred to the grand jury. A $1,000 bond was posted and the Frank-Rich Company was free to continue operating.

* * *

Most coin machine owners were not "chamber of commerce" types, yet they weren't dangerous. But Ernest Harris, owner of

North Side Amusement Company, was a man not to be crossed. A source who observed him for a period of years described him as a "mean son-of-a-bitch." At his income tax evasion trial, Harris blamed his troubles on the fact that because his employees were stealing from him, he didn't know the true amount of his income. The source said it was more likely the employees would choose to play with rattlesnakes than take a chance of angering their boss.

Harris had his defenders. A club owner remembered Harris as a dependable businessman. He owned North Side Amusement machines, including slots, and he never had any problems with Harris.

Ernest C. Harris was only twenty-eight years old when he was charged with killing a man. Testimony revealed Harris fatally shot defense plant worker Horace Jones when he found him in an automobile with Edith Harris. Mrs. Harris caught a stray bullet, but the two other people in the vehicle were unharmed. The jury found Harris guilty. His attorney appealed the murder without malice verdict and the case was later dismissed. Mrs. Harris filed for divorce.

At least two more assault charges were brought against Harris, but most of his troubles stemmed from fencing stolen property and owning gambling equipment. Police found two automatic washing machines, two air conditioners, and other appliances, which had been stolen from Vergal Bourland's home appliance firm, at Harris' North Side business.

Telephones were not that expensive, but Harris chose to receive and conceal seven phones stolen from Southwestern Bell Telephone Company trucks in May 1961. A year later he was charged with receiving and concealing three stolen tires. He posted bonds totaling $15,000. He was already on bond for fencing stolen property, as well as and a February charge of owning a gaming machine.

Along with other coin machine operators, he was frequently charged with owning gambling machines. These charges were usually reduced to misdemeanors, and he paid his fines, continuing with business as usual.

It was the long arm of Uncle Sam that grabbed Harris. In 1964 he was sentenced to seven years for income tax evasion. He served his time and returned to Fort Worth. Still bitter over what he saw as being made a scapegoat, he went into another line of work.

* * *

The Loicano family came from Sicily shortly before the turn of the century. Nick and Lena had four sons and six daughters. They settled on the South Side near cousins, aunts and uncles. Nick pushed a vegetable cart until his death in 1912. They were a close-knit extended family. "Italians, like Jews, were not readily accepted by their neighbors and therefore depended on each other," a grand-daughter commented.[6]

Anthony "Tony" Loicano founded Big State Novelty Company in 1920. He was no-billed in 1934 on a gambling machine charge. He was charged November 5, 1937, with keeping marble boards used for gambling purposes. With brothers John, Frank, and Martin, he owned property in the 1600 block of Houston which housed Big State, a liquor store and office space. Tony died in 1950 after a lengthy battle against cancer.

John Loicano was charged with murder in the shooting death of bootlegger W. M. Loid in June 1932. Called to the door of his home on Simondale Drive, Loid was lured to a car by someone who "wanted to sell him something." He was felled by one of several shots fired before the car and its occupant sped away. Loid died the next day. Loicano, already facing a prohibition complaint, was arrested. He was released on $5,000 bond.

All the brothers and some of the sisters were joint business owners. They operated the Seventh Street Pharmacy, the Turf Club, a liquor store, and had various oil interests. John managed the Turf Club, which as the name implies, was a front for gambling. He was charged with bookmaking about an hour before the 1951 Kentucky Derby. Arrested at the Court Hotel on 111 E. 6th, he had in his possession racing forms from tracks across the country. Loicano posted $5,000 bond. Two men were arrested with him, L. D. Dawkins and Robert Stewart, and each posted $1,000 bonds. All were indicted by the grand jury.

Martin "Buster" Loicano had several brushes with the law, but was never convicted of criminal wrongdoing. In 1938 he was charged with receiving and disposing of 100,000 $.03 stamps from a robbery in Louisiana. Loicano denied guilt.

By 1947 he was primary owner and operator of Big State Coin Machine Company. In a lawsuit filed to regain telephone service, the feisty graduate of the old Central High School testified his company had cigarette, marble, and music machines. Telephones were needed to handle service calls. Police Chief Bob Dysart asserted the telephones were used for gaming purposes. Judge Thomas Renfro sided with the petitioner and ordered the lines be put back in service.

Throughout the 1940s and into the 1950s Buster was charged with operating gambling machines. He posted bonds, paid his fines and carried on business as usual.

Loicano never hesitated to fight city hall, although he didn't always win. When two of his marble tables were picked up by the police, he went to court. Contending he had paid state taxes on the machines, the comptroller's office said otherwise. Closer investigation found the state to be right. His lawyers dismissed the mistake as "careless" on their client's part.

Undaunted, Loicano challenged Police Chief Cato Hightower for confiscating his property. He blamed political pressure, and charged the police with harassment. He asked for a reimbursement of $25.00 per week for each machine taken out of circulation. Moreover, he argued his marble boards were for entertainment, not gambling. Judge Harold Craik, in a scathing opinion, cited testimony which showed the pinball machines came with illegal gaming devices when they arrived in Fort Worth from the manufacturer. "It's hard for me to realize anyone would play these machines for amusement,"[7] the judge said. Loicano vowed to appeal Craik's ruling.

A mere six months later Buster found himself in court again. The burning issue this time revolved around twenty-four cases of hot cigarettes found in the Big State Coin Machine store room. The more than 135,000 smokes had been stolen from a warehouse in Waco.

Unlike Ernest Harris, Loicano had a good working relationship with his employees. He treated them fairly and they were loyal to him, several staying with him for years.

As did other coin machine operators, Buster paid his fines. But he didn't hesitate to put up a fight over what he believed to be interference with a service to the public. He got out of every jam save one—the tax man nailed him.

* * *

According to the 1937 city directory, Benny McDonald operated a filling station at 1701 N.W. 21st. He later started the Star Coin Machine Company. More than any other operator, McDonald helped his marble table revenue by putting up the money for others to go into business. At times he would have money in as many as fifty enterprises. He would loan a man enough to rent and stock a cafe or tavern with the understanding that his juke boxes, cigarette machines, marble tables, and slot machines would be installed.

With the same regularity as other owners, McDonald's machines were confiscated. He paid his fines, made bond, and went back to replacing the lost machines. In August 1947 he paid $150 in fines and court costs for slot machines picked up on the Jacksboro Highway.

By 1956 McDonald was threatening to sue the city over the confiscation of his machines. Speaking for six other distributors of machines, he said, "If the police start picking them up they will have a lawsuit on their hands."[8] This was in response to a city council ordinance outlawing all coin operated amusement machines. Cato Hightower met the challenge, saying, "We are going to start picking up the machines just as soon as the ordinance becomes effective in about a week."[9]

Judge Harris Brewster placed a restraining order on the city's plans. Through his attorneys George Cochran and A. L. Wardlaw, McDonald argued his machines were neither gambling devices nor nuisances. They were skill or pleasure machines, he contended.

The skirmish continued until the state legislature made the matter a moot point by outlawing the machines. McDonald and the other coin machine operators concentrated on less lucrative, but legal, cigarette machines and juke boxes.

Punch boards provided another way for people to lose their money. Supposedly if a board had 500 chances and it claimed to have 100 winning punches, a player would have a one in five chance of hitting a winner. If eighty of the winners were for modest sums, the likelihood of a player making money dwindled considerably. This was if the board was on the up and up. In many cases the cafe or tavern owner would punch until he removed all the big winning punches. Thus, if he paid $25.00 for the board, used up 150 punches getting the big winners out, at $.10 a punch he still made as much forty percent profit. If it took less than 150 punches to get the twenty big winners out, his profit was even greater.

Another way the unsuspecting lost money on punch boards was for a bartender or counter man to "gamble" with the customer. Perhaps the bet was for who could punch the highest number. If the customer punched, say eighteen, the bartender would slip a higher pre-punched number into the play. The customer, especially if he had been drinking a bit too much, usually never caught on to the scam.

Punch boards were money makers. Reporter Mary Crutcher wrote of seeing two uniformed officers drinking coffee at a lunch counter. At the elbow of one of the men were two punch boards. When paying for the drinks, he flipped a dime to the cashier, tossing it over one of the boards.

The *Fort Worth Press* ran a front-page story of a $25,000 protection racket prior to the 1951 grand jury crackdown. Reporters noticed a sticker with gold lettering on some openly displayed punch boards. They asked how the boards could be out on the counters without fear of being picked up by the police. One woman pointing to the sticker said, "We buy the stickers, ... the money goes to the big shots and the cops don't bother 'em."[10] The stickers sold for $.50 to $1.50, depending on the value of the punch board. Who were the "big shots?" The woman didn't know, but surmised they were the ones at city hall and the courthouse.

A tavern owner who refused to buy the sticker kept her boards under the counter when customers weren't playing them. "I'll get rid of my lousy punch boards before I'll pay to keep from having them picked up," she was quoted as saying.[11]

Every autumn football cards were as common as falling leaves in the 1940s and early 1950s. Texas Christian University fielded a powerhouse team and even the sheriff bet on them. It was impossible to go into any barber shop, cafe, or drug store and not see the cards. Police Chief George Hawkins claimed he had never seen a football card. Two reporters got their picture on the front page when they presented the chief a bushel basket full of cards they gathered up within blocks of the station.[12]

Marble boards were seen occasionally after the crackdown, but they were not the cash cow as in the old days. Another machine to separate people from their money came on the local scene in 1958. Resembling a postage stamp machine, it was called the "Lucky Horoscope." Put in a nickel, dime, or quarter and out popped a cardboard with a horoscope on it. George Cochran, the machine owners' attorney, declared the machines were not for gambling. "If there's gambling going on the owners want to know about it . . . They would be the first to stop it,"[13] he assured the press. Evidently they didn't read the sales pitch put out by the manufacturer: "Lucky Horoscope pays off $180 out of every $250 it takes in."[14] Taverns displaying the machines were said to pay into a weekly "protection pot" to keep the machines from being picked up by lawmen.

Despite their initial appeal, the horoscopes never gained the widespread popularity of other gambling devices, and eventually faded away.

By the end of the 1950s the coin machine operators had retired or were involved in other ventures. In place of slots and marble boards, vending companies offered candy and cold drink machines. Video games swept the country. The industry born in the Depression to offer entertainment and the elusive hope of "hitting the big one" died in the prosperity of the post-war economy. Gamblers now could afford to go to Las Vegas to play the slots.

Chapter 15

And the Killin' Goes On

Eleven-year-old Sammy and his fourteen-year-old brother Jimmy still had a month of summer vacation. One morning in early August they were returning from fishing off Inspiration Point. Approaching Roberts Cut-Off Road, there was no hint they were about to experience the most excitement of their young lives. At 11:25 A.M. the house at 2806 exploded. They couldn't believe their eyes. Five, ten and twenty dollar bills were floating down from the sky. Quickly they began to stuff the greenbacks into their pockets.

Sam Atchley, who grew up to write such hits as "Coca Cola Cowboy," smiled as he recalled his momentary wealth.[1] Alas, the police made the boys give the money back. It was evidence, the lawman said, in the investigation of the attempted assassination of gambler Frank Cates.

Charles Frank Cates was no stranger to violence. He was suspected of killing Lon Holley, Nelson Harris, and Que Miller. Under the aliases Frank Thompson, Charles Frank Gates, and A. W. Collier, his police record went back to 1915 when he was imprisoned for white slavery. Bootlegging, safe cracking, robbery, and operating "con" games appeared on his rap sheet. At one time he served a sentence in Leavenworth for smuggling and tax evasion.

Cates was one of three men arrested in 1939 in connection

with a Beaumont post office burglary ring. This was about the same time Buster Loicano was charged with receiving stolen postage stamps, but Cates' involvement could not be proven.

Those who knew the big-time Fort Worth gamblers and gangsters of the 1940s and 1950s considered Cates to be a cut above the rest intellectually. Police detective A. C. Howerton believed Cates was the brightest and the meanest of the bunch. The pudgy gambler, who also dabbled in real estate, was always well dressed and cooperative when questioned by the police. Of course his cooperation did not extend to telling the officers anything about his activities or friends, but he was polite when not telling them anything.

Cates was a running mate of Jim Thomas. When Thomas was charged with the murder of a Littlefield, Texas, doctor, Cates was questioned as well. He was released for lack of evidence. Cates' next run-in with the police came in 1948 when he was a suspect in the slaying of Lon Holley. Again lack of evidence led to his release. The murder was never solved.

When Nelson Harris and his wife died in the explosion that shook city and county governments, Cates was one of twelve men taken in for questioning. The others met with police December 6, 1950. Cates cited being in Houston on his honeymoon as his excuse for not joining that august group. Escorted from his attorney's office by Lt. O. R. Brown, Cates told officers he knew nothing about the Harris bombing, "Pale but stubborn, Cates repeated the denials when detectives shifted the questioning

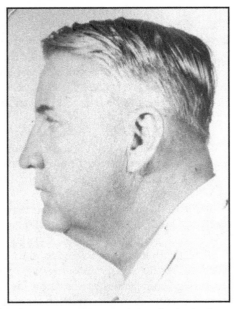

Frank Cates promised his bride he'd go straight. He should have kept his promise.
—Photo courtesy of Henry H. Wright

to the 1948 Lon Holley murder and other unsolved gangland exterminations."[2]

Frank Cates' bride and second wife, Jackie, begged her husband to quit the criminal and gambling activities. "I'm going to be the kind of guy who puts on his slippers and reads the evening paper in front of the fire,"[3] he once told a reporter. For a while it appeared he abided by her wishes. His Richland Hills neighbors spoke well of him. They believed his ample income came from rental property.

But the allure of big money and excitement was too strong. He began handling questionable diamond transactions. By the time of his death he was reportedly into bankrolling games in the Sansom Park area. This was believed to have led to the house bombing that almost cost him his life.

The blast sent Cates stumbling outside. His clothes were shredded and his body covered with wooden splinters. One missile about the size of a cigar lodged in his cheek. Huge chunks of flesh were blown from his legs.

Sansom Park Police Chief Bob McLaughlin was the first officer on the scene. He found the dazed and bleeding ex-convict sitting on the porch. Cates said, "Bob, I just had $1,800 blown out of my hand. Find it for me."[4]

He was rushed to All Saints Hospital. The once feared man now looked more like a pin cushion than a human being. He suffered burns and cuts on his arms, face, and stomach. Quickly doctors and nurses worked to save his life. As he was given four pints of blood, Cates declared he had no idea who might have tried to kill him.

Meanwhile sheriff's deputies investigated the scene of the blast. The explosion happened when Cates answered the telephone at the house. Every wall in the four-room home was split and twisted. The force ripped the door of a refrigerator off, but failed to disturb the half case of beer and quart of milk inside. The living room floor became a pile of toothpicks. Broken window glass was strewn about, as were the venetian blinds. Even the bathroom fixtures were disconnected by the blast. Playing cards, poker chips, and dice were scattered throughout the area. The telephone was found in the yard.

According to an article in the *Star-Telegram*, "Deputy sheriffs found lead wire from the bomb, planted under the living room floor, trailing 250 feet down the Jacksboro Highway."[5] The ends of the wire had been kinked as if they had been attached to a battery terminal. A hole had been drilled in the foundation of the imitation stone house, and the dynamite placed directly under the telephone stand.

The dwelling was behind Chenault's Dining Place. Witnesses told investigators two men were seen in the area the morning of the bombing. One drank five beers and made several trips to the outside telephone booth. The other sat in a blue 1956 Buick in an alley behind the restaurant. Lawmen theorized that one man called the house, and when the victim answered, signaled to the man in the Buick. The second man set off the charge that sent Cates' money floating up to the heavens.

Police believed a call from this telephone booth set up the bombing of Frank Cates' house on Roberts Cutoff Road.

—Photo by Ann Arnold.

With Cates not talking, officers relied on rumors to supply a motive: "Underworld reports said Cates became the target of assassins because he tried to dictate who could operate in the Sansom Park area."[6] This theory was based on word that Gene Paul Norris had moved into the Fort Worth suburb and banked games in the back room of Howard Dodd's tavern. There wasn't enough business for two big operators. Supposedly Cates suggested a merger, but the deal fell through.

Sheriff Harlon Wright believed the attempt went back to old

grudges. Cates reportedly lost some of his bravado in the under-world when his partner Jim Thomas was murdered. Both men had made enemies when they controlled the criminal activity, and now it was payoff time.

Cates' actions seemed to support the first theory. He spurned an offer for police protection, saying he would handle it himself. First, he wanted to talk to Howard "Junior" Dodd. But the five-foot, six-inch, 264-pound ex-con and Jacksboro Highway tavern operator was nowhere to be found. Friends said he left town "for health reasons."

Fort Worth Press reporter Carl Freund was told Dodd and Norris believed Cates informed Texas Rangers about their games as a way to stifle his competition. Whichever theory was correct, law-men were left with few leads and no suspects.

Frank Cates was released from the hospital after a three-week stay. He returned to his Hardisty Street home to complete his recu-peration and to look for the ones responsible for his injuries. They found him first.

On the night of October 8, 1956, Frank Cates received a tele-phone call late in the afternoon. He told his wife he "had to meet a man and would be back in a few minutes." There was no question Cates knew and trusted the caller. After the bomb attack he was even more wary about his safety and would not have agreed to meet with a stranger or known enemy. A source told reporter Carl Freund that Gene Paul Norris called Cates at least twice before two shotgun blasts did what the dynamite failed to do. His killer is still unknown.

According to reports, "The gambler apparently was shot to death between 7:30 and 8 P.M."[7] His body, slumped in his car, was found within a mile of where Tincy Eggleston's body was found the year before. Bandages were still on his healing legs.

According to the reconstruction by authorities, the killer strode to the right front window of Cates' automobile and fired twice with a .12-gauge double-barreled shotgun: "One blast struck him in the right arm and chest . . . the second almost blew his head off. It tore a big hole in his jaw and blew his brains out."[8] A veteran lawman said "it was the goriest sight he had ever seen."

At the funeral Evangelist Charles Fairchild spoke kindly of the sixty-one-year-old victim. He cited a long acquaintance of Cates who said, "Every time I met Frank he had something joyful to say."[9] What Cates never said was who wanted to kill him.

Chapter 16

Miscellaneous Murders

"Little Bo Peep has lost her sheep, and doesn't know where to find them. Leave them alone and they'll come home, wagging their tails behind them," the nursery rhyme goes. The gangland slayings, like spinning wheel strands of yarn, were so interwoven that to attempt to tease them out was futile. "Leave them alone and they'll kill themselves off," seemed to be the unofficial sentiment of the homicide department. They investigated; they made statements to the press. But not one murder resulted in an arrest or conviction.

Elston Brooks, in his book *Don't Dry Clean My Blackjack*, likened the gangland killings in Fort Worth to the story of the "Ten Little Indians," and then there were none. Between 1940 and 1960 sixteen gangsters were murdered (Mrs. Nelson Harris and Darlene Hauer are included).

James (Red) Cavanaugh disappeared in December 1943, and has never been found.

Ray Sellers, burglar and safe cracker, was not as well known as his brother-in-law Clyde Barrow. While serving a ten-year sentence in Oklahoma, Sellers donned civilian clothes and escaped into a crowd of 5,000 people watching a prison rodeo.

He was on the outside just two months when he was shot and critically wounded. Dumped from a car, Sellers staggered to a dairy farm in a sparsely populated area of eastern Tarrant County. The escaped convict refused to say who shot him. He died December 2, 1943. Police questioned Lois Green, another Dallas gangster, but no charges were filed.

* * *

Rodeo performer and gambler Louis Tindall was next. In the early 1940s Tindall appeared in domestic court almost as often as the roping arena or the roulette table. Velda, his first wife, sued him for divorce and child support. Their relationship was one of charges and counter charges. Once in a fit of rage he destroyed the furniture and Mrs. Tindall's clothes.

Velda's mother Anna Callahan claimed he held her prisoner and beat her with a Bible and a pistol and threatened to kill her. She suffered a broken arm. He received a two-year assault to murder sentence. Given a number of reprieves, and benefitting from technical delays, he never actually served time.

The one-time trick rider was ambushed in the driveway of his Arlington Heights home in November 1944. A shotgun blast from a hedge blew out the car window. Then two pistol shots rang out, one striking him in the back and the other coursing through his body from side to side.

Tindall's second wife Opal told police she and her husband had returned from a downtown movie. As she got out of the car, her gun in her hand, the first shot rang out. He thought she was shooting at him. "I started to tell him I hadn't fired and as he was turning around toward me a second shot hit him in the back,"[1] she said. Both emptied their pistols at the assassin. Tindall was critically wounded. A hemophiliac, he required massive amounts of blood. He rallied, then took a turn for the worse, and died a few days later.

"I would give up my life, but not my money," Tindall was quoted as saying after he disarmed and severely beat a would-be robber some years earlier.[2] It seems he did just that.

Tindall always carried a great deal of money—money made from big-time policy game operations. An attempted burglary of their home in 1943 was foiled when Mrs. Tindall turned on a light and saw two men in the house. She screamed and Tindall's gunfire scared them off.

At the time of the driveway shooting, Mrs. Tindall explained to police she always got out of the car first, gun in hand. She would search the house, then her husband would enter. Neither she nor Tindall would tell police why they were so cautious or who might want to harm them. Word on the underworld grapevine was that Benny Binion wanted to move into Fort Worth's policy racket and that Tindall, the local boss, opposed him. Binion supposedly put out a contract, but police had no clue as to the identity of the hit man.

At the time of his death Tindall was under indictment for gambling. A native of Eastland, he was buried there.

* * *

Like a scene from a Western movie, in the early 1940s two Jacksboro Highway characters shot it out on Exchange Avenue in the stockyards. Lon Holley and Elmer Sharp argued over a business deal gone sour. Sharp didn't explain to officers what caused the dispute, but the two combatants had at one time jointly owned a bar in Lawton, Oklahoma.

One of Holley's bullets hit Sharp in his left side; another hit his right thigh. Yet another bullet hit a bystander. Lon Holley was pistol whipped by Sharp. All three recovered.

Holley was charged with several robberies after leaving Oklahoma. At the time of his death, he was out on $30,000 bond for robbery. Shortly before he was to stand trial, he was shot in the head at close range.

Police speculated Holley was trying to plea bargain and that had made someone nervous. In exchange for a lighter sentence there was talk he would finger some of his friends. One friend, Jim Thomas, had been tried twice for the murder of a Littlefield physician. He was out on appeal awaiting still another attempt by the state to prove his guilt. Some thought Holley had the murder weapon, which he would turn over to the authorities if the right deal could be struck. Others believed Holley knew too much about a recent $16,000 bank robbery in Rosebud, Texas.

On Saturday March 6, 1948, Holley received a telephone call at approximately 10:00 P.M. He handed his wife a note with the names Frank Cates and Jim Thomas written on it, saying to her, "If I'm not home by midnight, you will know something has happened."[5]

Something certainly did happen. Holley's body was discovered in his late-model auto-mobile the next morning by two men looking at some real estate. He had been shot twice in the head by someone appar-ently sitting in the back seat. One bullet emerged close to his right eye, the other on the left side of his head.

Police speculated Holley hadn't been ex-pecting trouble. It was a cold, rainy night, and he wore an overcoat, so it would have been difficult for him to reach his pistol in time to defend himself. His unfired .38 caliber revolver was still on his

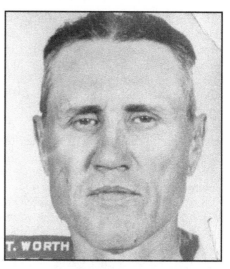

Lon Holley left his wife a note, "If I'm not home by midnight, you will know something happened." Something happened.
—Photo courtesy of Henry H. Wright

hip. There was no evidence of a struggle, and his wallet, containing almost $50 had not been touched.

Holley met his demise on a portion of Roberts Cut-Off Road near a bluff overlooking Lake Worth, just south of Inspiration Point. No houses were within two blocks of the area, and no one reported hearing gunfire.

Cates and Thomas were questioned by detectives and released—another unsolved murder for anyone who was keeping score.

Seven months later the police had yet another body on their hands. Que Robert Miller, a fifty-one-year-old ex-convict and ex-sheriff, was found shot to death in his late-model automobile in a secluded area in late September of 1948.

A dozen years before his death, Miller was stripped of his badge and served time in the penitentiary for misapplication of pub-lic funds. He was tax collector as well as sheriff of Foard County prior to his conviction. Following his release he continued to amass a long list of crimes ranging from counterfeiting to robbery.

Patrolmen W. O. Sharp and O. M. Carter, while making a rou-tine check of an East Side park, discovered the former West Texas lawman slumped in the front seat of his car. An empty pistol shell from a .45 caliber automatic pistol was found in the back seat. Another gun was on the ground near the left rear door. One bullet entered the right side of his neck and exited the left side before penetrating the windshield. The other bullet struck him slightly above the left eye. The position of the wounds and the body led investigators to believe he was shot by someone sitting in the back seat. The car's motor was still warm and there was no sign of a struggle. The only thing unusual was that the body was not found near Lake Worth.

Miller had been living off and on at the Westmoor Tourist Court at 5800 Camp Bowie for about a year before his death. A porter said the slain man made a telephone call about 4:00 P.M. the day he was killed. Although there were several similarities between Miller's slaying and that of Lon Holley, authorities could find no direct connection.

Que Robert Miller was buried in Rose Hill Cemetery. Sidney Miller, who made the arrangements, was out on bond for the slaying of a New Mexico man at the time of his brother's death.

* * *

Mrs. Herbert Noble was killed November 29, 1949, by a car bomb intended for her husband. A month later Dallas gangster Lois Green, brother of Cecil, was ambushed; then Mr. and Mrs. Nelson Harris were killed November 22, 1950, also by a bomb. Herbert "the Cat" Noble's nine lives ran out when he opened his wired mail box in August 1951.

Next to die was Jim Thomas. Tall, well built, usually wearing tailor-made grey suits, he was one of the heavyweights of the criminal world. Thomas began a twenty-five year sentence in the Nebraska, penitentiary in 1931 for the $27,000 robbery of a bank in Hastings. He did not go willingly. The day he was scheduled to be transferred, he sawed his way out of the Adams County, Nebraska jail. His liberty was short-lived. Captured the same day, he spent nine years in prison. Thomas worked in the hospital during that time and learned about the effects of anesthetics, knowledge he would put to use in a later crime. After his release by Nebraska authorities, he was taken into custody by Texas lawmen, who wanted him to serve time for a robbery committed before the Nebraska bank job.

Herbert "the Cat" Noble's car. Note ace of diamonds in the foreground.
—Courtesy of *Fort Worth Star-Telegram* Photograph Collection,
The University of Texas at Arlington Libraries.

He was soon in trouble following his release by Texas authorities. In 1942 he was severely wounded in a gun battle with Baxter Honey, a former Lubbock police officer. The shootout occurred when Thomas attempted to kill Maitland Jones. Honey, Jones' bodyguard, got the better of him, and Thomas found himself in Huntsville again. Thomas' wound caused a blood system complication which left him emaciated and weak.

While serving his term, Thomas was given a reprieve to obtain medical care in Galveston. Prison Dr. M. D. Hanson told the state board, "This inmate is now an invalid in the prison hospital. . . . If he doesn't receive surgical aid, in my opinion, he will not live more than a few months"[4]

Thomas had surgery and was removed from invalid status. Apparently he was well enough to travel to Littlefield in West Texas and allegedly kill Dr. Roy Hunt and his wife. Court evidence showed he first anesthetized the couple, then trussed them up. Hunt was shot in the eyes with a small caliber pistol. Mrs. Hunt died of a major brain concussion.

In Littlefield during Thomas' trial, witnesses testified that the knots that bound the doctor and his wife were made by a left-handed person. How did they know? Lawmen raised on farms and ranches, and familiar with cattle roping, recognized the "pull" being tighter on the left. The accused was left-handed.

Thomas was found guilty, but the judge declared a mistrial when it was discovered a juror discussed Thomas' prior criminal record. He was retried and again found guilty. The Court of Criminal Appeals ruled insufficient evidence to sustain a death penalty. This led to a third trial, in which he was sentenced to ninety-nine years in prison. In June 1947 the Court of Criminal Appeals reversed judgment and ordered a fourth trial. He was scheduled for that trial when he was killed by an Oklahoma livestock trader.

While out on bond between the trials and retrials, Thomas was questioned by Fort Worth police in the deaths of Lon Holley, Que Miller, and Mr. and Mrs. Nelson Harris. Lacking evidence, the police released him.

In August 1951 Thomas went to Durant, Oklahoma, to see longtime business and social acquaintance Hubert Deere. An argument erupted over the sale of a truck, and Thomas slapped Deere, prompting Deere to shoot Thomas.

A badly shaken Deere walked three blocks to the police station and gave himself up. He related the events to Police Chief Ben Risner. He told of shooting the underworld character twice with a .12-gauge shotgun. One blast caught Thomas in the upper stomach. The other ripped through his groin and nicked his wallet in his right hip pocket. Deere claimed this was the first time he ever shot anyone.

Back in Fort Worth, neighbors on Hill Crest Street expressed surprise at the notoriety of the man who lived at 2117. They described him as a quiet man who liked to work in his garden. "A mild, soft-spoken man who did not drink, smoke or swear. . . ."[5] Gambler Frank Cates said Thomas was "an awfully nice fellow." Attorney Byron Matthews doubted Thomas had been in trouble in the "past few years," but added his record could not be denied. A detective remembered him as a suave, polite man. Police, however, saw him as half of the team that killed Lon Holley and Que Miller, as well as a strong suspect in the Nelson Harris bombing.

At the time of his death, Thomas owned a nightclub in Odessa, a Midland trailer court, the home on Hill Crest, and several vehicles. He bequeathed his assets to his children by a previous marriage and the bulk of his estate to his twenty-five-year-old widow.

Sid Foley — 1957
. . .dumped on 'boot hill'

Sid Foley was a running mate of Eggleston and Green before the three had a falling out over Foley's wife.
—Photo courtesy of Henry H. Wright

Jim Thomas, while out on appeal for a Littlefield murder, was shot by a business associate.
—Photo courtesy of Henry H. Wright

* * *

Sid Foley, a one-time stockyards worker and partner of Tincy Eggleston and Cecil Green, had fallen on hard times. He was out on bond for the theft of a diamond ring when he was killed. He had been making ends meet by selling dyed rabbit skins as expensive fur stoles. Officers found three bottle caps, and only $2 in his pockets.

An argument over the division of stolen diamonds was the probable motive for his death. Police also theorized a barroom brawl with George Kean led to his execution.

A thirteen-year-old boy who lived near the Lake Worth garbage pit discovered Foley's badly beaten body. The hoodlum's face was so mangled police at first didn't recognize him. He had been shot in the back of the head with a .38 caliber pistol. His skull was fractured in two places in addition to the bullet wound. Some said it was poetic justice that his body was found at the county dump.

A sister from California, who had not seen him in fourteen years, claimed Foley's body. She planned his burial without services, but women friends of the slain man arranged for a minister to deliver a graveside message. Elston Brooks noted, "Only 11 mourners gathered at Foley's graveside that raw, wind-whipped afternoon."[6]

* * *

Gene Paul Norris, one of the "Big Three" in criminal circles, was gunned down by lawmen April 30, 1957.

According to Elston Brooks' *Don't Dry Clean My Blackjack*, the next to go was Jack Nesbit. George Rennie (Jack) Nesbit was a man of many talents, according to the police. He was adept at bomb making, forgery, theft, robbery, and murder. He claimed to make his living as an electrician. As early as 1927 Kansas police arrested him for forgery. Oklahoma police wanted him for grand larceny. He served time in both states. Twenty years later Fort Worth authorities knew him as a bodyguard, club bouncer, and nitro expert. He was a suspect in the deaths of Mr. and Mrs. Herbert Noble, Mr. and Mrs. Nelson Harris, the attempt on Tincy Eggleston's life, and numerous other Fort Worth crimes.

On one of his later escapades something went amiss in the West Texas town of Paducah. The Goodwin Implement Company store, located on the town square, had been splashed with gasoline.

A 200-watt light bulb was placed in a box of kitchen matches. The plan was for Nesbit and his helper, S. C. Stewart to be in a public place with plenty of witnesses when the heat of the bulb ignited the matches. But even the best laid plans . . . They were caught leaving the building. Nesbit was out on bond for "placing inflammable material in a building, and burglary with intent to commit arson" when he was killed.

He didn't go out in gangland style. He was shot by his attractive, thirty-one-year-old mistress Lois Stripling, who claimed self-defense. She shot Nesbit four times with a pistol he had given her for protection. She used it against him when he came at her during an argument at her Riverside area apartment. "I was afraid he was going to kill me,"[7] she told police.

Lois, the widow of gambler Howard Stripling, had been trying to break off the affair, but Nesbit would have none of it: "I wanted to leave him and he told me that I'd stay away only long enough for him to throw a stick of dynamite at my folks' house. Then I'd be back."[8] The grand jury believed her story. She was no-billed.

Mrs. Nesbit had an entirely different story to tell about the deceased man. Standing by her man, Lucille Nesbit called him a good provider and the "best husband a woman ever had." Concerning the arson attempt in Paducah, she explained, "We had no income at the time. I was in an arthritic condition. We needed the money."[9] At the time of his death, Nesbit was a bouncer at Boston Smith's Tarrant-Parker county line gambling establishment. Mrs. Nesbit opted not to have a funeral for the greatest husband a woman ever had.

✳ ✳ ✳

Three more killings made the front pages of Fort Worth newspapers as the decade came to a close. Willard and Darlene Hauer's deaths led investigators away from turf battles over gambling and into the murky world of drug dealing. The Hauers were associates of Harry Huggins of the Clark murder case. Cecil Green was another associate of Hauer's. Forty-four-year-old Willard, a five-time loser and underworld "wannabe," was brought up from Huntsville for questioning in the Clark case.

Both Willard and Darlene had long police records. His went back to the 1930s for such offenses as assault, burglary, drug dealing, forgery, and theft. Hers listed drug possession, prostitution, and shoplifting. After his latest release from prison he sold a few cars. Darlene was so dependent on drugs she could no longer lure the businessmen who once supported her lifestyle.

The Hauers were shot to death in their Southside apartment in early 1959. Police had no motive and no suspects. A neighbor reported seeing a man running from the apartment the previous night. A week after the slayings, police said they had no suspects, but believed the couple was killed over a narcotics deal gone bad.

No relatives claimed the bodies. A few friends gathered for the graveside services. An Owens and Brumley Funeral Home staff member read from the Scriptures.

One could say it was a sad but fitting end to the decade, as well as an era. For all the gambling, crime, and bloodshed of the previous years, only the defense lawyers and dirty cops seemed to come out ahead.

Chapter 17

Good Guys Wear White Hats

Until Cato Hightower became Fort Worth chief of police in 1953, that office had a revolving door. Chief Karl Howard went into the service in 1942. He wanted his old job back when he returned after the war, but was given a captaincy instead. T. G. Curry was the wartime chief. He retired in 1945.

Next, R. E. Dysart was appointed to lead the department. He was well respected by the citizenry, but some on the force thought him too strict. They objected when he demoted, suspended, or fired fellow officers. After four and a half years, Dysart handed over the reins because he felt the job wasn't worth the cost to him and his family. There was an outcry from ministers and others who appreciated his tough stance. They said he was the best chief Fort Worth ever had.

George Hawkins lasted eighteen months, then R. R. Howerton succeeded Hawkins in 1951. Cato Hightower was chief from 1953 to 1964.

* * *

Kids going to the Saturday matinee at the New Isis on North Main knew who the good guys were. Gene Autry and Roy Rogers always wore white hats. Most of the law enforcement officers in

Fort Worth and Tarrant County wore "white hats." Those who didn't had some real explaining to do when Nelson Harris' "little black book" was made public. It started with the police chief and sheriff and worked its way down.

From time to time the city council and county commissioners railed against gambling and other forms of illegal operations, but breast beating was about as far as it went.

As the 1951 grand jury delved deeper into the gambling morass, newspapers reported damning evidence of police corruption. Delbert Willis' front-page story on February 26 outlined a $500,000 annual payoff to law enforcement officers. This figure equaled the monthly salaries of more than 200 patrolmen. It was not the men on the beat who got the money, it was the men at headquarters who benefited handsomely for allowing gambling and other vice operations to flourish.

Broken down to a monthly cost, the *Fort Worth Press* itemized what gamblers called the "law nut," bribery expenses: "Here's the way they break down the 'nut' total for one month during peak operations last year: 20 big dice games at $1,000 each . . . $20,000; 30 firms, 3,000 marble boards . . . $6,000; 12 big policy wheels . . . $13,000; 20 bookies . . . $15,000. Total monthly law nut . . . $54,000."[1] This monthly payout occurred at a time when city and county officers swore there was no gambling anywhere in Tarrant County.

At the time of Hawkins' elevation to chief, reporter Bill Haworth noted that veteran police force and city council members publicly described tall, dimpled-cheeked George Hawkins as "a firm, fair and independent cop."[2] When Hawkins took over the department in 1949, only a few insiders knew the reason he was promoted from lieutenant to chief. That reason wasn't a noble one—unlike Dysart, Hawkins would wink at vice activities in the city.

Hawkins placed the vice squad under his direct supervision, saying, "I want to keep my finger on that business."[3] Each time a reporter inquired about the running of slot machines and other gambling devices, Hawkins denied any knowledge of the illegal activity.

Fort Worth Press reporters played a joke on the chief concerning the wide-spread betting on football cards, one retired reporter laughingly recalled. Texas Christian University Coach

L. R. "Dutch" Meyer urged police to put an end to college football gambling cards. Chief Hawkins declared he didn't know much about them. "He had heard about the betting cards, but had never seen one," he said.[4] The reporters deposited a box full of the bingo-size cards on Hawkins' desk. No longer able to say he had never seen one, he announced that possession of the cards was not illegal, but if he ever saw anyone betting on one he would arrest him.

A *Press* story on open Sunday illegal liquor sales in the downtown area, complete with a picture of a known bootlegger leaning into a squad car talking to officers, brought Hawkins' usual comment. He said he knew nothing about the practice. Moreover, the officers told him they didn't know the man they were talking to was a bootlegger. That satisfied the chief, who said he would order a crackdown on bootlegging anyway.

Police chief George Hawkins was called before the grand jury investigating payoffs.

—Courtesy of *Fort Worth Star-Telegram* Photograph Collection, The University of Texas at Arlington Libraries.

Two weeks after Hawkins took over the vice squad he assured Mayor Edgar Deen, "There is no open gambling inside Fort Worth at this time."[5] The chief angrily denounced a report that some local gamblers were complaining the cost of protection had risen sharply. He attributed the report to gamblers unhappy with his strict enforcement of the law.

If the mayor bought that, the grand jury didn't. Hawkins appeared before that body in March. He emerged grim faced, telling reporters he was still convinced there was no big-time gambling in the city. When asked about the 2222 Club on the Jacksboro Highway, the chief admitted he had never raided the place. "But my men have and they've found no gambling there recently,"[6] he said. Pat Kirkwood said his father, the owner of the 2222 Club, was always forewarned about the raids.

The Nelson Harris payoff card played an important role in the grand jury investigation of the police department. Following the indictment of thirty-two gamblers and coin machine owners, Ray Finney was asked if more indictments were on the way. His response was, "Not at this time." A reporter caught a glimpse of a secret document listing indictments of thirty-seven top-level city and county lawmen.

A compromise was worked out wherein all those to be indicted would be transferred to other duties. This led to a massive overhaul of police department supervisors under newly appointed chief R. R. Howerton. Hawkins was demoted from chief to lieutenant and placed in the traffic bureau.

However, his usual denial of any knowledge why the notation "C H–100" was found in the slain gambler's payoff papers did not ring true. Everyone in the department, as well as police reporters, knew that "C H" referred to "Chief Hawkins."

* * *

Roland R. Howerton immediately reorganized the detectives' office, the vice squad, and uniformed platoons. Two glaring transfers indicated the new chief's determination to clean house. He sent Karl Howard to the warrant division, and Capt. R. H. (Rip) Burks, a former vice squad head, became custodian of police equipment. These and other changes rankled officers accustomed to Hawkins' lenient style.

Chief Howerton led the department for two years. During his watch, he tried to elevate the morale of police officers not involved in the scandal. He enjoyed limited success. "The reason for tendering my resignation is to attempt to create peace and harmony within the department,"[7] he wrote to the city manager.

Howerton was named head of the police training school. Despite underhanded obstructions to the reorganization, he had paved the way for his successor.

* * *

In April 1953 Cato S. Hightower got the nod from city fathers. In one of his first official actions, he denied re-instatement of officers fired by Howerton, telling them to re-apply and take the civil service exam.

Department inside sources told a *Star-Telegram* reporter of a plot to discredit the new chief by encouraging known prostitutes to saturate the area: "Motive of the alleged plot was to attempt to show that . . . (Hightower) had permitted the town to 'open up,' the sources said."[8] Hightower showed his class by dismissing the matter without retaliation against the disgruntled officers.

The Somervell County native became popular with policemen in all departments. Because he was considered fair in his dealings, even detractors respected him. Cato Hightower's leadership brought the department to higher standards. Friends described him as "just about the nicest guy they ever knew;" felons described him as "tough."

* * *

In the last quarter of the nineteenth century, when Hell's Half Acre was at its zenith, the infamous Wyatt Earp was a frequent visitor. He and Sully Montgomery would have had a lot in common. Both made more money from gambling and protection rackets than from wearing a star. Both were unsuccessful as tavern owners. They differed in that Earp's violence resulted in foes' deaths, while Montgomery's violence resulted in enemies lying prone on the boxing ring canvas.

As a youngster Sully Montgomery boxed in Golden Gloves competition and Al "Cotton" Farmer was his sparring mate. They would go three rounds in an open air arena at Casino Beach. Each received $1.00 and tips. Later the six-foot, three-inch, 225-pound

North Sider played high school and college football. For three years he was a professional football player, then a pro boxer for twelve years. Although Jack Dempsey clobbered him in the ring, Sully considered the champion a good friend. When Dempsey visited Fort Worth, Montgomery showed him around the town.

Montgomery's first public office was as constable of Precinct 1. The year was 1942. After two terms at that post, he won election as sheriff. A consummate "good ole boy" politician, he was twice re-elected before the bad publicity of kickbacks, gambling, and an income tax evasion trial brought his career to an end. Like Chief Hawkins, the sheriff ran a lax department, and stated repeatedly he knew of no open gambling in the county.

Sully Montgomery at his income tax evasion trial
—Courtesy of *Fort Worth Star-Telegram* Photograph Collection,
The University of Texas at Arlington Libraries.

Reporter Carl Freund recalled how the sheriff kept some of the money from confiscated slots and other sources of cash in a green pillow case. It was dubbed the "little green bag." When a woman came in complaining her husband deserted her and she had no money to buy food for the children, Sully would bring out the pillow case and tell the distraught woman to help herself. Certainly not legal, supporters admitted, but unquestionably compassionate.

Montgomery received a great deal of criticism when he bought the Rockwood Inn at 1816 Jacksboro Highway while in office. The previous owner was under sodomy charges at the time of the sale. The sheriff paid $9,000 for the club, saying he wanted to turn it into a "nice cafe." Public outcry caused him to sell the club a month later. He made $1,000 profit from the sale.

The sheriff was also the object of the grand jury investigation. The *Press* lead story February 23, 1951 detailed a witness' account of frequent visits by the police chief and the sheriff to Nelson Harris' dice game. Sully Montgomery escaped indictment, but it was a bittersweet victory.

The publicity over bribes and payoffs alerted internal revenue agents. Montgomery was charged with income tax evasion and found guilty.

Montgomery was sentenced to seven years in prison. A petition was circulated urging the removal of the sheriff from office. Instead, he forestalled such action by announcing he would resign five days after the primary election determined his successor.

His lawyers appealed his conviction and won a new trial. The U.S. Fifth Circuit Court of Appeals at New Orleans ruled Judge T. Whitfield Davidson had made a reversible error by not allowing Sully's lawyers to examine some of the state's documents.

He got a new trial and this time was cleared of criminal intent to evade his taxes. He was a free man, but things would never be the same. He later ran for re-election and lost. Resigned to remain in the private sector, he bought a franchise for coffee, tea, and chocolate vending machines.

* * *

Harlon Wright was sworn in at 12:01 A.M., September 1, 1952. A Mason and a resident of the Riverside neighborhood, the new sheriff was seen as friendly and outgoing. James McGraw, president of the General Ministers Association, sent a telegram saying, "Congratulations. Your election is a victory not only for you but for the people of Tarrant County who want law enforcement."[9]

Wright didn't keep a "little green bag," but he was every bit as controversial as his predecessor. In office less than twenty-four hours, he got in trouble over "a lot of bologna." His side of the flap was that prisoners had been forced to eat bologna for two days. With offices and stores closed for Labor Day, they faced two more days of "poor man's round steak." Wright called his meat company and ordered delivery of seventy-five pounds of veal. The prisoners were happy with their stew, but county purchasing agent Walter Bell was unhappy that the new sheriff failed to follow purchasing regulations. "I told him I realized all purchases should go through his office," Wright declared, "But the matter was an emergency. The prisoners were getting rambunctious."[10] A month later the picky eaters went on strike to protest too much mustard greens.

The sheriff tore up the $46.50 bill for the stew meat. His company, now run by his sons, discontinued submitting bids to the county to avoid a conflict of interest.

Three months into his term, Wright and the commissioners court were at loggerheads over cigarette and candy vending machines. He won the argument and used profits from sales to buy coveralls for inmates.

Of a more serious nature was the matter of jailbreaks. On February 18, 1953, ten prisoners escaped. One was Floyd Hill, a guest of the county following his arrest in the $248,000 Western Hills robbery. The infamous fugitive declared his cell door was open and he walked out. He claimed he had been within four blocks of the jail for ten days before he was captured in a Dallas County farmhouse.

The official story of the jailbreak had the jailer overpowered when he entered a cell to give a prisoner some medicine. The unofficial story making the rounds told of a poker game between a deputy and prisoners that led to the break. Whichever version was true, two deputies lost their jobs over the lapse in security.

Wright often disagreed with federal marshals and Texas Rangers concerning the way he ran the jail and his efforts to fight crime in the county. But there were exceptions when the departments relied on each other. For example, one day when Deputy E. N. Buie was questioning a suspect who, along with two others, had stolen some trays of donuts off a delivery truck. Two had already confessed, but the third had a lapse of memory concerning the activity. Buie was getting nowhere with the suspect when Ranger Captain Jay Banks came into the interrogation area. Banks had been down on the Trinity riverbank searching for evidence in an unrelated case. He paid no attention to Buie and the youth. Banks' hands were muddy and his only interest was to get cleaned up. As Banks rolled up his sleeves, Buie pointed to him and said to the suspect, "That's Texas Ranger Captain Banks, I think I'll just turn you over to him." Seeing only the rolling up of the sleeves, the suspect decided he wanted no part of more interrogation and said, "Mr. Buie, it's all coming back to me now. . . ."[11]

Despite his inability to get along with other county officials, Wright was recognized in 1957 as one of four outstanding sheriffs by the Texas Law Enforcement Foundation. He was praised for upgrading technology in the sheriff's department, such as placing two-way radios in all county patrol cars.

Gambling was not a big problem, but all was not well. The January 1960 grand jury noted "highly reprehensible, irregular and perhaps illegal conduct" in the sheriff's office. Wright was criticized for the unprofessional conduct of some of his deputies. They were charged with collusion with certain defense attorneys and tipping off criminals about impending vice raids. The jury also denounced him for allowing a man with a lengthy criminal record to serve as a trustee.

Wright attributed his troubles to politics. He maintained District Attorney Doug Crouch was working behind the scenes to enhance Lon Evans' chances of unseating the two-term sheriff. The feud between the two top county lawmen continued unabated through 1960.

Lon Evans won the election and was sworn in as sheriff on January 1, 1961, but Harlon Wright still made headlines. Another grand jury investigated the disappearance of guns and evidence needed in the prosecution of pending criminal cases. Wright returned two armloads of weapons he took with him when he vacated his office. He insisted he thought he was right in holding them for safekeeping until they were needed as court evidence. No further action was taken.

Former sheriff Harlon Wright joined Southwestern Petroleum as a sales representative. He died of a heart attack in 1970.

* * *

Stewart Hellman would have made a perfect television series district attorney. Tall, with thick, wavy, silver hair, he looked like he wore the "white hat." Looks can be deceiving.

From the time Hellman first took office in 1948 there was turmoil in the district attorney's office. He was slow and sometimes refused to bring to trial certain indicted individuals. Rumor had it he did not want to prosecute the gamblers indicted by the 1951 grand jury for fear they would reveal embarrassing information about himself or his staff.

The assistants he hired caused no end of controversy. Hellman allowed his staff to take on private practice cases. One assistant reportedly refused to help a woman collect child support from her estranged husband, but did offer to represent her, for a fee, in getting a divorce. This raised such an uproar in the press, Hellman personally interceded for the woman to secure the money for her children.

A.L. Wardlaw, another assistant, was charged with income tax evasion. As in the Sully Montgomery case, he was acquitted on appeal.

But the biggest problem during Hellman's tenure was the problem with the 1951 grand jury. Hellman was ejected from his own grand jury post and replaced with a man whose reputation was that he couldn't be bought. Did that mean Hellman could be bought?

Like other officers of the law, Hellman denied any knowledge of gambling or payoffs. He informed the jurors that Texas law clearly specified that bribery or payoffs must be witnessed by a third person. This, he said, meant he would not prosecute any policemen or deputies named in Nelson Harris' records.

The reduction from felony to misdemeanor status for the indicted gamblers angered the citizens. Hellman contended he was trustworthy and had "labored honestly and conscientiously to that end and performed [his] job according to the lights [he] had before [him], and the record reflects that fact."[12] No one believed him. Hellman was never charged with any wrongdoing, but the voters didn't like what they learned during the grand jury investigation, and he was defeated in the 1952 election.

Hellman was ousted in favor of Howard Fender. The former district attorney entered private practice. Two years later he and his first wife were slapped with a lien against their property for unpaid taxes in 1952. The couple was divorced and in 1956 he married his private secretary. Hellman died suddenly of a heart attack in late January 1958. He was forty-nine years old.

* * *

The knight in shining armor to restore credibility to the district's attorney's office was Howard M. Fender. The Paschal High School graduate brought an impressive resumé to the office. He attended Kemper Military School, U.S. Military Academy at West Point, and was a graduate of Washington and Lee University School of Law.

The thirty-two-year-old announced his intention to "fight a stepped-up campaign against crime" even before he took the oath of office. Within a week of being sworn in, Fender was considering cases that had been passed over by Hellman.

The murder of Dorothy Matthews by her husband caught his attention. Wilcie Turner Matthews, a Jacksboro Highway tavern operator, had been indicted by the grand jury, but not prosecuted for the crime. Pretty, dark-haired Dorothy Marie was shot at her home on August 15 the previous year. Hellman recommended dismissal because there were no witnesses to the crime. Fender disagreed. "Fender said he also will check into cases dismissed by his predecessor for possible resubmission to the county grand jury," the *Star-Telegram* reported.[13]

The respectable district attorney did have his off moments. Gambling was not as open after Fender took office, but it was still a problem. A well-orchestrated raid that went awry was led by the district attorney himself. Fender was determined that news of the raid would not be leaked. He summoned law officers from city and county jurisdictions, as well as Texas Rangers. After locking the door, he outlined his intent to raid the Sportsman's Rod and Gun Club near Katy Lake. He assigned two teams, one to approach from the front, the other to come in from the back of the property. Watches were synchronized and the would-be raiders marched single file out of the office.

There was just one small flaw in the plan. To get to their cars they walked past the sheriff's radio room. Eight men, single file, following the district attorney—whatever could they be up to?

Someone in the radio room put two and two together, and word went out all over town about the raid. When Fender and his raiders slogged through the heavy mist and burst into the club, they beheld a rare sight. Men in suits, whose athletic activities had for years been limited to dealing cards and throwing dice, were trying their best to hit a ping pong ball back and forth across the netted tables. One playing card was found on the floor. The raid became known in Fort Worth newsrooms as "Fender's Fizzle in the Drizzle."[14]

Fender complained of being short staffed and often tried cases himself. In one instance, the judge asked a defendant, "How do you waive?" The man looked puzzled, hesitated, then slowly moved his hand back and forth. Even the stern, no-nonsense judge could hardly stifle a laugh.

Fender served two terms as district attorney. One of his fondest memories of his days in that position was being able to look from the courthouse across the Trinity River to the historic Oakwood Cemetery. "My grandparents are buried there," he said.[15] After leaving county office Fender served in the enforcement branch of the State Attorney General's Office. He later became a judge.

Chapter 18

Here Comes the Tax Man

The Government Printing Office sold 356,585 copies of *Your Federal Income Tax Guide* in 1949. The 144-page book, with drawings scattered throughout to make it more clearly understood, cost forty cents. Several gamblers and politicians should have bought one.

Money from gambling, payoffs, robbery, and other illegal sources usually did not show up on 1040 tax returns. But the money was spent, and that's when the IRS agents got nosy. Many gamblers and gangsters who easily handled local lawmen with under the table "gifts," and whose attorneys used all the technical wiggleholes to avoid guilty pleas in local courts, met their match with the Feds.

Eugene O'Neill's 1939 *The Iceman Cometh* was an example of the pessimistic playwright's treatment of the inevitability of fate. Many characters chronicled in this book found, to their chagrin, that if attention was brought to them by the grand jury they inevitably got a letter from the IRS.

Benny Benion, Ernest Harris, Les Hutt, Buster Loicano, Asher Rone, and W. D. Satterwhite were called in to justify their tax payments.

Elmer Sharp, a man of more brawn than brain, went down to see the local tax agent. In a voice loud enough to be heard all over the office, he said, "Well, I got a bill from you for $75.00. I just can't pay it. Preachers raisin' hell and the town's all closed down.[1]

Some city and county officers also got into trouble. Those pesky agents wanted to know how James Ralph "Sully" Montgomery could spend more than he reported. During the tax evasion trial, testimony brought to light what many courthouse observers had known for years—the sheriff was making rounds.

Sheriff Sully Montgomery's trial was typical of the government's attempt to prove evasion of income taxes. First, Sully's lawyers requested a continuance due to the ill health of his wife. They claimed her testimony would be crucial to establishing the innocence of their client. They produced a statement from the Montgomery family physician declaring Mrs. Montgomery needed sixty to ninety days to recover from surgery.

His lawyers contended that, upon her recovery, Mrs. Montgomery would testify that her husband made considerable money in boxing and professional football. He also loaned $30,000 to a friend, Paul Suggs, to start a meat market business. Suggs "prospered and he became a very wealthy man; that Suggs always felt greatly indebted to the defendant and to this witness for this particular favor," the continuance plea noted.[2] Montgomery's counsel further stated Mr. Suggs gave money to Montgomery for furniture and donated to his campaign. The continuance was granted.

The sheriff's tax evasion case was widely covered by the media. In a 1952 federal district court hearing, records showed Montgomery declared a 1948 income of $10,112.79. The government contended his income was actually $16,422.23 and he owed $3,204.28 in taxes, fines, and interest. The next year he said he made $9,903.97; they said it was $19,295.53 and he owed $2,036.58.

Where did he get the income above his county salary? He said from rental property and investments. Almost 1,000 pages of testimony showed that was not the whole story.

The May 14, 1952, trial started with an opening statement by R. Daniel Settle, Assistant United States Attorney: "Gentlemen of the Jury: You have heard the indictment read to you. The defendant is charged with having willfully attempted to defeat and evade the income tax due and owed by him to the government for the years, 1948, 1949 and 1950. He has done this by failing to report all of the income he received during each of those years."[3]

At this point Clyde G. Hood, one of Sully's lawyers, objected,

"We object to the statement 'he has done this.' We think the attorney for the government should state that the government intends to try to prove that he did."[4] The judge suggested changing the wording to read "we allege" or "we charge."

Mr. Settle rephrased his statement. "We will attempt to prove, and I believe we will prove to you gentlemen —." He didn't finish the sentence before Hood objected to "I believe we will prove." Settle countered, "Well, we do."[5] And so it went for the rest of the opening day.

Later in the proceeding, W. H. Getzendaner, an admitted bookie, gave damaging testimony:

> Q. Did you pay Sheriff Montgomery any moneys?
> A. Yes, sir.
> Q. And how much money would you pay him on the occasion for his visit, or visits?
> A. Did you ask me about the dice game or the horses, or —
> Q. All right, do you recall when you started your dice game there, Mr. Getzendaner, in what year?
> A. Well, it was in '50, in the latter part, it was only operated four or five months, and part of the time then.
> Q. All right. Now, before you opened your dice game, did Sheriff Montgomery come by your place of business, in 1950?
> A. Before?
> Q. Before you opened your dice game?
> A. Yes.
> Q. Did you pay Sheriff Montgomery any money?
> A. Yes, sir.
> Q. How much?
> A. Fifty dollars.
> Q. Was that fifty dollars—will you give us, to your best impression, as to how many visits Sheriff Montgomery paid you before you opened your dice operations?"[6]

At this point the defense lawyers argued against "best impressions." On cross-examination they weakened Getzendaner's testimony by showing he was vague on details such as dates of operations and alleged payoffs.

Another interesting witness to take the stand was Ernest Cavitt. The African-American taxicab and restaurant owner told of his visits to the sheriff's office:

Q. What did you go up there for?

A. I went in there in the case of trying to hire a nigger deputy sheriff.

Q. What else did you go up there to see him about?

A. I done some other things, I gave him distributing.

Q. What is that?

A. I gave him some distributing—some money.

Q. Distributing?

A. Money.

Q. You gave him some money?

A. Yes, sir.

Q. How much money?

A. About $25.00.

Q. How often?

A. About every month or two months.

Q. Where would you give him that money?

A. In his office.

Q. What did you give it to him for?

A. Just to tell you the truth, I don't know why I gave it to him, I will be honest, I will tell you why—will you allow me to say?

Q. Yes?

A. As far as craps is concerned, the nigger shooting dice, he wouldn't have to pay nothing, because he can run too good, he wouldn't have to pay off.[7]

The judge gavelled the court back to order and testimony resumed. As they had with Getzendaner, Montogmery's lawyers contended Cavitt was too vague, and moreover, giving money to a "friend" was not against the law.

Treasury agent W. D. Wilson told of being in the sheriff's office. He was offered a drink of whiskey which Montgomery produced from his office safe. The agent said he declined, then said, "He then took a green cloth bag."[8] That was as far as he got before defense attorney Clyde Hood was on his feet, objecting. The judge ruled the jury could not consider Sully's "little green bag" in determining his guilt or innocence in the tax case. But the little green bag was the talk of the town. In further legal maneuvering, Sully's two Dallas and three Fort Worth attorneys laid the groundwork to disqualify damaging testimony about the sources of extra money. In a legal document they stated:

Now comes J.R. Montgomery, Defendant in the above cause, and moves the Court to grant this, his specially requested charge number six:

Gentlemen of the Jury:—You are charged that the Court allowed certain testimony introduced by the government to go to you tending to show, if it did show, that the defendant accepted certain payments for protection of unlawful businesses. Whether or not it did so show such transactions is for you to determine beyond a reasonable doubt. You are charged that testimony has been submitted to you only for the purpose of showing, if it did show, that certain monies came into the possession of the defendant for which he did not account in his income tax return, and you will consider that testimony, if you consider it at all, for no other purpose.[9]

In other words, if he took payoffs, the jury shouldn't hold it against him.

Sully testified much of the money beyond his salary was gained by betting on local high school football and college bowl games. He said he was a member of a group of Fort Worth businessmen who placed bets. The sheriff couldn't recall where the bets were placed.

Fort Worth merchants recounted furniture, jewelry, and clothing purchases made by Mr. and Mrs. Montgomery. Robert Koslow of Koslow's Furs told of Sully making four cash payments totaling $550 for a coat for Mrs. Montgomery. M.S. King of Haltom's Jewelry Store said the sheriff bought his wife a $2,832.42 anniversary ring and paid for it in cash. This was a year in which $6,000 would buy a four-room frame house on a twenty-year FHA mortgage.

Defense lawyers asked the jurors to disregard testimony about money obtained from betting. They contended taxes were paid on winnings, and the morality or immorality of a sitting sheriff illegally gambling on athletic events should not prejudice them against the defendant.

Montgomery was found guilty and sentenced to seven years in prison. His team of lawyers immediately filed an appeal based on charges that federal agents did not inform Mrs. Montgomery that financial data she shared with them in their initial investigation could be used in a criminal trial. She contended she showed agents W.D. Wilson and Robert E. Baskett bank and other documents because they claimed it was a civil tax settlement. Both agents denied they discussed civil vs. criminal matters with Mr. or Mrs. Montgomery. Agent Wilson "admitted he did not tell Montgomery his records would be used in a criminal case, declaring he did not know at that point how they would be used."[10] The sheriff's lawyers requested all evidence supplied by the government be suppressed on the grounds the agents misrepresented themselves.

The appeals trial was as contentious as the first. Defense attorneys succeeded in keeping identification of contents of the infamous "green cloth bag" from being revealed. They cast doubt on Getzendaner's testimony by showing that he sought to evade his own tax troubles.

In his defense, the sheriff presented himself as a simple lawman who understood street criminals. He claimed he didn't know how to fill out a tax form. Two deputies handled his financial records and he just signed them, he said. He also disputed the testimony of Getzendaner, Cavitt, and others who reportedly "went to see the sheriff once a month." The tall, broad-shouldered former athlete made a favorable impression on the jury. Dressed in a gray suit, white shirt and red tie, he appeared somber and somewhat baffled by the legal technicalities surrounding him. This time he scored a touchdown. He won his case on appeal.

Sully was not a mental giant. Notified by telephone of the verdict, at first he didn't understand. According to the source, a Fort Worth newsman, the conversation went something like this:

"Sheriff, we just got the news on the wire. Your case has been remanded." The reporter expected to hear whoops of joy, instead there was a dead silence.

"What did you say?" Montgomery queried.

"I said your case has been remanded." More silence.

Finally, a weak voice asked, "Does that mean I have to go to jail now?"[11] Sully was accustomed to the term "remanded" meaning he should lock a prisoner up; he did not know what it meant in terms of court systems. He was cleared of all charges, but did not get off unscathed. He lost his office and his influence, and faded from the public scene.

Chapter 19

The Michigan Connection

eorge Kean considered himself the heir apparent to Tincy Eggleston as the number one tough guy in Tarrant County crime circles. But to reporters he modestly referred to himself as "just a small-timer." Like Elston Brooks' other "Ten Little Indians," Kean was an ex-con who kept bad company.

He was arrested five times in 1957. Early in the year police questioned him about the death of Sid Foley. He sneeringly told investigators they were wasting their time, "I'd rather take a murder rap than be a stool pigeon."[1] Perhaps he knew it was safer. Another police character summed up the situation by saying if anyone snitched, it would be out on the streets before the snitch got out of jail.

Police Chief Cato Hightower ordered his officers to pick up Kean after the ex-con allegedly threatened a traffic patrolman when Mrs. Kean was stopped for a routine violation. An angry Kean supposedly called the patrolman and said, "I'm tired of you bothering me and my family. If it doesn't stop something's going to happen to you and your family."[2]

In June he was arrested as a suspect in several jewelry burglaries in New Mexico which netted the thieves an estimated $20,000. When police picked him up at his Mansfield Highway janitorial supply company, they found three back rooms equipped for gambling.

Following this arrest Kean found his car rigged with a bomb. He didn't reveal to his wife who might want to kill him, but he sent her and their three children to stay with his brother in North Carolina.

Kean was last seen in Fort Worth in December 1957. After six months passed and none of his cohorts had talked to him, the police began to suspect he had been killed. They were right.

Mrs. Kean told officers she last talked by telephone with her husband in late November. He said he would join his family for Christmas, but didn't show up. When she didn't hear from him for several weeks, she returned to Texas and settled in Midland.

George Kean's death ranks as one of the most bizarre gangland slayings. In the summer of 1958 a dairy farmer reported finding what looked like a fresh grave in his pasture. Sheriff's deputies investigated the recently dug up area north of Haltom City, but no body was found.

A month later Detective H. L. Stephenson received an anonymous long distance telephone tip. The caller described the location of a shallow grave and said Kean was buried in it. The spot was easily found in a field near Lake Worth. Deputies supervised the opening of the grave, which was not far from where gambler Edell Evans' body was buried. They found a badly decomposed body and pulled it up by the belt. Pieces of black trousers and a corduroy jacket still clung to the corpse. The bones of the feet were encased in black shoes and black socks. An autopsy revealed the skeleton belonged to a man who had been shot through the brain.

A tearful Mrs. George Kean inspected scraps of rotting clothing. "After seeing the clothes, I felt like it was him,"[3] the twenty-nine-year-old woman said.

Detectives George Hawkins and H. L. Stephenson believed the body was that of the missing hoodlum. The estimated weight and hair color matched Kean's, but the skeleton was five inches shorter than Kean's height. Dental records proved the body was not George, and Mrs. Kean returned to Midland.

With additional word from an informant, local authorities realized they had been sent on a wild goose chase to give the killer time to destroy Kean's corpse. Texas Ranger Jay Banks, Sheriff Harlon Wright and Fort Worth Detective O. R. Brown flew to northern Michigan where the informant said Kean was buried.

The source told them to look for a hotel with an outside

George Kean, a wanna-be bad guy, was buried near a lake in Michigan.
—Photo courtesy of Henry H. Wright

staircase, with a Standard service station next door, and a real estate office across the street. After driving 800 miles, all the while checking several small towns, they finally found the right one. The Texans trudged deep into a muddy marsh along with five Michigan officers who aided in the search.

The eight men found the nude body buried five miles from Lake Huron. An icy spring flowing into the grave and the cold ground temperature kept the corpse from total decomposition. Brown and Wright identified Kean from his still recognizable facial features and scars.

For the second time in just over a week, Mrs. Kean was stunned at the news of her long-missing husband and hoped the officers were wrong again. But if they were right, she wanted the father of her three children buried in Texas. An Azle Funeral Home hearse was dispatched to Alpena, Michigan, to return the corpse.

Investigators found that George Kean had been accidently shot by one of his own gang members. Jimmie Tsermengas, nicknamed "the Greek," admitted to Detroit police he killed Kean. Tsermengas, a Galveston ex-convict, told how he, Kean, and two others wanted to go to Michigan because they were too well known by police in Texas. In Collinsville, Illinois, they were stopped on suspicion by two officers. They overpowered the policemen and handcuffed them to a tree. Kean wanted to kill them, but Tsermengas didn't want to deal with the aftermath of a cop killing. They left without harming the men and drove on to Michigan.

Near Pontiac, in a hideout owned by Donald Chandler, Kean and Tsermengas were planning a robbery when Kean got drunk and started a fight over who was the toughest. The Greek said he tried to subdue Kean by hitting him on the head with the butt of a gun. They struggled for the gun and, "The weapon discharged, and a bullet hit Kean above the eye."[3] The three loaded the dead man into the trunk of the car and drove several days until they found a suitable place to dump the body.

Fort Worth police speculated it was one of the gang members who had given the initial false tip, hoping to end the search for Kean. The identity of the body found in the Lake Worth grave was later determined to be a missing Dallas hoodlum.

At the Michigan trial of Jimmy Tsermengas, the other members of the gang were identified as Lowell Everett McComb and Tommy Smith. McComb, known as Danny, was the owner of the Jacksboro Highway tavern where Kean worked as a bouncer.

Donald Chandler testified Kean bragged of killing ten men, including a Texas Ranger. Texas authorities scoffed at the assertion. They maintained Kean was exactly what he said he was—"just a small-timer."

Smith was tried in Texas on a robbery charge and sentenced to five years in prison. Tsermengas was convicted of second-degree murder and received a twenty to forty-year sentence.

Chapter 20

Crime, a Family Tradition

Of all the Fort Worth gangsters, the Norris brothers were the most feared. Both Gene Paul Norris and older brother Pete made the FBI's most wanted list. Gene Paul, who went by his middle name, was also at the top of several Texas lawmen's lists until gunned down in 1957. Police Chief Cato Hightower labeled him a madman who killed for money.

Paul was just twenty-one when he first made the newspapers. His notoriety came about after he helped Pete escape from Ferguson Prison Farm at Huntsville. The two, along with a sixteen-year-old girl, were caught in a ramshackle farmhouse twelve miles southeast of suburban Kennedale. Officers recovered loot from previous robberies and a cache of firearms in the tin-roofed house.

The Feds sent Pete off to Alcatraz. He still had 436 years, less time off for good behavior, to serve for robberies in three Texas cities.

Jeanette, Paul's bride of one month, claimed she grew up in the same Houston neighborhood as her husband. Yet she told police she didn't know Pete was Paul's brother, and swore she knew nothing about the jailbreak. "Whatever he and his brother have done to others, they've been swell to me," she said.[1]

Paul, the slender, good-looking younger brother was charged with car theft in Dallas County, the robbery of a supermarket in

Jeanette Lyles, shown here with Pete Norris and Gene Paul, said "They've been swell to me."
—Courtesy of *Fort Worth Star-Telegram* Photograph Collection,
The University of Texas at Arlington Libraries.

Fort Worth, and draft evasion. Although he was acquitted on the robbery charge, he later got in trouble impersonating an FBI agent. Acting as a federal agent, Paul conned a Chicago couple out of $7,400. They discovered the scam, identified Gene Paul, and it was off to the pokey for him. He was jailed in Conroe.

Two months later he escaped from prison. The Montgomery County sheriff, state police, and FBI agents searched the rain-swollen swampland of the San Jacinto river bottoms. Three days later Norris, chin deep in Cypress Creek, surrendered.

Paul's story of the escape differed from the official version. He alleged Sheriff Rodney Chambless suggested the break in exchange for $900 cash and the promise of $7,000 more. He escaped from the Montgomery County Jail, he said, by walking out when the jailer left the door open for him. It took a jury only thirty minutes to absolve the sheriff.

The sentencing of Norris took longer. Opposing lawyers argued more than six hours. The defense pleaded with the jury not to convict on the stories of his cell mates' renditions of the jailbreak. The prosecution contended, "Ministers and respectable businessmen could not be expected to testify in jailbreak cases, since they were not usually in jail."[2] The state won its case, and Norris was sentenced to thirteen years in prison.

In 1949 he was released on a conditional out-of-state pardon and moved to Oklahoma.

An international headline-generating brush with the law occurred in 1952. Norris was identified as one of three men who robbed two Cuban nationals of almost a quarter of a million dollars at Fort Worth's Western Hills Hotel on Camp Bowie.

The robbery was described as more outlandish than fiction. Bill Haworth wrote, "A daring ex-convict, a former flying bootlegger and a one-time college football player and auto racer (were accused) in the spectacular $248,000 robbery. . . ."[3]

Orville Chambless, (supposedly no relation to the Montgomery County sheriff) was a longtime Oklahoma bootlegger. What made him unique was, rather than an automobile with a loaded-down trunk, Chambless flew merchandise to waiting customers in his private plane. When arrested, he announced he wasn't taking the rap by himself. He named Norris, a Fort Worth car salesman, Sam Brown Cresap, and local hoodlum Floyd Hill as his partners in crime.

Norris proclaimed his innocence and likened the whole thing to a "bad movie" plot. He was transferred from Chickasha, Oklahoma, to a fifth-floor cell by U.S. marshals. Before he could be released on bond, a jail-house snitch alerted the authorities of a planned escape. Norris was moved to "an undisclosed" location.

Federal charges against Norris and Cresap alleged they transported stolen money across state lines. Those charges were dropped when the government was unable to link them with the money. However, they still faced robbery charges.

Cresap denied having anything to do with the crime. He was released on bond paid in part by the former sheriff of El Paso County.

Investigators believed Floyd Hill rented a house at 2712 Skyline Drive to be used for the division of the stolen money. But they couldn't ask the Fort Worth hoodlum because he was still missing from the county jail.

After the usual legal delays, the case was heard in Judge Willis McGregor's Criminal District Court. Security was tighter than any in courthouse history. Dallas County deputies and federal agents joined Tarrant County deputies and Fort Worth police. Even District Attorney Howard Fender was believed to be armed.

The cheerful, soft-spoken Norris scoffed at the need for so many guns.

On the witness stand, Cubans Manuel Madareaga and Candido de la Torre testified they had come to Texas to buy guns for an anti-Batista counter-revolution. Instead of meeting with promised arms dealers, they were robbed by men with machine guns.

Madareaga and de la Torre pointed to Norris as the man they knew as "Johnny," the liaison between them and the arms dealers. Federal prosecutors contended there never was an arms deal, and that the Cubans were set up. The defense charged there never was a robbery; the Cubans kept the money and framed their clients. The state's case was weakened when the victims were unable to positively identify Chambless in court.

As one of the principals in the matter described it, Paul smilingly hobbled into court wearing a back brace and using a cane. He claimed to have hurt his back prior to the Western Hills affair, and produced a letter from his doctor stating he was under medical care for a back problem.

Paul's case was bolstered by his elaborate alibi. He supplied eye witnesses and written evidence that he was in his Duncan, Oklahoma, machine shop at the time of the robbery.

A man who knew Norris recalled the ex-convict's skill in setting up alibis. Once, he said, Norris went to a Western Union office in order to talk with the clerk so that he would be remembered. But after distracting the clerk's attention, he kept a telegraph form. Then he had a confederate send the telegram the day of the crime, thus he had "proof" he was far away from the scene.

Relatives and friends swore Paul was in Duncan before and after the time of the robbery. The defense offered a sales slip supporting their contention. An unnamed source, in speaking of the trial, noted that to put down the wrong date was a simple matter and rarely was the exact date remembered weeks later when sales slips were introduced as evidence.

Norris was no-billed in the case, but the 1949 conditional pardon granted by Governor Allen Shivers was revoked. He returned to Huntsville to finish his sentence for burglary and helping his brother to escape.

Again out of prison, Norris moved to Fort Worth and began

robbing gamblers and other criminals who dared not report the thefts. He teamed up with Cecil Green, with whom he later had a falling out over the division of money stolen in robberies. As recounted elsewhere, Green was gunned down at the By-Way Tavern owned by Norris' sister Dorothy Amyx. Police theorized, but were unable to prove, that Paul was the trigger man.

Always a charmer with the ladies, and having shed or been shed by his first two wives, Rita Davis, moved in with the smooth-talking Norris. This was after her week of mourning Cecil's death, of course.

Tincy Eggleston escaped that execution, lowering Norris' reputation in the criminal world. Also Tincy was thought to be hounding Paul's sister, trying to find out where the robbery money was stashed.

Homicide detectives suspected Paul soon rectified the matter and Tincy's body was found in a well.

Reporter Mack Williams re-created the scene: "Pistol in hand, Eggleston answered his doorbell one day. At the door stood Norris, unarmed and ready to offer Eggleston a deal. No one ever found out the details, but a week later, Eggleston's phone rang. . . ."[4]

Sources said "Norris became a killer for hire in Fort Worth."[5] Police believed he killed bootlegger Orville Chambless for fingering him in the Cuban robbery.

Authorities believed Norris' next victim was drug dealer Edward Eugene Townley and his wife. Another drug dealer, Olen Ray Raylor, annoyed Norris and was found shot to death. Then he went back to Oklahoma where it is thought he filled several murder contracts.

In the spring of 1956 he and his wife, Rita, returned to Tarrant County to live in River Oaks, out of the reach of Fort Worth officers. With them came William Carl "Wimpy" Humphrey, Paul's bodyguard. It wasn't long before Frank Cates' gambling house on Roberts Cutoff Road was blown to bits. Later Cates unwisely agreed to meet someone on the lonely Watauga Road where the Townley bodies had been found.

Police believed Norris made yet another attempt to honor a promise to brother Pete. Houston policy king Johnny Brannon helped send Pete to prison. Norris' 1957 automobile was seen near Brannon's home shortly before the Houston man and his wife were found bludgeoned to death. Described as one of the most brutal scenes police could recall, the couple's heads had been beaten to pulp. Several thousand dollars and the man's "lucky" diamond ring were missing. As one reporter later wrote, "Police were certain Norris was the murderer. They also knew he was now on dope and more vicious than ever."[6]

Paul told Wimpy to get rid of the ring, but greed got the better of the bodyguard. Instead, during a drunken spree he bragged about the crime and showed admirers the ring. An informer relayed the information to Fort Worth police.

Norris, meanwhile, was planning the biggest job of his career: robbing the Fort Worth National Bank branch located on the air force base. To gain entry to the well-guarded base, he would kidnap a bank employee and use her as his hostage. Norris would insure her cooperation by also holding her young son until after the robbery. He planned to drive her car, which had a Carswell Base sticker on the windshield, and enter at 8:00 A.M. when employees were going to work. Once inside the gate, Norris and Humphrey would use the hostage's keys to enter the bank and wait for the expected payroll. They would shoot their way out if anyone crossed them.

Police got word of the impending crime, one source said, by questionable wiretaps. They staked out the ex-convict and his bragging bodyguard for several days prior to the planned half million dollar heist.

On the last day of April 1957 Norris and Humphrey set out to make a practice run of the route to be used. In unmarked cars, Texas Rangers Jay Banks and Johnny Klehaven, Sheriff Harlon Wright, Police Chief Cato Hightower, and Detectives Andre Fournier and Chick Matlock were close at hand. The chase was on when Norris' souped-up Chevrolet sped around a police roadblock and headed down the Jacksboro Highway. Shots were exchanged before Humphrey lost control on a country road and crashed into muddy Walnut Creek. Officers pursued and the pair was riddled with bullets.

When the smoke cleared, everyone had their own versions of the story. Police felt sure Norris was responsible for nine murders. In addition to the ones already described, Chief Cato Hightower named Norris as the primary suspect in the murder of a Negro man killed before he was to testify against Paul in an oil well swindling case. Some put the total murders as high as forty. "There are a lot of shysters and gamblers breathing easier today with Norris gone,"[7]

Detective A. C. Howerton noted. The Tarrant County grand jury in a special report lauded the work of officers in stopping the criminal activities of Norris. Judge Willis McGregor called him the "No. 1 badman of the Southwest."[8]

A bondswoman who had worked with Norris many times in the past, labeled him as a "gentleman outlaw." Paul's mother Mary Norris said of her son, "I loved Paul—he was a good boy."[9] Among the mourners who accompanied his body to Healdton, Oklahoma, for burial were two sisters and his daughter.

Many years later a reporter who covered Norris' death was asked if he thought it was a police execution, since there was no effort made to take Norris alive. The reporter explained that such might have been the case, but if officers had not acted and the Carswell robbery went on as scheduled, the woman and her son, and perhaps innocent bystanders as well, would have been killed. "It was a bad thing done to prevent a worse thing," he said.

*Gene Paul Norris, the baddest of the bad, made
the FBI list of Ten Most Wanted.*
—Photo courtesy of Henry H. Wright

Chapter 21

Big Bands at the Casino

Before television, Fort Worthians flocked to rodeos and sporting events. For almost as long as there has been a Fort Worth, there has been a Fort Worth baseball team. In the early years it was the Cats. Shortly before the Wall Street crash of 1929, at a cost of $160,000, LaGrave Field was completed. For many years it was the only baseball facility in the Texas League that boasted a clubhouse for the visiting team.

Rogers Hornsby, a local boy, managed the Cats as part of the Brooklyn Dodger organization. Hornsby's .358 career batting average was the best in the league for years.

Another manager who became an adopted Fort Worth boy was Bobby Bragan. He managed the team from 1948-1952 and won two championships. His teams were the toast of the town, and the players were invited to all the important events. Once, Bragan and Bob Jones, son-in-law of Cats' owner Branch Rickey and business manager of the team, sat at the head table at a chamber of commerce luncheon. The master of ceremonies announced that Bob Jones would perform the invocation. Bob Jones turned ashen. He had regained some color in his face when Reverend Bob Jones, minister of First Presbyterian Church, stood up to pray. Manager Jones later said the only prayer he could think of at the time was, "Now I lay me down to sleep."[1]

For fans and players, a wedding to remember.
—Courtesy of *Fort Worth Star-Telegram* Photograph Collection,
The University of Texas at Arlington Libraries.

One August night in 1950 four members of the Fort Worth Cats team said their wedding vows at the pitcher's mound. The grooms, trading their baseball uniforms for tuxedos, and their brides in traditional wedding finery, marched down an "aisle" of arched bats held aloft by their teammates.

The Cats' games were well attended. Even the 1949 fire that destroyed the grandstands didn't keep fans away. Three thousand loyalists sat on the grass and on makeshift stands the next day and cheered their team. The bleachers, capacity 12,000, were ready for the 1950 season. In 1958 the Brooklyn Dodgers became the Los Angeles Dodgers and LaGrave Field was traded to the Chicago Cubs. A few years later the Cats had their last meow. LaGrave Field was scooped up by A. M. Pate and housed the expanded Texas Refinery Company.

Fans remembered such greats as Sparky Anderson, Chico Carrasquel, Carl Erskine, Billy Hunter, and Dick Williams as once being a part of Fort Worth.

Texas Christian University was a football powerhouse in the

pre-war years. Undefeated in 1938, the team, led by Heisman Trophy winner Davey O'Brien, tried to get in the Rose Bowl. They didn't make it. Dallas was miffed when they turned down the Cotton Bowl, but Fort Worthians thought all was sweet as their heroes played in the Sugar Bowl. O'Brien played for two years with the Philadelphia Eagles before he joined the FBI in 1940. Bob Lilly and Mike Renfro, who thrilled TCU fans, also went on to bigger and better things in pro football.

One of Fort Worth's most famous sons was Ben Hogan. At age twelve, he worked as a caddy at Glen Garden Country Club. He learned his game well and led the field in earnings five times, winning sixty-one tournaments. The crowning stroke was winning the 1953 Masters Tournament.

Fort Worthians also flocked to the stock show every year, usually in miserably cold weather. W. R. Watt presided over the Southwestern Exposition and Fat Stock Show from 1946 to 1977. Joseph Googins, long-time Swift Packing House manager, was a regular at the show. When his daughter, Ruth, married Elliot Roosevelt, the president's son, a box was always reserved for any visiting Roosevelt who happened to be in town during the show.

The first live radio broadcast of a rodeo emanated from the stock show in 1958. An estimated eight million people tuned in to NBC affiliate WBAP to experience the thrill of bronc riding and calf roping.

Gene Autry, Roy Rogers, Dale Evans, George "Gabby" Hayes, and the Sons of the Pioneers were some of the big name stars who appeared in the arena.

Gamblers Fred Browning and Boston Smith owned horses and cattle and hence had more than a passing interest in the Fat Stock Show. Tincy Eggleston was interested in livestock and at times owned horses. Club owners J. D. Farmer, Bill Walton, and George Wilderspin were also well-known rodeo performers.

In addition to rodeoing, George Wilderspin and gambler Tom Daly at one time operated the Ringside Club. This club, located at N. University Drive and the Jacksboro Highway, had dice games and roulette wheels. It also featured bands and entertainers. Paul Whitman aired several of his Sunday night radio shows from the Ringside and even the Andrew Sisters sang there. Daly once had the chance to hire Edgar Bergan, but turned him down because he didn't want a "corny ventriloquist." A few months later Bergan's act was the biggest in the country.

The Ringside had quite a history. "On this site during World War II," wrote Jack Gordon, "the late Bobby Peters sang his unforgettable 'Rum and Coca Cola'—demanded every night by wartime crowds that jammed the club."[2]

During Prohibition bootleg gin was served in china teacups, complete with saucers. That truly must have fooled the government raiders. The club was dynamited three times in the '30s and after one bombing Pete Ford repaired the damage, then ran the club during the '40s. Fire gutted the building in 1951, and it was finally renovated into a new car showroom and dealership.

In addition to the Ringside and the original Casa Manana, there were two other places where the big bands played on the Jacksboro Highway. The Casino Ballroom on the shore of Lake Worth was the oldest, but the Skyliner, a neighbor of the 2222 Club, had the most colorful history. Charlie Applewhite went from the Milton Berle television show to singing at the Skyliner. Candy Barr went from stripping at the Skyliner to prison.

The Casino complex included the ballroom and an amusement park. For most of the ballroom's glory years, George T. Smith was at the helm. Starting in 1928 he welcomed such big names as Tommy Dorsey, Eddie Duchin, Wayne King, Kay Kyser, Artie Shaw, and Ted Weems.

The Casino was a strange move for Smith, who had been a salesman for a Los Angeles ambulance and casket company. But dealing with live bands and even livelier dancers took hold of him, and he stayed for twenty-one years.

Hogan Hancock led the first band to play during Smith's tenure. There was a trumpeter in the band named Harry James who was so loud that Smith complained, "You either put that trumpeter in the back row of the band or hide his horn. He's driving me nuts."[3] Hancock dutifully sent him to the back of the bandstand.

Tommy Dorsey's last gig at the Casino was in the fall of 1949. With the autumn leaves he blew into town in his new pride and joy, a $40,000 bus. It featured its own bedroom, complete with mobile telephone and a refrigerator to keep his passion, tuna sandwiches.

Al Norris sang at the Casino. He was pretty good, but it wasn't until he changed his name to Tony Martin that he became famous.

Dorothy Lamour once graced the bandstand at the Casino.

Before she put on that daring sarong, she was a singer with Herbie Kay's orchestra.

Kay Kyser also played a memorable stand there. Kyser, the "Ole Professor" from the "Kollege of Knowledge" radio show, was at the height of his movie and radio fame when he played a one-nighter. Due to the earlier collapse of the casino boardwalk, the amusement park's shooting range had been moved indoors and the noise competed with the dance music. The band leader stood it as long as he could. Kyser made the concessionaire a deal. Shut the shooting range down for the night and he, Kyser, would pay him what he would take in if he stayed open. For the rest of the evening the band played on.

Ben Bernie, whose trademark was an upbeat "Yowsuh, yowsuh" was definitely not his usual cheerful self the night his band played the Casino. It seemed that before show time he spent several hours and a painfully large amount of money at Fred Browning's Top o' Hill Terrace. As a result, Bernie's cry between sets was, "Nawsuh, nawsuh, no more dice for me." He stuck by his vow—until the next day.

In September 1949 Jack Gordon, *Fort Worth Press* amusement columnist, reported big crowds danced to the music of Ray McKinley at the Casino Ballroom. McKinley, speaking of the last fatal flight of Glenn Miller, noted, "The weather was terrible. Even the birds were walking that day."[4]

Native son Tex Beneke brought his big band sound to the Casino, as did Billy May and almost every other name band in the period immediately following World War II.

By 1965 the ballroom was in need of repair. Smith remodeled at a cost of $90,000, which gave the landmark a few more years of life. Eight years later Gordon wrote the obituary for one of the most notable clubs on the Jacksboro Highway:

> Last tango at the Casino:
> The wrecking of Fort Worth's storied old Casino Ballroom began early yesterday, with workmen in the hard hats first ripping away part of the roof.
> Then at 4:30 P.M., as debris which rained down from the ceiling had covered most of the dance floor, Jerry Starnes and his partner, Reba Smith, danced what had to be the last dance at the Casino.

Starnes, manager of Casino Beach for 24 years, and Miss Smith, a First National Bank secretary, found a patch of dance floor still clear of wreckage. And to the music of a portable radio brought by Starnes,the two did their dance together.

It was a final, sentimental salute to the thousands of couples who since 1926 had danced away dreamy hours at the big ballroom on Lake Worth. Never again, after this brief dancing in a lonely, stricken ballroom late yesterday, would any couple ever dance at the Casino again.[5]

* * *

George Campbell, with too many musical compositions to count, plus a platinum record, reminisced about entertainment on the Jacksboro Highway. Following college he played at the Casino and in clubs around the world. It seemed to him the owners were awash with money. The logical thing to do was to open his own club. With partner Gene Hames he did just that. The Skyliner Ballroom was born.

Reporter Eleanor Wilson described their white stucco club as having 2,500 square feet of dance floor. Five hundred couples could do the fox trot, waltz, or form a conga line. It was by far the largest dance hall in the city. The maroon plastic floor was surrounded by blue carpet. Blue and rose mirrors reflected the wine and rose furnishings. The entrance was decorated with a skyline view of Fort Worth. It was a beautiful club, and catered to an upper income clientele, featuring such favorites as Benny Beckner, who packed the house with his routines, "The Deacon" and "Mr. Bach and Mr. Boogie."

At the beginning, quality entertainment was the order of the day. However, Campbell and Hames discovered what many other entrepreneurs learned the hard way—overhead took most of the profit. Even Satchmo Armstrong pulling in 2,000 people didn't ease the bottom line. Realizing they were on the slow road to starvation, the two sold the Skyliner to F. A. Florence.

Florence in turn sold it to W. D. Satterwhite, and it was downhill from then on. One of the new acts, the Jewel Box Revue, raised eyebrows all over North Texas. The cast, amusement editor Jack Gordon mused, were all female impersonators. Owner W. D. Satterwhite's only comment was, "Boys will be girls, you know."[6]

The owner of a beer joint down the highway approved of the show. When not performing, the entertainers hung out at his place. Dressed in drag, they danced and flirted with the more conservative patrons at the bar. Business tripled, but so did the fights when the macho guys discovered their dancing partners used urinals.

Satterwhite then built the Annex Club, a small, sparsely furnished gambling room and hired such notables as Tincy Eggleston, Nelson Harris, and Howard Stripling to run it. The latter, known as "Strip" was also a used car salesman who liked big diamond rings.

Stripling and his wife Lois got into trouble when he used his 5.26-carat ring and Mrs. Stripling's 3.5-carat ring as collateral for a $5,000 loan. He defaulted on the payments to a Grand Prairie bank. The rings were sold at auction for $4,850. Stripling didn't get to spend any of the money. The tax man was waiting with his hand out.

Satterwhite and Eggleston were charged by the 1951 grand jury with operating a gambling house. Essie Graham's testimony, described in a previous chapter, led to a not guilty verdict against Eggleston and dismissal of charges against Satterwhite.

Gangster Tincy Eggleston awaiting indictment
—Courtesy of *Fort Worth Star-Telegram* Photograph Collection,
The University of Texas at Arlington Libraries.

Satterwhite then brought suit against the *Fort Worth Press* for stories about the grand jury investigation. He alleged the newspaper's stories pictured his business as a "gambling house," which brought the club into "disrepute." On cross-examination the newspaper's attorney Spencer Shropshire asked, "Mr. Satterwhite, isn't it a fact you were convicted of a felony charge in the state of Oklahoma?" Satterwhite was not pleased with this line of questioning. Appealing to the judge, he responded, "He can't make me answer that, can he?" When told by the judge that he must answer the question, Satterwhite turned to his lawyer and said, "You didn't tell me all this. Let's forget the whole thing," and stalked out of the courthouse.[7]

In November 1953 the big news event at the Annex was the showing of an X-rated movie. A tip prompted the police chief to plant two undercover men in the audience. In addition to the pornographic flicks, eight nude live performers entertained those who paid $3.50 admission charge. Just as the show was getting really interesting, at the prearranged signal, the police burst in, surprising the 200 men crowded into the club.

From the city jail Satterwhite explained he ". . . rented the club to a private organization on the understanding there would be a strip tease act and a business film."[8] Misdemeanor and indecent exposure charges were filed against the actors and employees. Satterwhite and two others were charged with displaying lewd and lascivious pictures in a public place.

The day of the trial, civic-minded citizens, anxious to see their court system in action, packed Judge W. H. Tolbert's County Criminal Court. Dr. Chang Wook Moon, a social science professor, was there in the interest of academe. A mistrial was declared when a juror became ill during the noon recess and the film was not shown. Citizens lost interest, and a new trial date was set for March 1954.

Satterwhite pleaded guilty to a lesser charge of serving beer without a license, and the state dropped an open saloon charge against him. He paid a $200 fine and went back to business as usual—minus the movies.

In March at the rescheduled trial, "Spectators and jurors in County Criminal Court were treated to a triple feature movie Thursday,"[9] Bill Hitch reported to newspaper readers. Snippets of "Prescription For Love," "Sleepwalker," and "Peek-A-Boo" gave viewers a taste of the films.

A newspaper photographer scanned the courtroom, taking shots of the audience. This caused a man to rush up to the city editor's desk, pleading, "Man, you'll ruin me if you run that picture." Identifying himself as a minister of the Gospel, he sputtered, "I just went up there to see what type of people went to see that sort of obscenity . . . just out of curiosity . . . I wasn't one . . . that . . . please don't run my picture."[10] He examined the photograph and lofted a little thank you prayer heavenward upon not finding himself in the shot.

At the trial, officer W. F. McGill testified seeing the live performers after the movies were shown. He told the six-man jury that at one point Satterwhite had stood up and cheered. By now the former owner of the Skyliner, Satterwhite was found guilty and fined $750. The others involved in the action were fined and given ten-day jail sentences.

Attorney Hal Lattimore appealed the verdict. He contended Satterwhite was merely the landlord at the Annex, and did not know the nature of the films or live performance. Citing insufficient evidence to prove his client sold tickets to the two undercover officers, Lattimore asked that the ruling be overturned. He admitted, "if it were an offense to be a fool, Satterwhite ought to pay a fine."[11] Judge K. K. Woodley was not swayed and Satterwhite was ordered to pay up for showing the movie.

Jimmy Levens was the next Skyliner owner of note. With partner Emmett Spinks, a Central Airlines pilot, Levens changed the Annex to a milk bar for teens. Spinks, whether a comedian at a night club mike or at the controls of a plane, regaled his passengers with such comments as, "Ladies and gentlemen, there is a large city ahead. We aren't sure whether it is New Orleans or Dallas. The best thing is to drop in and ask somebody."[12]

Levens hired Charlie Applewhite, characterized as Fort Worth's latest singing sensation, to do a gig. However, Charlie, the All-American boy to millions of teenage fans, objected to another performer hired by Levens—stripper Sherry Lynn. The owner supported the exotic dancer in the dispute. Levens noted, "After all, Applewhite knew he was booked in a night club and not a Sunday School."[13] A compromise was worked out. Charlie sang first, then Sherry stripped.

Applewhite's life consisted of extreme highs and lows. Applewhite and his high school sweetheart, Joan Loicano, eloped when both were in their teens. They moved to New York when Charlie landed a spot on the Milton Berle television show. The marriage soured and ended in divorce.

About that time he was drafted. Jack Gordon quoted Applewhite as saying, "When I came out of the Army two years later the Berle show was off the air and a whole new crop of singers had taken over—like Andy Williams, Tony Bennett, Paul Anka."[14]

Applewhite sang in clubs, both his own in Dallas and wherever he could get a booking. Sources said drinking had become a problem and his financial woes were mounting. In September 1961 he, his wife Nancy, and friend Robert McGannon left Dallas in his light plane bound for Midland. The craft plunged into the ground 300 feet from Midland Air Park's runway. Nancy Applewhite and McGannon were killed. Charlie received a skull fracture, crushed chest, mangled legs, and smashed facial bones. A musician who had known the singer since he was a ten-year-old child star at the old Worth Theater, said Charlie was drunk and should never have tried to pilot the plane. He recovered, and, as Jack Gordon noted, "He lived to sing again . . . to fly again . . . and to marry again."[15]

In late 1958 Levens and Spinks sold the Skyliner Club to Billie Gale. Miss Gale planned to turn the troubled dance spot into a country and western hall. The sale proved stormy. Strippers Georgia Storm and Sherry Lynn demanded to appear during the holiday season according to their signed contracts with Levens. Miss Gale's rejoinder was "not in my club." Levens argued Gale's non-payment canceled the bill of sale, and the strippers would perform. An altercation between Storm and Lynn on one side and one of Gale's waitresses on the other became a hair-pulling, punching melee. The strippers went to St. Joseph's Hospital for treatment of minor bruises and bumps.

Levens regained control of the entertainment emporium, promising two floor shows nightly that included comedians and exotic dancers. One stripper ended her act wearing only a python snake. But the Skyliner's days were numbered, and when Levens died so did the once celebrated night club.

Jack Gordon reminded his readers of the twenty years of glory days for the Skyliner. George Campbell, in black tie with his fourteen-piece orchestra, had accompanied Nick Lucas opening night. Lucas, a popular nightclub and theater singer, sang "Tiptoe Through the Tulips" before Tiny Tim had progressed from crawling to toddling. Sally Rand performed at the club, and Rudy Vallee sang there.

A teenager named Candy Barr was a Skyliner stripper. Campbell told of the first time he met Candy: "She came to rehearsal dressed in jeans, an old flannel shirt, her hair in rollers and no make-up. My first impression was 'Ugh.' She cussed like a sailor as well." The next time he saw her she was in costume, complete with "those 45s" make-up, the works. His second impression was "Wow."[16]

Candy became the girlfriend of Las Vegas gangster Mickey Cohen. In what many believe was a set-up to get her to testify against the reputed mobster, she was charged with possession of a small amount of marijuana. She refused to cooperate and was sentenced to fifteen years in prison. Upon her release she resumed her real name and lived quietly in Brownwood.

The Skyliner knew bright moments and times best forgotten. Levens, its last owner, died of natural causes in 1966. The club, already on its last legs, needed massive renovation. It had been years since a big name entertainer played there. For three years the club remained dark and empty. Condemned by city inspectors, in April 1969 the wrecking ball put the Skyliner out of its misery.

* * *

When the North Side exhibit buildings were used for war production storage, the stock show moved to the Will Rogers Complex. It never moved back. In its place arose the North Side Coliseum. R. G. McElyea converted the old building into a combination dance hall, country concert hall, and wrestling arena. In 1956 he hired a former truck driver from Mississippi named Elvis Presley to appear for $500. By the concert date, Elvis had a number one hit on the charts. McElyea held him to the original fee. Sixteen years later "the Pelvis" played to a sold-out crowd at the Convention Center for considerably more than McElyea gave him.

Across town the Texas Wesleyan School of Fine Arts began producing annual musicals in 1955. For serious music lovers the Fort Worth Symphony and the Fort Worth Opera Association were established parts of the community.

* * *

A black-and-white ten-inch screen in a twenty by twenty-four inch consolette caught the attention of those who could afford it. This Philco "electronic magic entertainment center" cost $359.50 plus $1.50 federal tax in 1949. Children pondered how a man could fit into the thing, and adults were not much more sophisticated at understanding television. In 1954 WBAP-TV became the first all-color television station west of the Mississippi River. This was another Amon Carter contribution, but he didn't live to see Ed Sullivan and Carol Burnett in all their glory.

Wayne Brown was a pioneer in television news gathering. He recalled, "We went out and shot the pictures with a $200 Eastman camera. There was no sound. Then we went back to the station, wrote the script and read it on the air to match the pictures."[17] Many years and many awards later he used a $75,000 RCA mini-cam.

At first some people were wary of television. Brown covered one story where only print journalists were allowed to interview a subject. Elston Brooks told the story like this:

> "I'm Brooks, . . . from the *Star-Telegram*."
> Dick Growald went in next. "I'm Growald, . . . from the *Press*."
> Wayne tucked his camera under his coat, and was third through the door. "I'm Brown," he said, "from the sun."[18]

Brown had covered the discovery of the bodies of Tincy Eggleston and Edell Evans. Once, in a news van persuing the car of a kidnapper, Brown hung out the window to secure pictures of the chase. Covering another story, he was hit on the head by an angry crook. In another situation, a robber who didn't want to be on the evening news threw chunks of concrete at him.

That was entertainment, 1940s and 1950s style.

Chapter 22

The Other Side of Town

World War II was the most important event for Fort Worthians during the decade of the 1940s. From 1942 to 1946 a red star on a white banner hanging in the front window of a house told everyone a young man from that family was in the military. The newspapers were filled with stories of sons and husbands receiving medals, sometimes the purple heart. Readers anxiously followed the battles. After a long and exhausting war, the boys came home and attended Texas Christian University or Texas Wesleyan College on a new program called the "G.I. Bill."

The biggest industry in the '40s and '50s was defense, led by Convair. The company of many names—Consolidated Aircraft, Consolidated Vultee, Convair, General Dynamics, Lockheed, and now Lockheed Martin—was dubbed "the bomber plant." Housed on 526 acres, the almost five million square feet of assembly line was so huge workers regularly rode scooters or bicycles to get from one part of the plant to another. At its height during the war, 18,500 men and 11,500 Rosies riveted round the clock.

People flocked to the city from small towns and rural areas to work in the defense plants. Housing was so scarce homeowners with extra bedrooms rented to complete strangers.

Meacham Field was a busy place during the war. Both American and Delta Air Lines operated there. Government officials, movie stars on war bond tours, and those citizens daring enough to fly, could choose from thirty-four daily flights. American Air Lines left the field in the mid-fifties.

A young man who grew up near Meacham Field caught the flying bug. Major Horace Carswell, Jr., was posthumously awarded the Congressional Medal of Honor. He also had an Air Force base named in his honor.

On the South Side a manufacturing company, Williamson-Dickie, turned out more garments in 1940 in a half-day than it had during an entire month when it started in 1922. Movie actor Henry Fonda wore Williamson-Dickie work clothes in *The Grapes of Wrath*. Frank Sinatra's army khakis in the award-winning *From Here to Eternity* were made in Fort Worth. The manufacturer reverted back to making sturdy work clothes following the war.

Since the heyday of the 1920s Ranger oil fields, energy was the business that excited entrepreneurial gamblers. The Sid Richardson Gasoline Company was born in 1947. The next year he added carbon black. Nephew Perry R. Bass helped his uncle's company become one of the big success stories of the period. The legacy of his enormous wealth can be seen throughout the city.

Service industries sprang up to serve the needs of the 200,000 citizens of Fort Worth. L. N. Wilemon and Cleaves Rhea opened a bank on Exchange Avenue to help the blue-collar working people, where "Rough-edged cowboys, independent merchants, farmers, homemakers and people coming to a strange country to get a new start were their first customers."[1]

Not all attorneys defended gamblers and gangsters. Cantey and Hanger, established in 1882, handled tax matters and estate business. The McGown family of lawyers advised both prominent and ordinary citizens.

A working man's got to eat, and some Fort Worth restaurants became world famous. Theo Yardanoff, a Yugoslavian immigrant, opened Theo's Saddle and Sirloin Club on East Exchange. On the menu was "calf fries." He learned from a cowboy years earlier there was a market for "what separates the bulls from the cows."[2]

Multiple generations knew W. O. Chenault as "Pinky." While still in high school Pinky opened a drive-in on borrowed money. He hired North Side cheerleaders as carhops. After the war he opened the more famous restaurant on the Jacksboro Highway. Chenault's is still a popular place with residents and visitors in the 1990s.

Insurance man Jesse Roach established Cattleman's Cafe in the stockyards soon after the war ended. Few remember his insurance business, but Cattleman's became world famous for steaks. At various times Roach owned four other eating places. None could compare with Cattleman's.

President Harry S. Truman came to town September 1, 1948. He was the first politician to be interviewed on television news.

Four years later, the big story was that for the first time since the Civil War, Tarrant County voters cast their ballots for a Republican. War hero Dwight D. Eisenhower was elected president. He ushered in a new political era—thereby symbolically ending the era of corruption and violence.

Of course, crime did not disappear when the 1940s and 1950s bad guys were laid to rest. Random drive-by shootings and whole neighborhoods given over to gangs were unheard of forty years ago. The gamblers and gangsters of old would be scornful of today's "punks" who commit crimes as rites of passage.

Appendix A
Indictment Who's Who

The following is a list of indictments that ran on the front page
of the *Fort Worth Press* on March 31, 1951.

Gambling indictments were returned by the Tarrant County grand jury against
these men:

TIFFIN HALL, owner of Madoc Hotel and two Mexican Inn Cafes
> Hall, branded by a grand jury witness as the "kingpin" of gambling here, was
> named in three indictments. Two evolved from an investigation of dice games
> in the Commercial Hotel and accused Hall of maintaining a gambling house
> March 18, 1950, and November 4, 1950. The third accused him of renting to
> A. R. (Bob) Floyd and Clyde Neal space which they used for a dice game
> November 5, 1949.

FRED BROWNING, operator of Top o' Hill Terrace near Arlington (two indictments)
> Accused of maintaining a gambling house, permitting wagering on dice and
> card games, and keeping a slot machine October 7, 1950, and January 1, 1951.

GEORGE WILDERSPIN, operator of East Side Club in Halton City and personal friend of Nevada racketeer Benny Binion (two indictments)
> Accused of maintaining a gambling house, permitting wagering on dice and
> card games, and keeping a slot machine January 14, 1950, and December 23,
> 1950.

BERT WAKEFIELD, operator of 3939 Club on Jacksboro Hwy. (two indictments)
> Accused of maintaining a gambling house, permitting wagering on dice and
> card games, and keeping a slot machine March 25, 1950, and January 20, 1951.

W. C. KIRKWOOD, operator of 2222 Club (Four Deuces) on Jacksboro Hwy.
Kirkwood, whose club was included in a list of customers given to the Senate
Crime Investigating Committee by a manufacturer of gambling equipment,
was named in two indictments. They accused him of running a gambling
house and permitting betting on dice and card games August 12, 1950, and
February 3, 1951.

W. D. SATTERWHITE, operator of the Skyliner Club on Jacksboro Hwy. and its
after-hours addition, the Annex Club
Accused of keeping a gambling house, permitting betting on a dice game, and
exhibiting a slot machine January 7, 1950.

FRANK CATES, ex-convict arrested during a police round-up after the nitro
bomb slaying of gambler Nelson Harris and his pregnant wife
Accused of permitting gambling on premises November 4, 1950. The grand
jury says Cates rented space to the City Club—a partnership composed of
Hall, Floyd, and H. D. (Red) Oden—knowing the space would be used for a
dice game.

LES HUTT, associate of Wakefield at the 3939 Club (two indictments)
Accused of keeping a slot machine, permitting gambling on cards and dice,
and maintaining a gambling house March 25, 1950, and January 20, 1951. The
grand jury says Hutt rented space to Wakefield, knowing it would be used for
gambling.

IVY MILLER, associate of Browning at Top o' Hill Terrace
Miller, said to be a personal friend of Binion, was named in two indictments
accusing him of keeping a gambling house and permitting betting October 7,
1950, and January 1, 1951.

JERRY ROSENBERG, associate of Browning at Top o' Hill Terrace (two indictments)
Accused of keeping a gambling house and permitting betting October 7, 1950
and January 1, 1951.

A. R. (BOB) FLOYD, associate of Hall
Floyd, who was arrested during the round-up after the Harris bombing, was
accused in two indictments of keeping a gambling house and permitting betting on a dice game March 18, 1950, and November 4, 1950. The indictments
were an outgrowth of an investigation of Commercial Hotel dice games.

H. D. (RED) ODEN, associate of Hall and Floyd (two indictments)
Charged with keeping a gambling house and permitting betting on a dice
game March 18, 1950 and November 4, 1950.

OSCAR DONLEY, associate of Browning at Top o' Hill Terrace (two indictments)
Accused of keeping a gambling house, exhibiting a slot machine, and permitting gambling on dice and card games October 7, 1950, and January 1, 1951.

The grand jury charges Donley rented space to Browning, knowing it would be used for gambling.

PHIL LONG, associate of Wakefield at 3939 Club (two indictments)
Accused of keeping a gambling house and permitting betting on dice and card games March 25, 1950 and January 20, 1951.

AL CLARK
Clark was accused in two indictments which evolved from an investigation of Court Hotel dice games, with keeping a gambling house and permitting betting August 5, 1950, and September 29, 1950.

HOWARD LEE, associate of Clark at the Court Hotel (two indictments)
Accused of keeping a gambling house August 5, 1950, and September 29, 1950.

BILLY HUGHES
Hughes, an associate of Clark and Lee, was charged in two indictments with keeping a gambling house August 5, 1950, and September 29, 1950.

TOM DALY (two indictments)
Accused of keeping a gambling house and permitting betting on dice games August 5, 1950, and September 29, 1950. The grand jury says Daly rented Clark space for a dice game.

JACK DARBY, associate of Wilderspin at the East Side Club (two indictments)
Charged with maintaining a gambling house, permitting betting, and exhibiting a slot machine January 14, 1950, and December 23, 1950.

PAUL GARLAND
Garland, another Wilderspin associate, was accused in two indictments of maintaining a gambling house, permitting betting, and exhibiting a slot machine January 14, 1950, and December 23, 1950.

DEWEY INMAN
Inman, termed an associate of Hall, was charged with keeping a gambling house and allowing betting on a dice game March 18, 1950.

BO GREEN, JIMMY GREEN, and DUDE GREEN (two indictments each)
The three brothers were accused of running a gambling house and permitting betting on a dice game August 12, 1950, and February 3, 1951. They were indicted after an investigation of activities at the Town House Hotel.

L. J. McWILLIE, associate of Browning (two indictments)
Accused of keeping a gambling house and permitting wagering October 7, 1950, and January 1, 1951.

MACK TAYLOR, associate of Kirkwood at the 2222 Club (two indictments)
Accused of maintaining a gambling house and permitting betting August 12, 1950, and February 3, 1951.

WILLIAM JORDAN, associated with Wilderspin at the East Side Club (two indictments)
   Charged with operating a gambling house, exhibiting a slot machine, and allowing betting January 14, 1950, and December 23, 1950.

PETE FORD, associate of Kirkwood at the 2222 Club (two indictments)
   Accused of keeping a gambling house and permitting wagering August 12, 1950, and February 3, 1951.

LEE MOORE, owner of Lone Star Sales Co., 1153 Jennings (three indictments)
   Accused of owning and exhibiting three marble boards seized in raids last month.

ROY MOORE, 1441 W. Berry
   Moore, named in two slot machine indictments returned Tuesday, was indicted again as owner of another slot machine seized February 21.

BENNY McDONALD, Star Coin Machine Co., 1502 N.W. 25th
   McDonald, named in one slot machine and one marble board indictment Tuesday, was indicted again as owner of another slot machine picked up February 21.

JACK FRANKRICH, 2100 Warner Rd., operator of Ace Distributing Co., 102 W. 11th
   Accused of owning marble machine seized February 15.

Appendix B

Author's note: Fred Browning's indictment and defense is typical of all those cited by the 1951 grand jury. Legal documents pertaining to the Browning indictment follow.

INDICTMENT   D. A. 430

IN THE NAME AND BY THE AUTHORITY OF ⎱
    THE STATE OF TEXAS   ⎰

THE GRAND JURORS OF THE STATE OF TEXAS, duly elected, tried, empaneled, sworn and charged to inquire of offenses committed in Tarrant County, in the State of Texas, upon their oaths do present in and to the Criminal District Court/of said County that one Number Two ....

                    FRED BROWNING
....
                                                on or about the 1st
hereinafter styled Defendant, in the County of Tarrant and State aforesaid, ꜱ×ᴏᴛʜᴇ..................................

day of...January......, in the year of our Lord One Thousand Nine Hundred...Fifty-One.............did keep and exhibit a gaming table and bank for the purpose of gaming, AGAINST THE PEACE AND DIGNITY OF THE STATE.
                    SECOND COUNT
AND THE GRAND JURORS AFORESAID, upon their oaths aforesaid, do further present in and to said Criminal District Court Number Two in and for Tarrant County, Texas, that one FRED BROWNING, in the County of Tarrant and State of Texas, on or about the 1st day of January, A. D. 1951, did keep and was then and there interested in keeping a building and room there situate for the purpose of being used as a place to keep and exhibit a gaming table and bank for the purpose of gaming and as a place where people did then and there resort to gamble, bet and wager upon said gaming table and bank, AGAINST THE PEACE AND DIGNITY OF THE STATE.
                    THIRD COUNT
AND THE GRAND JURORS AFORESAID, upon their oaths aforesaid, do further present in and to said Criminal District Court Number Two in and for Tarrant County, Texas, that one FRED BROWNING, in the County of Tarrant and State of Texas, on or about the 1st day of January, A. D. 1951, did then and there knowingly permit property and premises there situate and then and there owned by him to be used as a place to keep and exhibit a gaming table and bank for the purpose of gaming, AGAINST THE PEACE AND DIGNITY OF THE STATE.
                    FOURTH COUNT
AND THE GRAND JURORS AFORESAID, upon their oaths aforesaid, do further present in and to said Criminal District Court Number Two in and for Tarrant County, Texas, that one FRED BROWNING, in the County of Tarrant and State of Texas, on or about the 1st day of January, A. D. 1951, did knowingly permit property and premises there situate and then and there under his control to be used as a place to keep and exhibit a gaming table and bank for the purpose of gaming, AGAINST THE PEACE AND DIGNITY OF THE STATE.
                    FIFTH COUNT
AND THE GRAND JURORS AFORESAID, upon their oaths aforesaid, do further present in and to said Criminal District Court Number Two in and for Tarrant County, Texas, that one FRED BROWNING, in the County of Tarrant and State of Texas, on or about the 1st day of January, A. D. 1951, did then and there unlawfully and knowingly permit certain property and premises there situate, and then and there owned and controlled by him to be kept for the purpose of being used as a place to bet and wager and to gamble with dice and cards then and there played and did then and there knowingly permit said property and premises to be kept for the purpose of being used as a place where people did then and there resort to gamble, bet and wager on games then and there played with cards and dice, and the said FRED BROWNING then and there knowingly permitted said property and premises to be kept and used for said purpose, AGAINST THE PEACE AND DIGNITY OF THE STATE.
SIXTH COUNT: And the Grand Jurors aforesaid, upon their oaths aforesaid, do further present in and to said Criminal District Court Number Two in and for Tarrant County, Texas, that one FRED BROWNING, in the County of Tarrant and State of Texas, on the 1st day of January, A. D. 1951, did then and there unlawfully keep and exhibit for the purpose of gaming, a gaming device, to-wit: a slot machine,

contrary to the form of the Statutes in such cases made and provided and against the peace and dignity

of the State.

Stewart Hellman.................................   ....Clay Finley...............................
                    Criminal District Attorney.   Foreman Grand Jury.

D. C. 141   WRIT TO SERVE INDICTMENT

THE STATE OF TEXAS

To the Sheriff of Tarrant County, said State—GREETING:

YOU ARE HEREBY COMMANDED, To immediately deliver to................................the defendant, in person, in

..........Fred Browning..........

the case of the STATE OF TEXAS vs...........Fred..Browning..........

..........No....30594-5 - 50617.18..........pending in the District Court of said

County, the accompanying certified copy of Indictment in said cause.

HEREIN FAIL NOT, and make due return hereof FORTHWITH.

WITNESS My signature and official seal, on this the...............

day of..........MAR 30 1951..........A. D. 19......

MRS. LEWIS D. WALL, JR. , Clerk

District Court, Tarrant County, Texas

By..., Deputy

Form D. C. No. 11—FELONY

THE STATE OF TEXAS
County of Tarrant

In the Criminal District Court No. 2.

To............ JAN...... 1951............ Term, 19........

To Any Sheriff of the State of Texas, Greeting:

You are hereby commanded to take the body of................................
Fred Browning

and him safely keep, so that you have him before the Honorable, the Criminal District Court No. 2 in and for the County aforesaid, at the Court House thereof, in the City of Fort Worth, instanter, then and there

to answer the State of Texas on a charge by indictment, with offense of...
Keeping and Exhibiting Gaming Table and Bank, Keeping a Gambling House, Permitting Place Owned to be Used for Gaming, Permitting Place Under Control to be used for Gaming, Permitting Place to be Used for Gaming, Exhibiting a gaming device for gaming
a felony.

Bail, $..1,000.00

Issued under my hand and seal of office in the City of Fort Worth, Texas, this
.... day of............ MAR 30 1951 .... 19........

GEO. LETTLE R. WALL, JR. ...., Clerk,

District Court, Tarrant County, Texas

By.., Deputy

S 45—Appearance Bond (Criminal District Court)

THE STATE OF TEXAS
COUNTY OF TARRANT } *Know all Men by These Presents:*

THAT WE, ... FRED BROWNING .... as Principal,

hereinafter styled Principal, and all signers hereto as Sureties, are held and firmly bound to THE STATE

OF TEXAS in the full and just sum of .... One Thousand _ _ _ _ _ _ _ .... DOLLARS,

and, in addition thereto, all necessary and reasonable expenses incurred by any and all Sheriffs or

other peace officers in rearresting the Principal in the event he fails to appear before the Honorable

Criminal District Court of Tarrant County, Texas, at the time stated herein, for the payment of which
No. 2

sum, well and truly to be made, we bind ourselves, our heirs, executors, administrators, jointly and sev-

erally, firmly by these presents.

WHEREAS, The above Principal stands lawfully charged by Indictment in the Criminal District

Court of Tarrant County with the offense of ....

Keeping and Exhibiting Gaming Table and Bank, Keeping a
Gambling House, Permitting Place Owned to be used for gaming, Permitting
Place under control to be used for gaming, Permitting Place to be used for
Gaming, Exhibiting a Gaming Device for Gaming
a felony against the peace and dignity of the State.

Now, the condition of the above bond is such, that if the above Principal shall make his personal
No. 2
appearance before the Honorable Criminal District Court of Tarrant County, Texas, at the term now in

session, at the Court House thereof in and for the County of Tarrant and the State aforesaid, instanter,

and there remain from day to day and from term to term of said Court, and not depart therefrom until

discharged by due course of law, then and there to answer said above described charge, then, the said

bond to be null and void, otherwise to be and remain in full force and effect.

Witness our signatures, this ...... 31st ...... day of .... March, ... A. D. 1951 ......

Fred Browning .... Principal.

SURETIES { *Jesse E. Martin*
Arthur Lee Moore
Leo Brewster

Taken and approved by me, this the ...... 31st ...... day of .... March ...., 1951 ......

.... Sully Montgomery ....
Sheriff, Tarrant County, Texas

By ...... *A B Carter* ...... Deputy.

NO. ___50617___

THE STATE OF TEXAS		IN THE CRIMINAL DISTRICT
VS.		COURT NUMBER TWO,
___FRED BROWNING___		TARRANT COUNTY, TEXAS.

TO THE HONORABLE JUDGE OF SAID COURT:

NOW COMES _____ FRED BROWNING _____, the defend-
ant in the above styled and numbered cause, and, at the first time this case is set
for trial and prior to filing any other pleadings of any character, makes this his
motion to quash the indictment returned against him in the above styled and numbered cause on March 30, 1951. In support of such motion to quash, he would show
to the Court that no character of criminal accusation and complaint had been filed
against him at the time the Grand Jury which returned this indictment was organized and impaneled, and this has been his first opportunity to question either the
legality of the Grand Jury's organization or the qualifications of its members, or
to attack the legality of the indictment returned against him. This defendant would
show that such indictments should be quashed upon the following grounds:

1.

This defendant would show to the Court that the Grand Jury returning
the indictment against him in this case was not selected, organized and impaneled in the manner required by law for each of the following reasons:

a. The Sheriff of Tarrant County, Texas, did not summons the pros-
pective grand jurors, who later composed the Grand Jury which returned the
indictment in this case, in the manner as required by law, and did not summons
them at least three days, exclusive of the day of the service, prior to the first
day of the term of Court in which they are to serve, by giving personal notice to
each juror, or by leaving at his place of business, or with a member of his
family over 16 years of age, a written notice to such juror that he had been
selected as a grand juror, and giving the time and place when and where the said
grand juror was to attend; and further the said Sheriff of Tarrant County, Texas,

did not make the return of the list of such grand jurors and prospe.
jurors as required by law.

      b. The Honorable District Court in which the Grand Jury in question
was selected and impaneled failed to administer to the Clerk of said Court and
each of his deputies, in open court, before the list of grand jurors was delivered
to the said Clerk, the following oath required by law:

> "You do swear that you will not open the jury lists now
> delivered to you, nor permit them to be opened until the time
> prescribed by law; that you will not directly or indirectly con-
> verse with anyone selected as a juror concerning any case or
> proceeding which may come before such juror for trial in this
> court at its next term. "

      c. After all of the testimony which is and was accessible to the Grand
Jury had been given in respect to the criminal accusation against this defendant,
and on which this defendant was indicted, and after the Grand Jury voted to
present an indictment, the Foreman of the Grand Jury failed to make a memorandum of the same with such data as would enable the attorney who represented
the State to write the indictment, and failed to deliver such memorandum to the
District Attorney of Tarrant County, Texas, or to any of his assistants, or to
any attorney legally representing the State of Texas, as required by law, in
order that said indictment might be prepared or written in this case.

      d. This defendant would further show that the members of such Grand
Jury did not have the qualifications required by law, particularly in that one or
more of such number did not possess a poll tax or legal exemption from payment
of poll tax, and consequently were disqualified, and the Grand Jury was not composed of the required number of qualified men, and such indictment returned
against this defendant should be quashed and the prosecution dismissed.

2.

      This defendant would further show to the Court that on numerous occa-
sions prior to the return of this indictment against him, the grand jurors would
ask for and receive advice and counsel from the Court touching matters before

them concerning the investigation and violations of the gambling laws generally,
and particularly by this defendant. In receiving such counsel and advice, the
Grand Jury did not go before the Court in a body, and so guard the manner of
propounding their questions as not to divulge the particular accusation that was
pending before them, or propound their questions in writing so that the Court might
give them the desired advice and counsel in writing, all as provided by the statutes
of this State; but the Grand Jury conferred with, and received advice from, the
Court touching the matters hereinabove set out singly or in small groups less than
nine, contrary to the manner provided by the statutes of this State.

3.

This defendant would further show that the indictment in this case should
be quashed on the further ground that a person not authorized by law performed all
the statutory duties of State's Attorney before the Grand Jury in question in connection with the investigation of this defendant that led to the indictment here sought
to be quashed, and was present during, and participated in, the deliberations of
the Grand Jury upon the accusation against this defendant which led to this indictment. In this connection, the defendant shows the Grand Jury in question was impaneled by the Court in the early part of January, 1951; and it returned the indictment against this defendant on March 30, 1951. Stewart W. Hellman was elected
Criminal District Attorney of Tarrant County, Texas, in the General Election in
November, 1950, for the term 1951 and 1952. He duly qualified as such officer
on January 1, 1951, and has been continuously at all times since that date the
duly elected, qualified and acting Criminal District Attorney of Tarrant County,
Texas. During the entire time the Grand Jury in question has been in session,
Stewart W. Hellman and his duly and legally appointed and qualified Assistant
Criminal District Attorneys have been the only persons authorized by law to perform the statutory duties of State's Attorney before the Grand Jury; and he and
his Assistants have been at all times present in his office in Tarrant County,
Texas, ready, able and willing to perform, and insistent upon performing, all
the statutory duties of State's Attorney before said Grand Jury, and not disqualified by law from performing any of their duties in connection with the investi-

gation of any accusations against this defendant. On or about February 27, 1951, this Court appointed John B. Honts as "Special Prosecutor", without the consent of Stewart W. Hellman, to perform the statutory duties of State's Attorney before said Grand Jury; and since such date the Grand Jury has excluded Stewart W. Hellman and his assistants from their sessions involving the investigation of all the accusations against this defendant and similar accusations against other persons. The said John B. Honts, insofar as this particular accusation against this defendant is concerned, has continuously performed all the statutory duties of the State's Attorney before such Grand Jury, has investigated and prepared the evidence to be submitted to the Grand Jury, has participated in the examination of witnesses before such Grand Jury and advised as to the proper mode of interrogation, has given to the Grand Jury his advice upon matters of law and other questions respecting the proper discharge of their duties, has participated in the deliberations upon the accusation against this defendant and advised the Grand Jury with respect thereto, and has prepared the indictment in question against this defendant, all without any legal authority whatever and contrary to the statutes of this State. The said John B. Honts has never been, at any time since the Grand Jury in question has been impaneled, Criminal District Attorney of Tarrant County, Texas, or Assistant, or other member of the staff of such Criminal District Attorney; and he has not been a secretary or stenographer in the District Attorney's office, or a reporter for the Grand Jury, or a witness, bailiff, or member of the Grand Jury. In all of his actions complained of the said John B. Honts has purported to act as and perform the duties of State's Attorney before such Grand Jury in connection with all of the investigation and proceedings leading to this indictment of the defendant, all without any legal authority whatever.

4.

This defendant would show to the court that at the time this indictment was returned on March 30, 1951, the Grand Jury returning the same was not a duly qualified, duly organized, and a legally existing Grand Jury, and if such body had ever been properly impaneled, organized and formed its legal existence had ceased at the time of the returning of this indictment.

WHEREFORE, premises considered, this defendant prays that upon hearing hereof, the indictment herein be quashed for one or all of the reasons set forth herein, and for such other relief as he may be entitled to under the law.

Martin, Moore, Brewster &

ATTORNEYS FOR DEFENDANT.

No. 50617

THE STATE OF TEXAS		IN THE CRIMINAL DISTRICT
VS.		COURT NUMBER TWO
Fred Browning		TARRANT COUNTY, TEXAS.

TO THE HONORABLE JUDGE OF SAID COURT:

Now comes _____ Fred Browning _____, the defendant in the above styled and numbered cause, and subject to motions heretofore filed to quash the indictment returned against him in the above styled and numbered cause, this defendant does except specially to the form and wording of the indictment against him, inasmuch as such indictment does not designate what character of gaming table or bank the defendant is accused of exhibiting, does not designate the location of such building or room which the defendant is alleged to have been interested in keeping for the purpose of being used as a place to exhibit a game table, does not describe the property and premises alleged to have been owned by him or under his control and used as a place to keep and exhibit a gaming table, and does not describe and locate the property and premises alleged to have been owned and controlled by him for the purpose of being used as a place to bet and wager and gamble with dice and cards, and such indictment is too vague and indefinite to put this defendant upon notice of what the State would seek to prove under any of the allegations in any of the counts, and of this exception the defendant prays the judgment of the Court and prays that the said indictment be quashed and the prosecution dismissed.

Wherefore, premises considered, this defendant prays that his special exceptions be sustained and that the indictment be quashed and prosecution be dismissed and he prays for such other relief as he may be entitled to under the law.

Martin Moore Brewster & Dean

by Jesse E. Martin

ATTORNEYS FOR DEFENDANT

NO. _____ 50617

THE STATE OF TEXAS		IN THE CRIMINAL DISTRICT
VS.		COURT NUMBER TWO
Fred Browning		TARRANT COUNTY, TEXAS.

TO THE HONORABLE JUDGE OF THE SAID COURT:

Subject to motions heretofore filed to quash the indictment in this cause and subject to special exceptions heretofore made, this defendant makes this additional motion to the Court:

This defendant would show to the Court that he is advised and has reason to believe that the Grand Jury heard other witnesses than those named on the back of this indictment concerning this alleged accusation against him and he now moves the Court to instruct the State to furnish to this defendant the names of all of the witnesses who appeared before the Grand Jury upon whose testimony such indictment was founded and to furnish to him the names of all the witnesses who were interviewed during such Grand Jury investigation and under its direction whether in the Grand Jury room or elsewhere concerning the subject matter set forth in this indictment and the names of all witnesses which the State does propose and expects to use on any trial of this case or any alleged companion case. In this connection this defendant would show to the Court that he is entitled under the provisions of Article 392 of the Code of Criminal Procedure and under the laws and constitution of this State to be furnished with a list of the names of all of such witnesses and is entitled to have such witnesses listed on the back of the indictment and he cannot safely prepare his defense to this accusation without being furnished such names and such list for a reasonable length of time prior to the trial of this cause.

Wherefore, he prays that the Court order State's Counsel to furnish him with a list of all such witnesses and that he have such other and further relief as he may be entitled to, this motion, however, being made subject to the action of the Court upon motions heretofore filed to quash the indictment and heretofore filed attacking the legality in which the Grand Jury was formed and

page 2

the legality of the returning of this indictment and subject to the special exceptions

heretofore made to such Bill of Indictment.

Martin Moore Brewster & Dan

by Jesse E. Martin

ATTORNEYS FOR DEFENDANT

APPLICATION FOR CRIMINAL SUBPOENA IN DISTRICT COURT—D. C. 187

To the Clerk of the District Court of Tarrant County, Texas:

IN THE CASE OF THE STATE OF TEXAS vs..

.....................FRED BROWNING..No.....50617................., you will please issue subpoenas in accordance with law for the following named witnesses, residing in the Counties as below set out, to-wit:

1. Leroy Quick..residing in........Tarrant..............................County, Texas,

whose avocation is that of...

and whose location is....301 Blandon, FA or VA 3870...

2................Billy Graham..............................residing in.............Tarrant................County, Texas,

whose location is that of...

and whose location is 3809 Washburn, Fort Worth, Texas...

3.........Phil Cohen..residing in Dallas..County, Texas,

whose avocation is that of...

and whose location is....2809 Purdue, Dallas, Texas, Emerson-5134...

4.....Morris Shapiro..residing in.....Dallas......................County, Texas,

whose avocation is that of...

and whose location is....4401 Stanhope, Dallas, Texas, Justin-3773...

5....Dr. William Tsukahara..............................residing in......Dallas......................County, Texas,

whose avocation is that of...

and whose location is....1400 Forest Ave., Hunter 6454 or 1209 Lausanne, Econ 7133.................................

6........Dr. K. B. Walborn..............................residing in........Tarrant....................County, Texas,

whose avocation is that of...

and whose location is.........Commercial Standard Building, Fort Worth, Texas...

7...........Dr. Hugh Beaton............................residing in......Tarrant.....................County, Texas,

whose avocation is that of...

and whose location is....1316 Medical Arts Building, Fort Worth...

8. Walter B. Griffin.....................................residing in Tarrant........................County, Texas,

whose avocation is that of...

and whose location is.....907 Houston, Fort Worth, Texas, ED 3244...

9....Abe Cohen...residing in.........Tarrant..................County, Texas,

whose avocation is that of...

and whose location is....Rt.10, Box 261, Fort Worth, Texas..

10..residing in..................................County, Texas,

whose avocation is that of...

and whose location is...

defendant 1

The testimony of said witnesses is believed to be material to the state.

W.H. Tolbert

Defendant —
Attorney for State

Sworn to and subscribed before me, this......10th......day of......October.......................................19 51.

Issued.....11.....day of......Oct......19 51

Lois E. Post

Deputy   Clerk, District Court, Tarrant County, Texas.

By..Deputy.

SUBPOENA—Criminal.   Form No. D. C. 9

THE STATE OF TEXAS

SUBPOENA

To the Sheriff or Any Constable of Tarrant County, Greeting:

YOU ARE HEREBY COMMANDED, That you summon

John B. Honts	W. T. Waggoner Bldg.
Ray Finney	2801 NW 30th
H. C. Vandervoort	900 S. Main
Ed S. Green	Mansfield, Texas
Raymond T. Gillentine	722 N. Main
P. W. Riggins	c/o Continental Oil Co., Fair Bldg.
Q. K. Wheeler	5917 Wall St
S. M. Graves	4539 Pershing
D. L. Brown	Burleson, Rt # 2
Homer Ladd	c/o LaddFurniture Co., 500 W. 3rd St.
Fred B. Porter	1109 Samuels Ave
J. E. Harper	2132 Park Pl
H. H. Monroe	1416 Stewart
Stewart W. Hellman	Crim. Court Bldg.
Mrs. Lewis D. Wall, Jr.	Tarrant County Courthouse
Sully Montgomery	Sheriff's Office
R. H. Stone	"
D. D. Dunning	"

how you have executed the same.

Issued under my hand at office, in the City of Fort Worth, this 14 day of June, A. D. 195 1.

MRS. LEWIS D. WALL, JR.

Clerk, District Court, Tarrant County, Texas

By..Deputy.

A DISOBEDIENCE of this Subpoena is punishable by a fine not exceeding $500, to be collected as fines and costs in other criminal cases.

SUBPOENA—CRIMINAL.   Form No. D. C. 9

SUBPOENA

THE STATE OF TEXAS

TO THE SHERIFF OR ANY CONSTABLE OF TARRANT COUNTY, GREETING:

YOU ARE HEREBY COMMANDED, That you summon

Leroy Quick   301 Blandin   VA-3870 *Shows-Res.*

Billy Graham   3809 Washburn

Dr. K. B. Walborn   Commercial Standard Bldg.

Dr. Hugh Beaton   1316 Medical Arts Bldg.

Walter B. Griffin   907 Houston   ED-8244

Abe Cohen   Rt 10 Box 261

to be and appear before the Criminal District Court No. 2 to be holden within and for the County of Tarrant, at the
Court House thereof, in the City of Fort Worth, on the 31st day of October at 9 AM, 196 1,
then and there to testify in behalf of   State   in a certain suit now pending in our said
Court, where THE STATE OF TEXAS is Plaintiff and   Fred Browning

Defendant, and that they continue in attendance from
day to day, and from term to term, until discharged by the Court.

HEREIN FAIL NOT, but have you then and there before said Court, this Writ with your return thereon, showing
how you have executed the same.

Issued under my hand at office, in the City of Fort Worth, this 11 day of October, A. D. 196 1.

MRS. LEWIS D. WALL, JR.
Clerk, District Court, Tarrant County, Texas

By_____Deputy.

A DISOBEDIENCE of this Subpoena is punishable
by a fine not exceeding $500, to be collected as fines
and costs in other criminal cases.

Appendix C
Text of Final Report of
Special Grand Jury

(From the *Fort Worth Star-Telegram*,
Thursday morning edition, August 23, 1951.)

Text of the Tarrant County special grand jury's final report, returned Wednesday, follows:

The special Tarrant County grand jury, now making its final report, impaneled on January 5, 1951, and has continued in session since that date. This grand jury was charged to investigate the gaming, bribery, and vice that might be existent in Tarrant County.

After several weeks of routine proceedings, we began investigation of the Nelson Harris bombing which occurred some time prior to our term of service. This city was shocked when one of its citizens and his wife, and an unborn child, lost their lives in a bomb explosion in their car. This was only one of several such continuing murders over the past 18 months in this same group. These murders apparently came from "someone getting in someone's way" in the gambling racket in this area.

After hearing a number of witnesses, it became very apparent that unbridled gambling was going on in Tarrant County; and with it, all the other undesirable elements that follow the breakdown of law enforcement. This jury was shocked at the testimony of many persons of this city and county about gambling and vice that seemed to grow so rapidly the latter part of 1949 and all of 1950. Some participants of gambling games, after an absence of a year or two, expressed amazement at what they found upon returning to Fort Worth during the period above mentioned. It appeared that some person or persons had "cut away" all law enforcement on gaming and other forms of vice.

JURY ADVISES OFFICIALS TO ENFORCE LAWS

Our investigation then turned to this gaming phase and also the purported bribery or pay-off angle that permits such operations. After some seven weeks of service, during which time we had received no offers of assistance nor any word of co-operation from any of the officers charged with law enforcement in Tarrant County, we decided the time for aggressive action had arrived.

It was then that the district attorney, sheriff, chief of police and all the constables were called before our body and were told that they should be entirely familiar with the laws they had taken an oath to enforce. They were told that it was our opinion—backed up by expressions from hundred of citizens and countless resolutions and letters from civic and religious organizations—that the people of Tarrant County, from this time on, expected the law enforcement officials to take over and run this county rather than allow the gamblers to be in charge. You are familiar with the closing of gambling games, the stopping of policy writing, the picking up of slot machines and marble boards which followed within a day or two.

We then entered into our investigation to seek those who were guilty of breaking our laws in the matters mentioned above. It is our understanding that the district attorney's office is charged by law to bring before the grand jury, not only evidence of law violations, but also evidence of any peace officer being in neglect of the enforcing of our laws.

JOHN HONTS ENGAGED AS SPECIAL PROSECUTOR

We were most fortunate in securing the services of John Honts, a former district attorney in another county of our state, and a resident of Fort Worth for several years. John Honts, in our opinion, accepted our invitation solely because he felt it his obligation as a citizen of the community in which he is making his home and rearing his family.

Following the extension of our term, made possible by a law passed by the Legislature then in session, we continued our gambling investigations and also entered into the alleged pay-offs which usually accompany such activities.

We are frank to admit that we are bringing our tenure of service to a close without being able to properly clear up all phases in which the citizenry was most interested; bribery is definitely in this category. Too much testimony was given for us not to realize how widespread and brazen such practices had grown, but we simply could not secure needed evidence and corroborated testimony.

UNABLE TO SECURE SUFFICIENT EVIDENCE

Bribery, almost unanimously, involves two people directly participating in the transfer of money or other thing of value. When a bribe is tendered and accepted, both parties involved are equally guilty; and consequently, neither can seldom be persuaded to divulge the offense against the other; though the grand jury interviewed and questioned hundreds of witnesses, scores of whom had general knowledge, yet the jury was unable to secure sufficient evidence to indict for bribery, though much direct testimony was received with reference to officers' demanding pay-offs of various and sundry kinds. In bribery cases, we learned, a conviction can not be secured on an accomplice's testimony alone; the requirement of the law to have other testimony in addition to an accomplice's testimony almost ruled out every case of bribery, since, as stated heretofore, a bribe is usually conducted between two individuals only.

We also found that perjury was most difficult to establish since the law requires two credible witnesses to a falsehood, or one witness strongly corroborated by other testimony. So we found, from the great number of witnesses brought before the jury, that though we were also conclusively convinced of one's participation in pay-off yet we could neither establish the bribery angle nor the perjury offense because of the stringent requirements of the law.

REPREHENSIBLE ACTS CITED BY GRAND JURY

This jury, though unable to secure sufficient evidence to return indictments, in convinced that the following, and similar acts, are not conducive to a more reputable, prosperous, a more desirable or a more beneficent city and should be stamped out so far as possible by its officials and should be condemned by its citizens:

1. Some police patrols and other law enforcement officials, for private gain, to knowingly permit gambling and gaming devices to be operated in stores, taverns and other public places.

2. For organized associations to collect monthly or other periodic sums—in some instances amounting to more than $1,000 per month—to be paid to those having authority to "keep the town open" for vice.

3. The practice of some law enforcement officials, elected or otherwise, to demand tribute or pay-off monty from operators in gambling, bookie and other gaming activities and rackets for the privilege of operating within the confines of the county.

4. The practice of some influential citizens and attorneys to get "no bills" for organized associations and groups operating in violation of the gaming and other laws against the morals of the community.

5. The practice of some elected and appointed law enforcement officials in taking a lackadaisical attitude toward law enforcement in flagrant disregard of their respective oaths of office.

6. The failure of some of those charged with the enforcement of law to vigorously pursue their responsibility because it is easier not to do so, and since they believe it is more calculated to get them re-elected to office.

7. The practice of some county and precinct officials in the loose handling of materials and equipment belonging to the county and the utilization thereof for private use, whether it be for getting votes or illegal private remuneration.

8. The practice of some public officials in covering up for gambling and other attendant evils, and shielding operators from indictment and prosecution.

TRUE BILLS RETURNED CHARGING BRIBERY

This jury is not revealing any secrets of the grand jury when it states that it did return 68 true bills for what it then thought, and now thinks, was bribery, since the newspapers secured the information from some source which was called upon to assist the jury. The district attorney's office declined to draw the true bills and the jury has acquiesced in that decision, since it would be an empty and expensive gesture to return indictments to which the district attorney has already expressed an adverse opinion, and which indictments could be prosecuted by no other agency.

Irrespective of the indictments not being drawn, practice on the part of some law enforcement officials in collecting the tribute should be condemned, and if the practice does continue, stringent measures should be promulgated and carried out to see that both city and county officials are stripped of the vicious privilege and practice of extracting money indirectly from the unsuspecting public, whether it be classed as "tips" or otherwise.

JURY THANKS CITIZENS FOR GIVING EVIDENCE

We certainly wish to thank the citizens, both white and colored, who have appeared before us, giving facts and information which helped, we hope, in bringing about some betterment in making our community the kind of place in which we want to live. We also know that many more people, both white and colored, had knowledge of numerous law violations and who should have, when requested, stood ready to come forward and help this community in which they have chosen to live. As time goes on, their withholding of these facts must be judged by their own consciences.

We most sincerely thank John Honts for the splendid, unselfish service he has rendered the people of Tarrant County in his role as special prosecutor for a period of six months. This service has only been performed at a personal sacrifice of time and remuneration. John Honts has at all times been ready and willing to take on any and all duties we have asked him to accept.

We also wish to thank the judges, bailiffs, court reporters and all others who have done everything within their abilities to make our term of service as comfortable as possible and productive of good for the community as a whole.

CHIEF HOWERTON PRAISED FOR SERVICE

We wish to thank Police Chief Howerton for the splendid cooperation we have received from him since his appointment. He appeared voluntarily before our body soon after his taking office, offered his full support to us and has most promptly and conscientiously carried out a number of requests we made for information and data.

In this connection, we think it but fair to say that we believe the great majority of men who wear the uniform of the Fort Worth police department and many deputies and assistants in the county government to be of a high type with the sincere desire to do the right thing to enforce the law, and who take pride in their work. However, these men can go only so far and are by expediency compelled to conform to the policies of the departments. There is, we believe, a trend toward better and more equitable law enforcement. This trend will continue so long as the people expect and demand it.

Judge Robert Young directed the district attorney to turn over to this grand jury the sum of $4,806.02 taken from slot machines seized in the city and county, and attached is a statement of the handling of these monies. You will note that since the end of the regular term of office, March 31, 1951, and the beginning of our term as a special grand jury, we have paid all expense of court reporters, court costs, witness fees, the major portion of legal advisors, investigation fees and other expenses incident to our operation, and hand you here with the balance to be passed on to present and/or succeeding grand juries.

MORAL BLINDNESS IN OFFICIALS CONDEMNED

Shortcomings in public officials is not a new phenomenon in this or any other community. What seems to be new—and alarming—is the moral blindness which allows those in responsible positions to accept practices which facts before us reveal. It is bad enough for us to have corruption in our midst, but it is worse if it is condoned and accepted as inevitable. Officials having to do with law enforcement must not only appear to be good—they must be good.

It is our feeling that there should be created a nonpartisan citizens commission to become a permanent body for the purpose of insisting upon ethical standards in the conduct of public affairs. This group should be representative of the best citizens of the community, selected without regard to race or creed, and should have ample funds, secured from public contributions, to carry forward any necessary activities. The body would under no circumstances undertake the business of law enforcement. Instead, it would concentrate upon the observation of those who are entrusted with the responsibility of the public trust, and keep the community reliably informed as to how well those entrusted with the offices of law enforcement were carrying out the obligations and oath they assumed when they entered their respective offices.

Respectfully submitted,
RAY FINNEY, Foreman.

Summary of Indictments
* major gambler

Gamblers Indicted 3/31/51
*Fred Browning—operator of Top o' the Hill Terrace, Arlington
*Frank Cates—ex-con, killed 10/9/56
Al Clark—Court Hotel dice games
Tom Daly—worked with Clark
Jack Darby—with Wilderspin, East Side Club
Oscar Donley—with Browning
*A. R. (Bob) Floyd—with Tiffin Hall, Commercial Hotel games
Pete Ford—worked for W. C. Kirkwood
Paul Garland—with Wilderspin
Bo, Jimmy, and Dude Green, brothers, Town House Hotel
*Carl Tiffin Hall—owned Mex. Inn Cafes, Madoc Hotel, Commercial Hotel
    games
Billy Hughes—with Al Clark and Howard Lee, Court Hotel
*Les Hutt—with Bert Wakefield, 3939 Club
Dewey Inman—worked with Tiffin Hall
William Jordan—with Wilderspin
*W. C. Kirkwood—2222 Club
Howard Lee—with Clark, Court Hotel, brother-in-law of Martin (buster)
    Loicano
Phil Long—with Wakefield, 3939 Club
L. J. (Chili) McWillie—with Browning
*Ivy Miller—with Browning; friend of Benny Binion (Las Vegas gambler)
Lee Moore—Lone Star Sales, slots and marble tables
Roy Moore—1411 W. Berry, slots
*H. D. (Red) Oden—Real estate, with Hall and Floyd
Jerry Rosenberg—with Browning
*W. D. Satterwhite—Skyliner Annex Club
Mack Taylor—worked for Kirkwood, 2222 Club
*Bert Wakefield—3939 Club
*George Wilderspin—East Side Club

Slot Machine / Pin Ball / Marble Table Operators
Martin (Buster) Loicano—Big State Coin Co.
Benny (also Bennie) McDonald—Star Coin Machine Co.
Ernest C. Harris—North Side Amusement Co.

Summary of Gangland Slayings

Gangsters killed in 1940s and 1950s
Ray Sellers, ambushed, 12/4/43
James (Red) Cavanaugh, disappeared 12/4/43
Lon Holley, "ride" 3/7/48
Que R. Miller, "ride" 9/30/48
Mrs. Herbert Noble, "mistake" 11/29/49
Lois Green (Cecil's brother), ambushed, Dallas 12/24/49
M/M Nelson Harris, car bombed, 11/22/50
Herbert Noble, bombed, 8/7/51
James Clyde (Jim) Thomas, shot, 8/23/51
Edell Evans, disappeared, 4/5/55 (father of Sonny Evans)
Cecil Green, ambushed, 5/3/55
Leroy (Tincy) Eggleston, shot, 8/27/55
Frank Cates, shot, 10/9/56
John Sidney (Sid) Foley, shot, beaten, dumped, 2/2/57
Gene Paul Norris, shot by police, 4/30/57
Jack Nesbit, shot by Mrs. Howard Stripling, 5/22/57
Darlene and Willard Hauer, found shot in South Side apartment, 1/4/59

Endnotes

FWST = Fort Worth Star Telegram
Press = The Fort Worth Press

Introduction
1. Personal interview with Carl Freund.

Chapter 1
1. Richard Selcer, *Hell's Half Acre* (Ft. Worth: TCU Press, 1991), p. 271.
2. Personal interview with B. M. Kudlaty.
3. Personal interview with Joan Loicano.
4. Jerry Flemmons, *Amon: The Life of Amon Carter, Sr. of Texas.* (Austin, Jenkins Publishing Co., 1978), p. 300.
5. Personal interview with J. D. Farmer.
6. Flemmons, op. cit. p. 322.
7. Personal interview with George Campbell.
8. Flemmons, op. cit. p. 318.
9. Flemmons, op. cit. 86.
10. Mack Williams, *The Fort Worth Press*, June 25, 1993.
11. Personal interview with R. R. Howerton.

Chapter 2
1. Personal interview with Pat Kirkwood.
2. Mike Cochran, *FWST*, March 20, 1988, Section 3, p. 1.
3. *Ibid.*
4. Personal interview with Pat Kirkwood.
5. Mike Cochran, *FWST*, March 20, 1988, Section 3, p. 1
6. Personal interview with Pat Kirkwood.
7. *Ibid.*
8. Personal interview with George Wilderspin.
9. Personal interview with Pat Kirkwood.
10. Jacquelynn Ford, *Dallas Times Herald*, February 4, 1988, p. B5.

Chapter 3

1. *FWST,* January 14, 1937.
2. *FWST,* August 10, 1937.
3. Personal interview with Louie Lancer.
4. *FWST,* November 4, 1944, Evening Edition.
5. *Ibid.*
6. Personal interview with Louie Lancer.
7. Personal interview with Carl Freund.
8. *Ibid.*
9. *FWST,* May 12, 1949, Evening Edition.
10. *FWST,* May 13, 1949, Morning Edition.
11. *Dallas Morning News,* October 8, 1950.
12. *FWST,* October 9, 1950.

Chapter 4

1. Allan Carney, *Press,* July 18, 1940.
2. Bill Hitch, *FWST,* November 23, 1950, Morning Edition.
3. Mack Williams, *FWST,* November 22, 1950, Evening Edition.
4. *Ibid.*
5. Mack Williams, Unpublished draft of story December 5, 1951.
6. Blair Justice, *FWST,* November 22, 1950.
7. Carl Freund, *Press,* February 17, 1951, p. 1.
8. Bill Haworth, *FWST,* November 22, 1950.
9. Madeline Williams, *FWST,* December 7, 1950.
10. Robert Hilburn, *FWST,* February 8, 1951.
11. Carl Freund, *Press,* February 7, 1951, p. 1.
12. *FWST,* February 27, 1951, Evening Edition.
13. *Press,* February 16, 1951, p. 1.
14. Carl Freund, *Press,* February 22, 1951, p. 1.

Chapter 5

1. *Press,* February 7, 1951, p. 1.
2. Bill Rudd, *FWST,* February 14, 1951, Evening Edition.
3. *FWST,* February 16, 1951.
4. Carl Freund, *Press,* February 17, 1951, p. 4.
5. Marshall McNeil, Washington Correspondent. *Press* February 17, 1951, p. 1.
6. *Press,* February 21, 1951, p. 4.
7. Personal interview with Pat Kirkwood.
8. *FWST,* February 17, 1951, Morning Edition.
9. Bill Rudd, *FWST,* February 19, 1951.
10. *FWST,* February 23, 1951, Morning Edition.
11. *Press,* February 22, 1951.
12. *Press,* February 27, 1951, p. 2.
13. Personal interview with Carl Freund.
14. *FWST,* March 1, 1951.

Chapter 6

1. *FWST,* March 16, 1951.
2. Personal interview with Carl Freund.
3. Robert Hilburn, *FWST.* March 31, 1951, Morning Edition.
4. Carl Freund, *Press,.* March 31, 1951.
5. Carl Freund, *Press* June 23, 1951.
6. *Press,* April 18, 1951, p. 3.
7. Carl Freund, *Press,* April 19, 1951, p. 1.
8. *FWST,* June 19, 1951.
9. Abigail Van Buren, "Dear Abby," *FWST,* November 1, 1996.
10. Indictment D.A. 430, County Clerk's office.
11. Subpoena, Criminal #50617-8, County Clerk's office.
12. *FWST,* June 19, 1951.
13. *Ibid.*
14. *Press,* June 19, 1951.
15. Robert Hilburn, *FWST,* June 20, 1951, Morning Edition.
16. *Ibid.*
17. *FWST,* June 20, 1951, Evening Edition.
18. Robert Hilburn, *FWST,* June 20, 1951.
19. Personal interview with George Wilderspin.
20. Carl Freund, *Press,* June 20, 1951 p. 2.

Chapter 7

1. Ed Reid, and Ovid Demaris, *The Green Felt Jungle* (New York: Trident Press, 1963), p.157.
2. Op. cit. p. 155.
3. *Ibid.*
4. Bill Rudd, *FWST,* March 6, 1951.
5. Mabel Gouldy, *FWST,* December 15, 1953.
6. Bill Hitch, *FWST,.* May 29, 1951.
7. *FWST,.* August 15, 1951.
8. *FWST,.* August 6, 1943.
9. *Press,* February 15, 1951.
10. Mexican Inn Menu.
11. Personal interview with Carl Freund.
12. Personal interview with George Wilderspin.
13. *Ibid.*
14. *Ibid.*
15. *Ibid.*
16. *Ibid.*

Chapter 8

1. Personal interview with Pat Kirkwood.
2. *FWST,* February 16, 1955, Morning Edition.
3. *Press,* March 15, 1955, p. 7.
4. Bill Hitch, *FWST,* April 5, 1955, Morning Edition.

5. *FWST,* April 6, 1955.
6. Carl Freund, *Press,* November 2, 1955.
7. Bill Hitch, *FWST,*. November 1, 1955.
8. *Press,* November 1, 1955.
9. Carl Freund, *Press,* November 3, 1955 p. 1.
10. Carl Freund, *Press,* November 2, 1955 p. 3.

Chapter 9

1. Lisa Black, *FWST,*. November 13, 1995.
2. Mike Cochran, *FWST,*. May 7, 1991.
3. *Ibid.*
4. *Ibid.*
5. Brian Howard, *FWST,*. June 1, 1983, Evening Edition.
6. Lisa Black, *FWST.,* November 13, 1995 Section A, p. 20.

Chapter 10

1. *FWST,*. May 29, 1953.
2. *FWST,*. June 10, 1953, Morning Edition.
3. Bill Hitch, *FWST,*. April 8, 1955.
4. Bill Haworth, *FWST.,* April 7, 1955, Evening Edition.
5. *Ibid.*
6. Bill Haworth, *FWST,*. April 11, 1955, Evening Edition.
7. *FWST,*. November 26, 1955.
8. *FWST,*. November 28, 1955.

Chapter 11

1. Ed Reid, and Ovid Demaris, *The Green Felt Jungle*, p. 158.
2. Press, December 30, 1953.
3. Carl Freund, Personal interview.
4. Bill Hitch, FWST, May 6, 1955, Morning Edition.
5. Bill Haworth, FWST, May 4, 1955, Evening Edition.
6. Bill Hitch, *FWST*, May 4, 1955, Morning Edition.

Chapter 12

1. *FWST,* May 26, 1938, Evening Edition.
2. Personal interview with Pat Kirkwood.
3. Dillon Graham, *FWST,*. May 12, 1940.
4. *FWST,*. March 24, 1964.
5. Personal interview with Madeline Williams.
6. Jack Gordon, *Press,* June 9, 1952.
7. Personal interview with Pat Kirkwood.
8. *FWST,*. June 15, 1954.
9. Gloria Van Zandt, University of Texas term paper quoted in *FWST*, May 18, 1994.

Chapter 13

1. Bill Feather, *FWST*, September 1, 1955.
2. *FWST*, August 28, 1947, Evening Edition.
3. Jack Douglas, *FWST*, November 23, 1950, Morning Edition.
4. Personal interview with J. D. Farmer.
5. Personal correspondence of Louis Tassione.
6. Robert Hilburn, *FWST*, December 11, 1951
7. Personal Interview with Carl Freund.
8. Personal Interview with Bobby Morton.
9. *FWST*, December 31, 1953.
10. Personal interview with Carl Freund.
11. Bill Haworth, *FWST*, April 12, 1955, Evening Edition.
12. *FWST*, April 11, 1955, Evening Edition.
13. Bill Haworth, *FWST*, April 13, 1955, Evening Edition.
14. Bill Haworth, May 3, 1955, Evening Edition.
15. *Ibid*.
16. Pat Kirkwood, Personal interview.
17. Harley Pershing, *FWST*, August 31, 1955.
18. *Ibid*.
19. *FWST*, August 27, 1955, Evening Edition.
20. *Ibid*.
21. Carl Freund, *Press*, September 1, 1955. p. 2.
22. Personal interview with Mrs. W. M. Young.
23. Caroline Hamilton, *Press*, September 2, 1955.
24. *FWST*, September 2, 1955.

Chapter 14

1. Marshall Fey, quoted in *Slot Machines, A Pictoral History of the First 100 Years*, Reno: Liberty Bell Books, p. 4.
2. *FWST*, October 25, 1935, Morning Edition.
3. *FWST*, November 17, 1941, Evening Edition.
4. *Ibid*.
5. Personal interview with B. J. Walton.
6. Personal interview with Joan Loicano.
7. *FWST*, September 6, 1957.
8. *FWST*, February 23, 1956.
9. *Ibid*.
10. Mary Crutcher, *Press*, March 5, 1951 p.1.
11. *Ibid*., p. 2.
12. Personal interview with Carl Freund.
13. *Press*, January 12, 1956.
14. *Ibid*.

Chapter 15

1. Personal interview with Sam Atchley.
2. *FWST*, December 10, 1950, Morning Edition.

3. *Press*, October 9, 1956, p. 2.
4. Elston Brooks, *FWST*, August 2, 1956, Evening Edition.
5. *Ibid.*
6. Carl Freund, *Press*, August 3, 1956, p. 3.
7. Harley Preshing, *FWST*, October 9, 1956, Evening Edition.
8. Carl Freund, *Press*, October 9, 1958, p. 2.
9. *FWST*, October 10, 1956, Evening Edition.

Chapter 16

1. *FWST*, November December 44, Morning Edition.
2. Obituary Draft, Special Collection of *FWST* materials, UTA Library.
3. *FWST*, March 9, 1948.
4. Byron Utecht, *FWST*, November 4, 1943.
5. Russ Hurst, *FWST*, August 23, 1951.
6. Elston Brooks, *Don't Dry Clean My Blackjack* (Ft. Worth: Branch-Smith, Inc., 1979), p. 23.
7. Phil Record, *FWST*, May 22, 1957.
8. *FWST*, May 23, 1957, Morning Edition.
9. *FWST*, May 22, 1957, Evening Edition.

Chapter 17

1. Delbert Willis, *Press*, February 26, 1951 p. 1.
2. Bill Haworth, *FWST*, December 7, 1949.
3. *FWST*, October 2, 1950.
4. *Press*, September 27, 1951 p. 1.
5. *FWST*, October 14, 1950.
6. *Press*, February 21, 1951 p.4.
7. Jim Vachule, *FWST*, May 5, 1953, Morning Edition.
8. *FWST*, May 29, 1953, Evening Edition.
9. Personal interview with Henry Wright.
10. *FWST*, October 21, 1952, Evening Edition.
11. Personal interview with Carl Freund.
12. *FWST*, May 6, 1952, Morning Edition.
13. *FWST*. January 6, 1953 PM
14. Personal interview with Carl Freund.
15. Personal interview with Howard Fender.

Chapter 18

1. Personal interview with George Wilderspin.
2. Box 357, Criminal Court Files 12958-1300.
3. Box 357, No. 13,000 Criminal Court Files, *US vs. J. R. Montgomery*.
4. *Ibid.*
5. *Ibid.*
6. Box 357 Criminal Court Files. pp. 410, 411.
7. Box 357 Criminal Court Files. p. 517.
8. Mabel Gouldy, *FWST*, February 1, 1954, Evening Edition.

9. Box 357, No. 13,000 Criminal Court Files. p. 8.
10. Mabel Gouldy, *FWST*, February 5, 1954, Evening Edition.
11. Personal interview with Carl Freund.

Chapter 19

1. *FWST*, February 5, 1957, Morning Edition.
2. *FWST*, March 30, 1957, Morning Edition.
3. Ed Johnson, *FWST*, September 22, 1958, Morning Edition.
4. *FWST*, September 30, 1958, Evening Edition.

Chapter 20

1. *FWST*, March 4, 1943.
2. *FWST*, December 1, 1943.
3. Bill Haworth, *FWST*, October 6, 1952.
4. Mack Williams, *Press*, June 25, 1993, p. 4.
5. *Ibid.*
6. Mack Williams, p. 16.
7. Elston Brooks, *FWST*, May 2, 1957.
8. *FWST*, April 30, 1957.
9. *FWST*, May 1, 1957.

Chapter 21

1. Bobby Bragan, *You Can't Hit the Ball with the Bat on Your Shoulder* (Fort Worth: The Summit Group, 1992), p. 164.
2. Jack Gordon, *Press*, August 25, 1968, 13B.
3. Jack Gordon, January 23, 1972 p. 1B.
4. Jack Gordon, September 19, 1949.
5. Jack Gordon, January 31, 1973.
6. Jack Gordon, April 21, 1969.
7. Personal interview with Carl Freund.
8. *FWST*, November 14, 1953.
9. Bill Hitch, *FWST*, March 19, 1954, Morning Edition.
10. Personal interview with Carl Freund.
11. Sam Kinch, *FWST*, October 27, 1954, Evening Edition.
12. Elston Brooks, *FWST*, January 24, 1985.
13. *Press*, March 20, 1954 p. 1.
14. Jack Gordon, *Press*, October 14, 1964.
15. *Ibid.*
16. Personal interview with George Campbell.
17. Personal interview with Wayne Brown.
18. Elston Brooks, *Don't Dry Clean My Blackjack*, p. 78.

Chapter 22

1. Michael Pellecchia, *Fort Worth, Catching the World's Attention* (Montgomery, Alabama: Community Communications, Inc., 1995), p. 228.
2. J'Nell Pate, *North of the River, A Brief History of North Fort Worth* (Fort Worth: TCU Press, 1994), p. 65.

Bibliography

Books

Bragan, Bobby, as told to Jeff Guinn. *You Can't Hit the Ball with the Bat on Your Shoulder*. Fort Worth, TX: The Summit Group, 1992.

Brooks, Elston. *Don't Dry Clean My Blackjack*. Fort Worth, TX: Branch-Smith, Inc., 1979.

Fey, Marshall. quoted in *Slot Machines, A Pictoral History of the First 100 Years*. Reno, NV: Bell Books.

Flemmons, Jerry. *Amon: The Life of Amon Carter, Sr. of Texas*. Austin, TX: Jenkins Publishing Co., 1978.

Mills, Susie. *Legend in Bronze the Biography of Jay Banks*. Dallas, TX: Ussery Printing Company, 1982.

Pate, J'Nell. *North of the River: A Brief History of North Fort Worth*. Fort Worth, TX: TCU Press, 1994.

Pellecchia, Michael. *Fort Worth: Catching the World's Attention*. Montgomery, AL: Community Communications, Inc., 1995.

Reid, Ed, and Ovid, Demaris. *The Green Felt Jungle*. New York, NY: Trident Press, 1963

Selcer, Richard F. *Hell's Half Acre*. Fort Worth, TX: TCU Press, 1991.

Sloan, Bill (William J.). *In and By*. Honey Creek Press, 1987.

Newspapers

Fort Worth Press
Fort Worth Star-Telegram
Dallas Morning News

Documents

National Archives Records
Tarrant County Criminal Court Records

Interviews were conducted by the author with the following people:

Reporters:

Wayne Brown, retired WBAP television reporter.
Carl Freund, retired *Fort Worth Press*.
Harley Pershing, retired *Fort Worth Star-Telegram*.
Madeline Williams, retired Fort Worth *Star-Telegram*
Bill Fairley

Law Enforcement:

Howard Fender, former Disctrict Attorney, retired judge
Byron Matthews, former defense attorney, retired judge
Herbert Hopkins, retired Fort Worth Police Chief
R. R. Howertown, retired Fort Worth Police Chief
Cecil Stoker, Sheriff's Deputy
Bobby Morton, retired Sheriff's Deputy
Kenneth Adcock, retired Fort Worth policeman
Mrs. Donna Young, widow of Sheriff's Deputy

Club owners:

George Campbell, former owner of the Skyliner
Pat Kirkwood, son of owner of 2222 Club
J. D. Farmer, former owner of North Fort Worth Club
B. J. Walton, former owner of Longhorn Lounge
George Wilderspin, former owner of East Side Club

Entertainers:

Joan Loicano, former wife of Charley Applewhite
Perry Sandifer, musician
Leon Rausch, musician
Carroll Hubbard, musician

Others:

Sam Atchley, songwriter, friend of Pat Kirkwood
Bob Bolen, former mayor
Al "Cotton" Farmer, friend of Pat Kirkwood
B. M. Kudlaty, longtime Fort Worth resident
Louie Lancer, son of pool hall owner
Ben Rubin, longtime Fort Worth resident
Rick Selcer, author
Louis Tassione, former employee of Tincy Eggleston
Jim Gordon gave me access to his father, Jack Gordon's columns

Index

A

Albatross Club, 11
Alcatraz, 155
All Saints Hospital, 119
Alpena, Michigan, 153
American Air Lines, 174-175
Amyx, Dorothy, 159
Anderson, Sparky, 163
Andrew Sisters, 164
Andujar, John, 74
Anka, Paul, 171
Annex Clubs, 97, 168, 169, 170
Applewhite, Charlie, 165, 170-171
    Nancy, 171
Arlington, 84
Arlington Bible College, 86
Arlington Country Club, 86
Arlington Downs, 8, 85
Arlington Heights Methodist
    Church, 39
Armour and Swift, 12
Armstrong, Satchmo, 167
Atchley, Sam, 117
Audie Murphy Rodeo, 99
Austin, 80, 99
Austin, Albert D., 36
Autry, Gene, 70, 133, 164
Avalon Courts, 15, 52, 53
Avalon Night Club, 52
Azle, 10, 153

B

Bailey, Norman D., 22
Ballard, Dave, 6
Bally Manufacturing, 108
Banks, Jay, 141, 152, 160
Barr, Candy, 165, 172
Barrel Club, 11
Barrow, Clyde, 122
Baskett, Robert E., 149
Bass, Perry R., 175
Bates, R. H., 74
Bean, Juanita, 25, 28
Beaumont, 118
Bell, Walter, 140
Belton, 93
Benbrook Dam, 98
Beneke, Tex, 11, 166
Bennett, Tony, 171
Bergan, Edgar, 7, 164, 165
Berle, Milton, 165, 171
Bernie, Ben, 166
Bevil, D. W., 30
Big State Novelty Company, 112
Binion, Benny, 10, 34, 36, 48-50, 57,
    58, 84, 86, 124, 145
"Binion Bullet," 49
Bishop, H. Clay, 31
Black Cat, 11, 15
Blackstone Hotel, 17
Bohmfalk, Rev. Erwin F., 83
Bolger, Ray, 7
Bonham, 71
Bourland, Vergal, 111
Bowling Green, Kentucky, 85

Boyd, Whit, 105
Bracker, Karl, 22
Bragan, Bobby, 162
Brannon, Johnny, 159
Breckenridge, 98, 99
Brewster, Harris, 114
   Leo, 41, 43, 45, 74
Brice, Fannie, 7
Brooklyn Dodgers, 162, 163
Brooks, Elston, 122, 130, 151, 173
Brown, Jesse, 45
   M. Hendricks, 41, 42, 46
   O. R., 118, 152, 153
   Wayne, 173
Browning, Fred, 34, 40, 43- 44, 48,
   50, 84-92, 164, 166
   Mary, 85
Brownwood, 172
Buck, Frank, 70
Buddie's Super Market, 58, 103
Buie, E. N., 140, 141
Burks, R. H. (Rip), 30, 136
Burleson, 95, 105
Burnett, Carol, 173
By-Way Drive-In, 82
By-Way Tavern, 159
C
Caan, James, 7
California, 107, 130
Callahan, Anna, 123
Callaway, Dick, 73, 74
Campbell, George, 167, 171-172
Cantey and Hanger, 175
Cantor, Eddie, 7
Carrasquel, Chico, 163
Carswell Air Force Base, 12, 52, 95,
   160, 161
Carswell Base Hospital, 96
Carswell, Horace, Jr., 175
Carter, A. B., 41
   Amon, 3, 4, 8, 85, 173
   Mrs. Amon, 70
   O. M., 125
Casa Manana, 4, 6-7, 8, 165
Casino Ballroom, 11, 165, 166, 167
Casino Beach, 137, 167

Cates, Frank, 41, 117-121, 124, 125,
   129, 159
Cattleman's Cafe, 176
Cavanaugh, James (Red), 122
Cavitt, Ernest, 147, 148, 150
Central Airlines, 170
Central High School, 112
Chambless, Orville, 157, 159
   Rodney, 156
Chandler, Donald, 154
Chenault, W. O. "Pinky," 175
Chenault's Dining Place, 120
Chicago, 156
Chicago Cubs, 163
Chickasha, Oklahoma, 157
Civil War, 1
Claiborne, Harry, 51
Clark, Mary, 74, 75, 76, 77, 78
   Phillip, 73, 75
   William P., 73-78, 82, 100, 102
Cleburne, 67, 100, 106
Cleere, Clarence, 40
Clemmer, Marcus, 52
Cochran, George, 76, 114, 115
   Mike, 13
Coconut Grove, 11
Cohen, Mickey, 172
Collier, A. W., 117
Collinsville, Illinois, 153
Commercial Hotel, 18, 56
Compton, Henry, 98
Connally, John, 86
Conroe, 156
Consolidated Aircraft, 9, 174
Consolidated Vultee, 174
Convair, 174
Cope, John, 99
Cosden, Josh, 8
Cotton Bowl, 164
Court of Criminal Appeals, 128
Cox, V. O., 30
Craik, Harold, 113
Cresap, Johnnie, 60
   Sam Brown, 157
Cribbs, A. B. (Ott), 92
Crouch, Doug, 141

Crownover, Dick, 29
Crutcher, Mary, 115
Curry, Foy, 61
   T. G., 133
Cypress Creek, 156
D
Dallas, 4, 8, 50, 60, 64, 83, 99, 100,
   104, 123, 126, 154, 164, 170, 171
Dallas County, 62, 140, 155, 157
Dallas Morning News, 12, 23
Daly, Tom, 22, 26, 164
Daniel, Price, 20, 34, 42
Davidson, T. Whitfield, 139
Davis, Rita, 80, 83, 100, 159
Dawkins, L. D., 112
de la Torre, Candido, 158
Decker, Bill, 62, 64
Deen, Edgar, 136
Deere, Hubert, 128, 129
Delta Air Lines, 174
Dempsey, Jack, 138
Denton, 51, 75
Derden, J. B., 30
Detroit, 153
Dickerson, S. D., 95
Do or Don't Lounge, 96
Dobson, Ben, 86
Dodd, Howard "Junior," 120, 121
Donley, Oscar, 48
Dorsey, Tommy, 11, 165
Duchin, Eddie, 165
Duncan, Oklahoma, 158
Dunwoody, John, 99
Durant, Oklahoma, 128
Dysart, R. E., 19, 20, 21, 23, 112, 133,
   134
E
Eagle Mountain Lake, 64
Earp, Wyatt, 137
East Fort Worth, 84
East Side Club, 17, 41, 58
Eastland, 25, 124
Eastland, Midland, and Odessa, 25
Eggleston, Carole, 98, 106
   J. W., 93-94
   Leroy "Tincy," 28, 29, 31, 51, 61,
      62, 64, 65, 67, 75, 76, 77, 78, 80,
      81, 82, 83, 93-106, 121, 130, 151,
      159, 164, 168
   Walterine, 99, 101, 106
Eighteenth Amendment, 2
Eighth Avenue Klub, 52, 54
Eisenhower, Dwight D., 176
El Reno, Oklahoma, 67, 99
Erskine, Carl, 163
Euless, 99
Evans, Clarence (Sonny), 67
   Clifton Edell, 67
   Dale, 164
   Dennis, 67
   Dorothy Jean, 59, 60, 62, 63, 64, 67
   Edell, 51, 59-67, 80, 81, 100, 102,
      105, 152, 173
   Lon, 141
Evans Livestock Company, 59
Everett, Jack, 56
Everman Cemetery, 67
F
Fairchild, Charles, 121
Fairtrace, George, 18
Farley, James, 4
Farmer, Al "Cotton," 94, 137
   J. D., 6, 164
FBI, 155, 156, 161, 164
Fender, Howard, 100, 101, 142, 143-
   144, 158
Ferguson Prison Farm at Huntsville,
   155
Fey, Charles, 107
Finney, Ray, 29, 32, 36, 37, 38, 39, 40,
   41, 45, 46, 47, 136
First Presbyterian Church, 74, 162
Fisher, Georgia, 35
Florence, F. A., 167
Floyd, A. R. (Bob), 29, 48
   Jim, 100
Foard County, 125
Foley, Sid, 80, 100, 129, 130, 151
Fonda, Henry, 175
Ford, Pete, 48, 165
Fort Worth, 1, 154, 162
Fort Worth Cats, 162-163

Fort Worth Club, 4, 8
Fort Worth National Bank, 160
Fort Worth Opera Association, 172
Fort Worth Press, 21, 27, 30, 31, 33,
    54, 65, 106, 115, 121, 134, 139,
    166, 169, 173
Fort Worth Recreation Club, 19
Fort Worth Star-Telegram, 3, 4, 7, 18,
    23, 27, 28, 30, 35, 40, 85, 109,
    119, 137, 143, 173
Fort Worth Stockyards, 58
Fort Worth Symphony, 172
Four Deuces, *see* 2222 Club
Fournier, Andrew, 160
Fox, John, 6
Frank-Rich Distributing Company,
    110
Franklin, Arthur W., 106
Frankrich, Annie, 110
    family, 109
    Jack, 41
    Kalman, 110
    Leslie, 38, 109
    Sammy, 109-110
Freiden, B. W., 49
Freshair, Frank, 19
Freund, Carl, 20, 30, 31, 106, 121,
    139
G
Gale, Billie, 171
Garrison, Homer, 21
Gates, Charles Frank, 117
General Dynamics, 174
General Ministers Association, 22,
    140
Gensberg, Sam, 108
Getzendaner, W. H., 147, 148, 150
Glen Garden Country Club, 164
Goodman, Benny, 11
Goodwin Implement Company, 130
Googins, Joseph, 164
    Ruth, 164
Gordon, Jack, 2, 86, 165, 166, 167,
    171
Government Printing Office, 145
Graham, Dillon, 85

Essie, 97, 168
Grand Prairie, 168
Grant, Howard, 27-28
Grayson County, 36
Green, Cecil, 51, 64, 65, 67, 75, 76,
    77, 78, 79-83, 93, 99, 100, 101,
    103, 104, 106, 126, 130, 131, 159
    Claud, 17
    Hollis DeLois "Lois," 79, 123, 126
    Joan, 83
Green Dragon Dope Syndicate, 24
Greenwood Cemetery, 54
Gross, J. C., 39
Growald, Dick, 173
Gusher Cafe, 19
Gussy, 89
H
Haire, Grady, 99
Hall, Helen, 56
Hall, Tiffin, 10, 18, 29, 34, 41, 43, 48,
    54-57
Haltom City, 41, 49, 58, 152
Haltom's Jewelry Store, 149
Hames, Gene, 167
Hammond, W. J., 17
Hancock, Hogan, 165
Handley, Texas, 84
Hanson, M. D., 128
Hardin, Doss, 28, 32
    Ross, 28, 30, 32
Harris, Austin, 30, 31, 36
    Edith, 111
    Ernest, 109, 110, 111, 113, 145
    Jay, 31, 33, 34, 54
    Jesse, 29, 34
    Juanita, 1, 26, 32, 34, 79, 94, 122,
    126, 128, 130
    Nelson, 1, 9, 23, 24-38, 53, 56, 79,
    94-95, 96, 97, 117, 118, 126, 128,
    129, 134, 136, 139, 142, 168
Harrison, Ardie, 88-89
Hauer, Darlene, 122, 131-132
    Willard, 131-132
Hawkins, George, 20, 21, 29, 30, 34,
    35, 41, 42, 115, 133, 134, 135,
    136, 138, 152

Haworth, Bill, 101, 134, 157
Hayes, Ernest, 29
  George "Gabby," 164
Healdton, Oklahoma, 161
Heisman Trophy, 164
Hellman, Stewart, 22, 23, 36, 38, 42,
  43, 45, 46, 47, 52, 58, 71, 97,
  142-143
Hell's Half Acre, 1, 2, 137
Henry, Lee, 45
Hightower, Cato, 65, 76, 100, 113,
  114, 133, 137, 151, 155, 160
Hill Crest Street, 129
Hill, Floyd, 140, 157
Hitch, Bill, 169
Hogan, Ben, 164
Holley, Lon, 117, 118, 119, 124-126,
  128, 129
Honey, Baxter, 128
Honts, John B., 38, 39-40, 43, 45, 46,
  47
Hood, Clyde, 146, 148
Hopper, Marion, 26
Hornsby, Rogers, 162
Horseshoe Casino, 50
House, Boyce, 6
Houston, 4, 155, 159
Howard, Karl, 30, 36, 133, 136
Howerton, A. C., 80, 83, 118, 161
  R. R., 9, 23, 41, 133, 136, 137
Hubler, Willard, 99
Hudgins, Velma, 96
Hudspeth, Clinton Earl, 104
Huggins, Harry, 75, 76, 77, 100, 131
Hull, H. A. (Salty), 35
Humphrey, William Carl "Wimpy,"
  159, 160
Hunt, Roy, 128
Hunter, Billy, 163
Huntsville, 99, 158
Hutt, Helen, 52
  Lester, 10, 40, 51-52, 145
I
Inman, Dewey, 48
Inspiration Point, 117, 125

J
James, Harry, 11, 165
Jenkins, Lew, 85
Jewel Box Revue, 167
Johnson Act, 107
Johnson County, 100
Johnson, Vernon, 105
Jones, Bob, 162
  Horace, 111
  Maitland, 128
  Mrs. P. E., 67
  W. O., 29
K
Kansas, 130
Kansas City, 82
Katy Lake, 143
Kay, Herbie, 166
Kean, George, 130, 151-154
  Mrs. George, 152
Kefauver, Estes, 28
Kemper Military School, 143
Kemper, Robert, 23
Kennedale, 155
Keystone Novelty and
  Manufacturing, 108
King, M. S., 149
  Wayne, 165
Kinney, James, 57
Kirkwood, Pat, 12, 13, 34, 69, 70, 71,
  72, 85, 136
  William C. (Pappy), 10, 26, 28, 33,
  34, 41, 43, 48, 52, 68-72
Kleberg, Dick, 70
Klehaven, Johnny, 160
Koslow, Robert, 149
Koslow's Furs, 149
Kyser, Kay, 165, 166
L
LaGrave Field, 162, 163
Lake Huron, 153
Lake Worth, 10, 64, 125, 126, 130,
  152, 154, 165
Lamour, Dorothy, 165-166
Lanzarotti, E'gildo, 18, 19
Las Vegas, 36, 48, 50, 51, 58, 72, 84,
  116
Lattimore, Hal, 170

Lawton, Oklahoma, 124
Leberman, Faye, 69
Lee, Ed, 30
Levens, Jimmy, 170, 171, 172
Lilly, Bob, 164
Littlefield, Texas, 118, 124, 128
Lockheed Martin, 174
Loicano, Anthony "Tony," 17, 109,
    112-113
  brothers, 109, 112
  Buster, 118, 145
  Frank, 112
  Joan, 170
  John, 112
  Martin, 112
Loid, W. M., 112
Long, Phil, 40
Los Angeles, 165
Los Angeles Dodgers, 163
Love Field, 51
Love, Jack, 76, 77, 100, 101
Lucas Funeral Home, 65
Lucas, Nick, 171
Luttrell, Bill, 16
Lyles, Jeanette, 155, 156
Lynn, Sherry, 170, 171
M
MacArthur, Douglas, 41
Madareaga, Manuel, 158
Madoc Hotel, 56
Malone, Buddy, 49
  Double-O, 96
Maloney, Jack, 109
Markum, Buddie, 58
Marr, Dr. J. H., 83
Martin, Jesse, 41, 45, 46
  Mary, 6
  Tony, 165
Massey's, 11
Matlock, Chick, 160
Matthews, Byron, 13, 41, 129
  Charles, 46
  Dorothy, 143
  Wilcie Turner, 143
May, Billy, 166
Mays, Clifford, 41, 42, 96, 97, 99

Clyde, 94
McComb, Lowell Everett, 154
McCormick, Harry, 23
McDonald, Benny, 38, 41, 109, 113-
    114
McElyea, R. G., 172
McGannon, Robert, 171
McGee, Dave, 32, 35, 39, 41, 45, 46,
    97
McGill, W. F., 170
McGown family, 175
McGown, Quenton, 72
McGraw, James, 139
McGregor, Willis, 78, 100, 157, 161
McKinley, Ray, 166
McKnight, M. M., 21, 22
McLaughlin, Bob, 119
McMurtry, Larry, 57
McWillie, L. J. "Chili," 48
Meacham Field, 174, 175
Meador, Paul, 20
Meriweather, Rev. Jim, 67
Metropolitan Hotel, 69
Mexican Inn, 10, 54, 56
Meyer, L. R. "Dutch," 135
Michigan, 152, 153, 154
Midland, 25, 129, 152, 171
Miller, Dave, 41
  Glenn, 166
  Ivy, 48, 49
  Que Robert, 117, 125, 126, 128,
    129
  Sidney, 126
Mills Novelty, 107
Moloney, Raymond T., 107
Monroe, H. H., 40
Montague County, 31
Montgomery County, 156
Montgomery, James Ralph "Sully," 6,
    20, 23, 27, 29, 35, 44, 47, 51, 138,
    139, 142, 146, 147, 148, 149, 150
  Mrs., 146, 150
Montgomery Ward, 22
Moon, Chang Wook, 169
Moore, Arthur Lee, 76, 84
  Lee, 38, 41, 51

Ray, 38, 41
Moslah Temple, 75
Montgomery, Sully, 137
Murphy, Edward P., 50
Murray, Sam, 49
N
Neal, Clyde, 23
Nebraska, 126
Nelson, Willie, 13
Nesbit, George Rennie (Jack), 26, 31, 130, 131
   Lucille, 131
Nevada, 49
New Isis, 133
New Mexico, 73, 151
New Orleans, 170
New York, 171
Noble, Herbert "The Cat," 28, 36, 49, 79, 127, 130
   Mrs. Herbert, 79, 126
Noles, E. L., 49
Norris, Al, 165
   Gene Paul, 82, 120, 121, 130, 155-161
   Mary, 161
   Pete, 155-161
North Carolina, 152
North Richland Hills, 59
North Side Amusement Company, 111
North Side Coliseum, 172
O
Oakwood Cemetery, 144
Oden, H. D. "Red," 10, 41, 48
Odessa, 25, 29, 129
Offield, Tom, 99
Oil and Gas Journal, 4
Oklahoma, 64, 122, 128, 130, 157, 169
Oklahoma City, 99
Olney, 69
Owens and Brumley Funeral Home, 132
O'Brien, Davey, 164
O'Neill, Eugene, 145

P
Paducah, 130, 131
Pandora Club, 63
Panther Novelty Company, 109
Parrish Inn, 61
Paschal High School, 143
Pate, A. M., 163
Paylor, Kathleen, 74
Pearl Harbor, 107
Peeples, Pete, 71
Penn, Boyd, 99
Pershing, Harley, 102
Peters, Bobby, 165
Petroleum Building, 18
Philadelphia Eagles, 164
Pinkard, R. E., 33
Pioneer Palace, 7
Power, Truman, 76, 77, 96, 100, 101
Presley, Elvis, 172
Prohibition, 165
R
Rand, Sally, 7, 172
Ranger oilfields, 175
Rausch, Leon, 12
Ray Crowder Funeral Home, 106
Ray, Jack, 61
Rayburn, Sam, 70
Raylor, Olen Ray, 159
Renfro, Mike, 164
   Thomas, 113
Renfro Wholesale Drug Company, 79
Rey, Jack, 67
Reynolds, John, 29
Rhea, Cleaves, 175
Rice, Ben H., 50
Richardson, Sid, 4, 86, 175
Richhard, C. L., 7
Richland Hills, 64, 67, 119
Rickey, Branch, 162
Riley, Randell, 60, 61
Ringside Club, 17, 26, 164, 165
Risner, Ben, 129
River Oaks, 11, 19, 159
Riverside, 139
Roach, Jesse, 176
Roberts Cut Off Road, 10, 120, 125
Robertson, Evelyn, 65, 76, 101

Rocket Club, 11, 16
Rogers, Henry, 60, 101
  Roy, 133, 164
  Will, 4
Rone, Asher, 15, 52-54, 145
  Grace Riggs, 54
Roosevelt, Elliot, 164
Roosevelt, Oklahoma, 54
Rose, Billy, 7, 9
Rose Bowl, 164
Rose Hill Cemetery, 86, 126
Rosebuds, 7
Rosenberg, Jerry, 48
  William Samuel, 4
Rouer, R. E., 110
Rubin, Ben, 7
Rum and Coca Cola, 165
Runyon, Damon, 7
Russell, Charles, 51
S
San Antonio, 4, 50, 52
San Francisco, 107
San Jacinto River, 156
Sansom Park, 10, 119
Satterwhite, W. D., 41, 97, 145, 167-170
Sayre, Oklahoma, 80
Scenic Drive, 65
Scoreboard Lounge, 13
Seibold Hotel, 17
Selcer, Richard, 2
Sellers, Ray, 122
Settle, R. Daniel, 146
Seventh Street Pharmacy, 112
Shannon Memorial Chapel, 106
Sharp, Elmer, 13-15, 29, 124, 145
  W. O., 125
Shaw, Artie, 165
Shepherd's Parking Garage, 56
Shivers, Allen, 51, 158
Showboat, 11
Shrine Hospital, 75
Shropshire, Spencer, 99, 169
Sinatra, Frank, 11, 175
Skyline Drive Motel, 10, 52

Skyliner, 11, 41, 97, 165, 167, 170, 171
Smith, Boston, 131, 164
  George T., 165
  Reba, 166
  Tommy, 154
Somervell County, 137
Sons of the Pioneers, 164
Southwestern Bell Telephone
    Company, 111
Southwestern Exposition and Fat
    Stock Show, 164
Southwestern Petroleum, 141
Spinks, Emmett, 170, 171
Sportsman's Rod and Gun Club, 143
Spring Creek Restaurant, 57
St. Joseph's Hospital, 53, 82, 171
Standard Oil, 8
Star Coin Machine Company, 113
Starnes, Jerry, 166-167
State Bar, 2
Stephens County, 99
Stephenson, H. L., 152
Stewart, Robert, 112
  S. C., 131
Storm, Georgia, 171
Stowe, Ross, 60
Stripling, Howard, 29, 131, 168
  Lois, 131, 168
Suggs, Paul, 146
Sullivan, Ed, 173
Sweetwater, 85
Swift Packing House, 164
T
Tarrant County, 134, 140, 151, 158, 159, 161, 176
Tarrant Field, 9
Taylor, Mack, 48
Terrace, Winton, 74
Texas Centennial, 18
Texas Christian University, 115, 163, 174
Texas Hotel, 87
Texas Rangers, 12, 20, 21, 74, 121, 140, 143, 154
Texas Refinery Company, 163

Texas Wesleyan College, 174
Texas Wesleyan School of Fine Arts, 172
Theo's Saddle and Sirloin Club, 175
3939 Club, 10, 12, 20, 40, 50, 51
Thomas, Jim, 29, 118, 121, 124, 125, 126, 128, 129
Thompson, Frank, 117
Tindall, Louis, 57, 123
  Opal, 123
  Velda, 123
Tiny Tim, 171
Tolbert, W. H., 169
Tomlin, Paul, 98, 99
Top o' the Hill Terrace, 17, 40, 50, 84-92, 166
Townley, Edward Eugene, 159
Trinity River, 98, 141, 144
Truman, Harry S., 41, 176
Tsermengas, Jimmie, 153, 154
Tulsa, Oklahoma, 68
Turf Club, 17, 112
2929 Club, 26
2222 Club, 10, 12, 26, 33, 34, 41, 70, 71, 136, 165
U
Upham, Hobart, 67
Urban, Harry R., Sr., 50
V
Vallee, Rudy, 172
Van Zandt, Gloria, 86
W
Wakefield, Bert, 10, 33, 34, 40, 43, 50, 51
Wall, Mrs. Lewis, Jr., 44
Wall Street Journal, 4
Walton, Bill, 164
Wardlaw, A. L., 22, 58, 114, 142
Washington and Lee University School of Law, 143
Water Valley, Mississippi, 68
Watt, W. R., 164
WBAP-TV, 164, 173
Weems, Ted, 165
Welch, Louis, 36
West Point, 143

West Side Recreation Club, 26
West Van Zandt Elementary School, 24
Westbrook Hotel, 18
Western Hills, 140, 157, 158
Western Union, 158
Westfall, Howard, 57
Westmoor Tourist Court, 126
Wheeler County, 94
White Settlement Fire Department, 105
Whitehead, Grady, 29
  Robert, 29
Whitewright, 57
Whitman, Paul, 164
Wilderspin, George, 15, 29, 41, 43, 49, 57-58, 62, 164
Wilemon, L. N., 175
Will Rogers Auditorium, 6
Will Rogers Complex, 172
Williams, Andy, 171
  Dick, 44, 163
  Mack, 9, 27, 159
Williamson-Dickie, 175
Willis, Delbert, 134
Wills, Bob, 12
Wilson, Eleanor, 167
  W. D., 148, 149, 150
  Will, 49
Woodley, K. K., 170
World War II, 8, 9
Wright, Harlon, 64, 65, 67, 105, 120, 139, 140, 141, 152, 153, 160
  Robert L., 99
Wynn, Carl, 38
Y
Yardanoff, Theo, 175
Yellowstone National Park, 57
Young, Bob, 36, 45, 74-75
  W. M., 105

CPSIA information can be obtained
at www.ICGtesting.com
Printed in the USA
LVHW091900160919
630974LV00005B/51/P

9 781571 682505